(

KE

J.

This edition first published in 2013 by:

Thistle Publishing
36 Great Smith Street
London
SW1P 3BU

ISBN: 978-1-909869-03-5

ACKNOWLEDGEMENTS

The origins of this book lie in a lecture given by James Douglas-Hamilton, now Earl of Selkirk, a few years ago at Fettes College about Rudolf Hess's flight to Britain in 1941, and the role played by his father in this extraordinary affair. I was riveted by what he had to say and later contacted him to see whether he would be at all interested in a biography of his father. He was and at every stage of this assignment Lord Selkirk, a historian of some repute, has been a fount of information and expertise, as well as answering my many queries with infinite patience. To him I owe my greatest debt.

I would also like to extend a special thanks to Lord David Douglas-Hamilton for his help, not least his work on the history of his family, and to other members of the Douglas-Hamilton family who shared their memories of the 14th Duke: Lord Patrick Douglas-Hamilton, Alasdair Douglas-Hamilton, Diarmaid Douglas-Hamilton and Mrs Diana Younger.

I also acknowledge the help and kindness I received from others who knew the Duke: Stuart Chalmers, Sir Charles Fraser, Dougal McIntyre, Dr Rosalind Marshall, Jimmy Miller and John Mutch.

I must pay a special debt of gratitude to Alexander, Duke of Hamilton, for granting me permission to use the family archives at Lennoxlove and to his secretary, Lindsay Stuart, and the staff at the Lennoxlove Estate Office for all their help.

I would like to thank the following for all their cooperation: the Scottish Conservative Party for permission to use its archive; Miss Allison Derrett, Assistant Archivist at the Royal Archives, Windsor: Dr Maria Castrillo, Curator of the National Library of Scotland; Mrs Rachel Hart, the Deputy Head of Special Collections, the University of St Andrews, Mrs Penelope Hatfield, the Archivist of Eton College Library, Ms Angela Logan and Ms Pearl Murphy of Hamilton Town House Library and Andrew Riley, the Archivist of Churchill Archives Centre, Churchill College, Cambridge.

I also acknowledge the help I received from the staff of Edinburgh Central Library, The British Library, Colindale, The National Archives, Kew, the National Library of Scotland and Victoria State Library, Melbourne.

I am grateful to the following for permission to quote from copy-right material.

Extracts from the Royal Archives are published by the gracious permission of Her Majesty Queen Elizabeth II.

Crown copyright material in the National Archives is reproduced by permission of the Controller of Her Majesty's Stationery Office.

Alexander, Duke of Hamilton, for letters written by the 14th Duke of Hamilton, and other material from the family archives.

James, Earl of Selkirk, for letters and notes written by the 14th Duke of Hamilton.

Alasdair Douglas-Hamilton for an extract from a letter written by his father.

Diarmaid Douglas-Hamilton for an extract from a letter written by his father.

The University of St Andrews Library, Special Collections, for extracts from the papers of Sir James Irvine and J.Steven Watson.

Andrew Lownie for an extract from *Ten Days That Saved The West* by John Costello and published by Bantam.

Mainstream Publishing for extracts from *The Truth About Rudolf Hess* by James Douglas-Hamilton.

Stacey International for an extract from *After You, Prime Minister* by James Douglas-Hamilton.

Woodfield Publishing for an extract from *Prestwick's Pioneer: A Life of David F.McIntyre* by Dougal McIntyre.

From *Flight from Reality: Rudolf Hess and his Mission to Scotland, 1941* edited by David Stafford, published by Pimlico. Reprinted by permission of the Random House Group Limited.
From *Fear God and Dread Nought: The Correspondence of Admiral of the Fleet Lord Fisher of Kilverstone: Volume 111 Restoration, Abdication, and Last Years, 1914-1920* by A.J.Marder, published by Jonathan Cape. Reprinted by permission of The Random House Group Limited.

Every effort has been made to contact copyright holders. In some cases this has not proved possible. Where any inadvertent infringement of copyright has taken place, the author and publishers would crave indulgence and will make the necessary acknowledgements in later editions.

I am deeply grateful to Dr Paul Addison, Dr Jeremy Crang, Allan Massie and Dr Harry Reid for reading the book and for their comments; to Gavin Lloyd for putting me right on a number of grammatical points, to Owen Dudley Edwards for writing the foreword and for being so supportive throughout; and last, but by no means least, to Andrew Lownie and David Haviland for bringing the assignment to completion.

Mark Peel, Edinburgh 2013.

FOREWORD

One of the greatest pleasures in University teaching is to renew links
with former students, especially when they have become teachers themselves. For them to become University teachers themselves makes for
the prospect of exciting future collaboration, and rethinking your ideas
through a fresh mind familiar with your own. Friendship with a graduate
of one's Department who has become a schoolteacher opens up equally
exciting futures. Here is the chance to see progress in young minds at
ages before they reach university: and in education it frequently hap-
pens that the best work done in the teaching of a student is at school
rather than university, provided the teacher can inspire. The University
of Edinburgh's former student Mark Peel was such an inspirational
force as History teacher at Fettes College {famed as *Alma Mater* of eminent English politicians and, more notably, of W.C.Sellar, co-author of
1066 and All That, perhaps the greatest history book ever written}. He
has carried this fascination with complexities of the past in his many
books, studies of unusual educators, a life of the great Socialist pastor
and preacher Donald Soper, a study of the leading woman intellectual
in modern British politics Shirley Williams, and the present biographi-
cal work, on a twentieth-century hero who was also perhaps Scotland's
best-loved Duke. It is very hard for the historian to capture a person's
loveable qualities and here as elsewhere Mark Peel has done nobly. There
was a rare beauty in the nature of Douglas Douglas-Hamilton, fourteenth

Duke of Hamilton. In such perception the programme for his memorial service in Edinburgh's St Giles' Cathedral began with a quotation from Edith Sitwell: 'Love is not changed by death, and nothing is lost, and all in the end is harvest'. Hamilton was a great harvester.

That service of celebration and thanksgiving for him was attended by representatives of more Christian faiths than Scotland may ever previously have brought together in common worship. Appropriately for them all, it took a took an emblem from St Polycarp, disciple of Jesus's beloved St John 'God the Father of Our Lord Jesus Christ increase our faith and our truth and gentleness'. To Hamilton's faith the differing Christians united in testimony. He was indeed valiant for truth, and it was the tragedy of his life that others were not. His gentleness I encountered before I met him, in the one who above all others by desire and by nature resembled him most: his second son James.

James's memoir, *After You, Prime Minister,* echoes his father's gift for reminiscence lightened by amusing self-deprecation. They leavened their lives with laughter. My meeting with him arose from the only sport of which I was capable – debating - in which for the first time I was asked to judge a round of the *Observer* Mace, known to me from days as combatant. I had very recently joined the University of Edinburgh as a historian, and the round happened there. The result was clear to all three judges, and as Chair I suggested I say a word on winner and runner-up and asked my colleagues to speak about the other contestants. It was a stupid idea, as to my horror became toxically evident when my first fellow-judge delivered individual castigations to each of the losing teams, contemptuous, dismissive, derisive. And then Lord James Douglas-Hamilton spoke. Any nurse could have studied him to great advantage. With no allusion to his appalling *confrere*, he went down the same shattered line of speakers, and in every case he found the perfect words in which to discover their strengths, their courage, their validity, and to help them recover their self-respect. I watched face after face lose its bitterness, misery and anger; shoulders straightened, jaws relaxed, eyes brightened. He shook his head over my later, private, whole-hearted thanks. He had only done what needed to be done, and was glad I thought he had done it right.

Reading Mark Peel's book brings an entire context for that incident: as always James Douglas-Hamilton had done instinctively what his father would have done. Charmingly, Mark Peel himself also embodies many of the Duke's qualities, including this strength through gentleness, making him peculiarly fitted for telling the story as well as he does. All three of them naturally enjoyed friendship with persons of very different politics from their own Toryism: as someone who would never vote Tory, I may be forgiven for saying that the need for gentleness and for healing must be particularly urgent in that party when its middle-aged young Turks are feeling their muscles.

James Douglas-Hamilton was shortly to publish a book *Motive for a Mission,* on Rudolf Hess's wartime flight to Scotland where he demanded to see the Duke of Hamilton, then a Squadron Leader in the RAF. Hamilton seems never to have met Hess, though he had probably been in the same room during receptions for international civilities of air-flying personnel. On identifying Hess, he communicated with Winston Churchill, a friend, and Prime Minister. H.M.Government announced Hess's Capture, but with some idea of keeping Hitler guessing made no explanation, and malice in the experienced hands of Lord Beaverbrook's *Daily Express* and elsewhere fed vague impressions that Hamilton had Nazi sympathies. It was a ludicrous hint. Think of a Nazi and you are thinking of everything that Douglas Douglas-Hamilton was not. The pivot of Hess's motivation was in fact Hamilton's acquaintance with Albrecht Haushofer, a friend of Hess's in spite of his being partly Jewish. James Douglas-Hamilton's book was a vindication of his father, but was also a moving exploration of the mind and career of Haushofer and his poetry, written in the months before the Nazis killed him. Hamilton had never written his own account of the matter. Lord James inherited his literary talents from his mother the Lady Elizabeth {as we all knew her in the Carlyle Society whose scholarship prompted her charming topographical study of Jane Welsh's Haddington and its influence on her before she married Carlyle — a fascinating book, but as yet unpub-lished}. I had much pleasure in reviewing *Motive for a Mission* for the *Irish Times.* It then occurred to James that I would enjoy meeting his father particularly because his boyhood meeting with Sir Roger Casement would interest an Irish historian.

Hamilton on Casement reminded me vividly of a folksinger, Frankie McPeake, whom I had interviewed for the *Irish Times* a couple of years earlier. Both of them had the ability to conjure up the past vividly, and to make you feel you knew the Casement of whom they spoke. I had not expected it in McPeake's case, for my quest with him sought memories of early twentieth-century Belfast poverty.

But his boyhood prowess in the uilleann pipes had interested cultural nationalists, and he was taken to play for a gathering none of whom had any interest in him save for his pipes, Casement alone taking the trouble to make the boy feel he was worth knowing in himself. The Duke of Hamilton told the same story, in very much the same way: he was then Marquess of Clydesdale, and as heir apparent to a Dukedom of passing interest to visitors, but Casement alone talked to him as though he were a person. Neither Frankie McPeake nor the Duke made a grievance out of it: they simply took pleasure in remembering the man who talked with them as themselves rather than social objects. They shared Casement's conversational classlessness.

Hamilton talked of Hess and ran over some details of the episode. He was clearly very proud of James's book: for a father to witness his son embattled for him is one of the greatest delights imaginable. He didn't say so, but was happy to smile an assent to my own admiration for *Motive for a Mission*. He had a charming, recessive sense of humour. I mentioned the former premier, Sir Alec Douglas-Home, formerly Earl of Home. The Duke nodded. 'We speak now', he said. 'We didn't for a hundred and fifty years.' This alluded to the famous 'Douglas Cause', but as an Irish veteran of family feuds I was awed by its grandeur. But was there a nuance behind it? Superficially it might be assumed Douglas-Home would also be politically akin to Douglas-Hamilton? As Mark Peel shows, Hamilton was a loyal though not particularly visible supporter of Stanley Baldwin and Neville Chamberlain. But politics for him seems to have been something one took on from a sense of duty and service. The fact that, when he realised Hess was now a British prisoner his first reaction {after being put on a very long civil service finger} was to get in touch with Churchill, is instructive. He served the Baldwins and Chamberlains: he doesn't seem a natural intimate for them. Baldwin was too English, and for all of his Macdonald ancestry spoke as though only concerned with England, and Hamilton was extremely quick to fight for Scottish rights under attack or in danger of erosion. It was appropriate that his son James should have become probably the most constituency-friendly Tory MP in Scotland, but it was also appropriate that his son Hugh joined the Scottish national party and wrote about the '45. As for Neville Chamberlain, Hamilton would have admired his conscientiousness but hardly have relaxed in his company. But Churchill was a natural friend for a former boxer and air-conqueror of Everest. What divided him from that fellow-aristocrat arose in part from Hamilton's Himalayan adventures. He really differed from Churchill on India. His friendship with Indians meant that support for progress towards self-government made sense to him, while Churchill was sneering at Gandhi as a 'naked fakir'. He wasn't about to go on hunger-strike or join the Congress party but he was glad to add his voice to Government steps towards ultimate Indian self-rule. The philosophy of goodwill towards opponents of goodwill permeated his political thought. With Germany, it was publicly asserted hopes that the Germans would repudiate and reject the anti-Semites after which Britain could rebuild friendship, with regret for the injustices of the Versailles Treaty as a common basis. But once at war, Churchill was his man, and he was Churchill's man, and in that war he, like his three airborne brothers, was ready to die. {Lord David did.}

James Douglas-Hamilton would marry John Buchan's granddaughter, and there is a touch of the Buchan hero in Hamilton. Not one of the Dukes — Buchan's Dukes were improbably Wodehousian — but a hero of the reflective, generous, courteous kind we know in Sir Edward Leithen, happiest in making friends with a rural boy vagrant and poacher, or in undertaking a dangerous quest for some comrade. That last word typifies his life. One reason why Hamilton was vaguely assumed to have Nazi links was because the American hero, Charles Lindbergh, first solo flier over the Atlantic, revealed Hitlerian sympathies during World War Two.

But Hamilton had not been that kind of hero. He was never interested in solitary glory. If he won boxing honours, it was by regarding himself as one in a sport, whose opponents and sparring partners might be among his closest friends. If he flew over Everest, it would be as a team man. {These are but two facets of Mark Peel's biography, admirably measured and realised.} He was ready, like Leithen, to bear his pain alone. But his life was given to working with others, and rejoicing in their friendship. James Douglas-Hamilton's *After You, Prime Minister* proudly placed on its back jacket a photograph of the boy Lord James facing his father in an early boxing lesson. It symbolises that father, teaching the skills, loving the opponent, and making a friend.

It will be ultimate justice if this book makes Hamilton many friends.

Owen Dudley Edwards.

$\mathcal{I}$NTRODUCTION

In his own understated way Douglas Douglas-Hamilton, Marquis of Douglas and Clydesdale, was something of a hero to those that knew him.

Born to the purple, he trod a gilded path through Eton, Oxford and the Conservative Party to his eventual destiny in the House of Lords as Scotland's premier peer. Yet aside from this life of pomp and privilege there was a more unconventional side to the Duke of Hamilton that marked him out from his fellow peers.

Imbued with the paternalist ethos of his parents, the young Marquis of Clydesdale had made every effort to become acquainted with the lot of his father's tenants and to mix with all types. His passion for boxing might well have been fostered at school and university, but it flourished in the crucible of South Lanarkshire where the sport offered a welcome distraction from the hazards of working-class life. Teaming up with a number of local boxers who went on to find fame in the professional arena, Clydesdale was inured enough by the experience to become Scottish Amateur Middleweight Champion in 1924. Already known as the 'Boxing Marquis', his mere presence in the ring guaranteed him many a headline, but although performing in alien surroundings his courage and chivalry won round all but the most cynical observers.

His popularity continued through his tough political baptism in the shipbuilding constituency of Glasgow Govan when even his opponent, the left winger Neil Maclean, publicly commended him for his upstanding character before urging electors not to vote for his party.

Clydesdale's profile was further enhanced not only by his charismatic leadership of 602 {City of Glasgow} Squadron, again an unusual choice for a leading aristocrat, but also by his participation in the Houston-Everest Expedition of April 1933. In an age when pioneering exploits in aviation were regarded as big news, his success, and that of fellow Scotsman David McIntyre, in becoming the first men to fly over Everest assured them a special place in the national consciousness.

His renown extended overseas so that when Clydesdale visited the Berlin Olympic Games in 1936 he was feted accordingly, not least by the highest echelons of the Nazi leadership. This privileged treatment was not simply the result of his aviation prowess; it stemmed also from his desire to cultivate closer ties with Germany.

It was during his stay in Berlin that Clydesdale became friendly with Dr Albrecht Haushofer, a foreign policy adviser to Rudolf Hess, Hitler's faithful Deputy, and over the course of the next several years they maintained contact in order to try and bridge the chasm that still existed between their respective countries.

Haushofer's initiative was reciprocated by Clydesdale in a public display of solidarity with those Germans opposed to Hitler. Although a serving officer he found the thought of a major European war with the German people a troubling prospect, and held out the possibility of peace with a democratic government devoid of Hitler and Nazi sympathisers. He articulated his views in a letter to *The Times* in October 1939 which, for all its good intentions, betrayed a certain naivety.

His words did not go unnoticed in Berlin as attempts by Hess to neutralise Britain continued in earnest. Although more refined in his personal lifestyle than most of his colleagues, Hess conformed to type in his ideological fanaticism and devotion to Hitler. Desperate to facilitate an invasion of the Soviet Union and avoid a two-front war by instigating peace with Britain, he sought various intermediaries to bring his plan to fruition. The reason he appears to have earmarked Hamilton {as he was from March 1940} was his friendship with Albrecht Haushofer and his perceived influence in high places. After the fall of France, Hess asked Haushofer to write to him proposing talks in neutral Portugal, a proposition with which Haushofer complied despite holding out little hope of success given Hamilton's status as a serving officer.

The letter, sent in September 1940 shortly after the conclusion of the Battle of Britain, was intercepted by British Intelligence a few weeks later. After satisfying itself that Hamilton was no renegade it summoned him to the Air Ministry in March 1941 to broach the possibility of his going to Lisbon, Haushofer's suggested venue, to obtain further information about Germany, a request to which Hamilton would only consent under certain conditions.

Hamilton's reservations about participating in such a foolhardy mission came to be shared by his superiors and it was subsequently aborted. By then it had been overtaken by events when Hess, in an act of desperation, flew into Scotland on the evening of 10 May 1941 specifically to meet Hamilton to talk peace. Such was the surreal nature of his mission and the floundering response of the British government that the true facts gave way to various conspiracy theories, many of which were detrimental to Hamilton's reputation. Because of his attempts to promote closer relations with Germany before the war, and his letter to *The Times* proposing peace under certain conditions, the rumours that he had been in contact with the Nazi leadership soon gathered momentum. Even Winston Churchill, the Prime Minister, and King George VI were among those disposed to believe that he might have met Hess at the Berlin Olympics when he had not, while others alleged he had actually befriended him and arranged his flight from Germany.

Keen to scotch such calumnies, Hamilton submitted various writs for libel, but despite winning complete retractions from two Communist publications in June 1942 the damaging innuendos continued, not least in the United States of America {US} and the Soviet Union. The longer the wall of secrecy remained intact and official government files closed, the more intense the speculation grew. During the 1990s the conspiracy theorists were out in force as book after book questioned the official version of the Hess flight. According to Peter Padfield in *Hess:*

The Führer's Disciple, the Deputy Führer was lured to Britain by British Intelligence, while to Lynn Picknett, Clive Prince and Stephen Prior in *Double Standards: The Rudolf Hess Cover-up*, Hess worked with pro-Nazi elements in the British establishment to procure peace.

As far as Hamilton is concerned, Padfield depicts him as an innocent stooge of British Intelligence, but to Picknett, Prince and Prior he is a far more disreputable figure. They contend that Hamilton had met Hess in 1936 and that he knew he was coming to Britain in 1941. To them it seems clear that immediately after Hess had landed Hamilton rushed to meet him that night and not the next morning as in the official accounts. They also allege that under oath he carefully took refuge in ambiguous phrasing and dissembling in order to toe the official line.

The strident nature of the allegations about a British establishment cover-up over Hess prompted an authoritative rebuff from David Stafford in a book entitled *Flight from Reality: Rudolf Hess and his Mission to Scotland 1941*. While accepting that some of the research had opened up new leads such as the connection between Mrs Violet Roberts, the widow at the heart of the Haushofer-Hamilton letter of September 1940, and her nephew who worked for Special Operations1, Britain's secret wartime 'black propaganda' agency, he cautions against reading too much into this.

The evidence, however, does not bear the weight of interpretation placed upon it by the authors, who have instantly leapt to a grand conspiracy theory replete with the all-too-predictable plot of Hess following Hitler's orders to meet a peace party in Britain followed by a massive official cover-up in Britain. Yet the monumental disarray and disagreement between Churchill and the Foreign Office over how to handle Hess's arrival in Scotland stands as overwhelming evidence against any such theory about some carefully plotted conspiracy. For why, if it was so cunningly prepared, was there no strategy in place to exploit it? [1]

The release of Foreign Office files relating to Hess in 1992, and MI5 ones in 2004, far from implicating Hamilton in any deliberate covert activity with Germany actually exonerate him by making clear that all his dealings with Albrecht Haushofer had been above board. Had British Intelligence known in November 1940 that he had shown Haushofer's peace letter of July 1939 to Churchill, then the leading anti-appeaser of Germany, it would have scotched any suspicions that lingered over his German activity pre-war.

The files also further demolish the age-old claim that Mrs Roberts, a long-standing friend of Haushofer's parents, General Professor Karl Haushofer, and his wife Martha, was somehow a veneer for British Intelligence in its machinations to lure Hess to Britain. She was not. She was very much in the business of writing humdrum letters to Martha Haushofer, and the one that arrived in August 1940 gave Karl Haushofer, Hess's mentor, the idea of using her as a conduit for a German peace initiative sent by Albrecht Haushofer to Hamilton but masterminded by Hess himself.

Thus the evidence belatedly coming to Hamilton's aid dismisses for all time the idea that the Duke was engaged in some dastardly plot to undermine his country. In saying this, one does not gloss over his part in the doomed attempts to foster closer relations with Germany through the mid-late 1930s, especially his support of the Munich Agreement of September 1938; there was also his underestimation of the crude dynamics of Nazi expansionism and his overestimation of the potential of the German opposition to destroy Hitler. In truth the world of political intrigue and international diplomacy was not his forte; he was a straightforward man of action and adventure with many accomplishments to his name and it is these accomplishments, as well as his part in the Hess affair, that this reappraisal of his life seeks to address.

1. A PROUD INHERITANCE

Douglas Douglas-Hamilton was born on 3 February 1903 at 71a Eccleston Square, Pimlico, into a family steeped in history. His father, the 13th Duke of Hamilton and 10th Duke of Brandon, was the premier peer of Scotland, only one of five British peers to hold more than one dukedom, and Hereditary Keeper of the Palace of Holyroodhouse, the official royal residence in Scotland.

The name Hamilton originated possibly from Hambledon in Northumberland and the arrival of Walter Fitz-Gilbert in 1294 to settle in Renfrew. During King Edward 1's wars against the Scots he supported the English, but following a change of allegiance to King Robert the Bruce after the Battle of Bannockburn in 1314 he was granted the barony and estates of Cadzow {later renamed Hamilton}, along with estates in Renfrew and the Lothians.

It was his grandson, Sir David Hamilton, the 3rd Baron Cadzow, who first used the family name, and Sir James Hamilton, the 6th Baron Cadzow and 1st Lord Hamilton, who was made a Lord of Parliament in 1445. His later marriage to Princess Mary, daughter of King James II of Scotland in 1474, was an astute one as it kept the family at the heart of Scottish affairs for the next two centuries. His son James, 2nd Lord Hamilton, became Privy Councillor to King James IV and helped arrange his marriage to Princess Margaret Tudor, daughter of King Henry VII of England, a diplomatic coup that gained him the earldom of Arran in 1503. His son James, 2nd Earl of Arran, as Regent of Scotland between 1542 and 1554, displayed similar finesse in securing the marriage of Mary, Queen of Scots to Francis of France and was created Duke of

1

Châtelherault by the French King Henri II, a title the Dukes of Hamilton still use to this day.

Arran was succeeded by his eldest son James, 3rd Earl of Arran, who failed in his attempt to marry Queen Elizabeth 1 of England, and was declared insane in 1561. His younger brother, John Hamilton, was Chancellor of Scotland under King James VI of Scotland {James I of England} and was created Marquis of Hamilton in 1599. The 2nd Marquis, as well as inheriting the earldom of Arran from his insane uncle, moved to England with James I and was appointed the King's representative to the Parliament of Scotland. His son James, the 3rd Marquis, performed a similar role as King Charles I's Royal Commissioner for Scotland, clashing with the Covenanters in 1638 over the King's unsuccessful endeavours to impose the new Prayer Book there. In 1643 Charles created him 1st Duke of Hamilton, making the dukedom the third oldest in Britain after Norfolk and Somerset, and during the Civil War he led the Royalist armies in a vain attempt to rescue the King from captivity. His defeat at the Battle of Preston in 1648 helped determine his fate, and that of the King, as both were beheaded by Cromwell's Roundheads.

The Duke's brother, a much more substantial figure, did not fare much better, dying from wounds at the Battle of Worcester in 1651 when supporting the future King Charles II's attempt to regain the throne. He left no heirs and the title passed to the 1st Duke's eldest surviving daughter, Lady Anne. She proved to be of stern mettle, paying off the family's large debts, reclaiming their estates confiscated by Cromwell and enlarging the magnificent Hamilton Palace, the main residence of the Hamiltons since 1591. She also married William Douglas, 1st Earl of Selkirk, who became 3rd Duke of Hamilton. He fell out with the Earl of Lauderdale, Charles II's chief minister in Scotland, over his persecution of the Covenanters and was dismissed from the Privy Council in 1676. Despite attempts by Charles's successor, James II, to restore him to favour, Hamilton played a leading part in enticing William of Orange to Britain and offering him, and his wife Mary, the throne of Scotland in 1689.

The Duchess Anne had thirteen children, and following her husband's death in 1694, she renounced all her titles in 1698 in favour of her eldest son, the 4th Duke. His opposition to the Act of Union of 1707 won him the admiration of the 14th Duke, although his stance was somewhat equivocal. In 1711 he was created Duke of Brandon to enable him, a Scottish peer, to sit in the House of Lords, and he was about to become Ambassador to France when he died needlessly in a duel with Lord Mohun in Hyde Park over a disputed inheritance.

With her elder son dead, it fell to the Duchess Anne to raise her grandson, the 5th Duke. He later commissioned the renowned Scottish architect William Adam to complete the extension of Hamilton Palace that his grandmother had begun and build the magnificent hunting lodge of Châtelherault on top of a hill overlooking the Palace.

The 6th Duke of Hamilton married the great society beauty, Elizabeth Gunning, and the 7th Duke inherited the title of Marquis of Douglas {although not the estates} by virtue of being a distant cousin of the 1st Duke of Douglas, who died childless in 1761. The Douglases were once the leading family in Scotland by virtue of the lands granted to Sir James Douglas, a staunch ally of Robert the Bruce and a sturdy champion of Scottish independence. In a turbulent history their power was such that they held the right to lead the van of the Scottish army in battle and carry the Scottish crown on state occasions, rights which now passed to the Hamiltons.

With the onset of the Industrial Revolution at the end of the eighteenth century, and the productive nature of the Lanarkshire coalfields, the Dukes of Hamilton stood to gain more than most from mining royalties. That wealth went into funding their already opulent lifestyle, including a major renovation of their various residences.

It was the 10th Duke, Alexander, married to the heiress Susan Beckford, who brought lustre to Hamilton Palace, the largest private residence in the country, by adding a splendid classical-style northern front and filling the interior with priceless treasures. Being a conceited man, he also constructed a mausoleum, complete with a massive dome, to house his remains in an Egyptian sarcophagus. It was during his stewardship that the Palace hosted a lavish reception for the wedding of his son William to Princess Marie Amelie of Baden in 1843, entertained Louis Napoleon, later Emperor of France, in 1847, and the virtuoso pianist Frédéric Chopin the following year. Later, in 1860, the 11th Duke played host to a lugubrious Empress Eugenie of France, and, in 1878, the 12th Duke entertained the Prince of Wales, the future King Edward VII, the Crown Prince Rudolf of Austria and the exiled Crown Prince Imperial of France for a weekend shoot that culminated in an exquisite ball. It was the high noon of aristocratic country house grandeur before Hamilton Palace's fortunes went sharply into reverse. While some of its decline could be attributed to eroding land values and the onset of death duties, the overriding cause was ducal profligacy. Most culpable was the 12th Duke who ran up huge debts by gambling on the horses. Despite selling off many of the family heirlooms at a great sale at Christie's in 1882 which fetched close to £400,000 {£36 million today}, he left debts of £1 million on his death in 1895. His demise without a male heir meant that the titles - but by no means all his estates - passed to Douglas Douglas-Hamilton, a distant cousin who was a great-great-great-grandson of the 4th Duke of Hamilton.

Douglas Douglas-Hamilton, born in 1862, was the only son of Captain Charles Douglas-Hamilton and Elizabeth Anne Hill, the only daughter of the Venerable Justly Hill, Archdeacon of Buckingham. Brought up with his three sisters – Helen, Flora and Isabel - at Shanklin on the Isle of Wight by their stepmother after both parents had died prematurely, he followed in the family tradition by enlisting in the Royal Navy at Dartmouth, aged thirteen, in the company of the future King George V. Three years later, in 1878, he went to sea in HMS *Pallas* under the command of Captain John 'Jacky' Fisher, later to become arguably the Royal Navy's greatest admiral since Nelson. The following March when the *Pallas* was anchored in the Dardanelles and Douglas-Hamilton and another midshipman, C.E.Munro, were reported missing, Fisher appeared concerned about Munro, not least for the promise he showed, 'but the other young devil was no loss - small as a rat, with a voice like a bosun's mate, and more oaths than one of Cromwell's troopers'. [1] The remark appears to have been made tongue in cheek because by the time the ship docked in Malta that May, Fisher, not renowned for his love of ball-games, was playing fives with Douglas-Hamilton and they went on to become lifelong friends.

One of the Navy's most daring officers, Douglas-Hamilton's strength and athleticism were such that he was known by his shipmates as the 'pocket Hercules'. An exceptional swimmer, he once dived under the *Pallas,* a second class Ironside, and came up the other side; more pertinently he thrice saved fellow shipmates from drowning, on one occasion diving into the freezing waters off Newfoundland and on another by braving the shark-infested waters of East Africa. It was thus with some regret that the Navy viewed his resignation in 1888, orchestrated by the 12th Duke, to concentrate on family affairs.

Greatly admiring of this handsome young naval officer with brilliant blue eyes who would succeed him, the Duke seems to have harboured hopes that one day he would marry his only child, Lady Mary, despite her being twenty years younger than him. Such hopes, however, were soon shattered when two years later Douglas-Hamilton was incapacitated by an obscure tropical disease sustained on his last tour of duty. Unconscious for six weeks, he was nursed with utmost dedication by his three sisters, and rallied sufficiently to live for another fifty years, but it left him partially paralysed with difficulties in movement, concentration and speech. Confined to a wheelchair for much of that time, and unable to take on business responsibilities, he rarely allowed his misfortune to weigh him down, inspiring all who knew him with his fortitude and good cheer.

Succeeding to the dukedom in 1895 was not quite the inheritance it might have been for the 12th Duke had left the bulk of his estates - his ones in Suffolk and those on the Isle of Arran - to his daughter Mary, later Duchess of Montrose, and had only bequeathed the life rent on the remaining ones. On top of that there emerged debts of £1 million and a home that was increasingly dilapidated and ultimately unsustainable given the prohibitive cost of its upkeep. Yet whatever the financial restraints, the 13th Duke, unlike his predecessor, proved a model employer with his genuine concern for the less fortunate. According to David Douglas-Hamilton, his grandson, the lack of apparent resentment against the family's opulent lifestyle is partly to be explained by them frequently attending the same church as the miners and steelworkers. This was even true of the profligate 12th Duke, a stickler for Sunday observance, a contrast with many other wealthy Scottish families who were Episcopalian, long regarded as the lairds' church and little better than popery.

The Hamiltons' support for the Reformed Church dated back to 1528 when Patrick Hamilton, cousin of the future Regent Duke of Châtelherault, became the first Scottish Protestant martyr. Thereafter the Hamiltons were members of the Protestant Church of Scotland from the Reformation of 1560, so that even the first two Dukes of Hamilton who sided with the Stuarts in the Civil Wars were fervently anti-episcopalian, while the 3rd Duke was President of the Convention at Edinburgh in 1689 which re-established Presbyterianism in Scotland. Against this background it is perhaps not surprising that the 13th Duke and, later, his wife renounced their Anglican upbringings and transferred their allegiances to the Church of Scotland, the Duke becoming an elder at Hamilton Old Parish Church in 1912.

In October 1901 the 13th Duke astonished his friends who thought him a lifelong bachelor by announcing his engagement to Nina Poore, the youngest of seven children of Major Robert Poore and his wife Juliana Benita Lowry-Corry, the daughter of a rear admiral. The Poores were an old established Wiltshire family whose collateral ancestry could be traced back to Roger le Poer, Bishop of Salisbury and Lord Chancellor under King Henry I in the twelfth century. The major was an enlightened Wiltshire landowner whose oldest son, Robert Montagu Poore, was not only a talismanic cricketer for Hampshire but also a high-ranking officer Mentioned in Dispatches three times during the Boer War. In 1898 he married Flora Douglas-Hamilton at Hamilton Palace, the marriage in time paving the way for a second union between the two families.

After inheriting Hamilton Palace in 1895, the 13th Duke lived there quietly and unostentatiously, cared for much of that time by his sister Flora while her husband was in South Africa. Weighed down by his infirmities and the trials of his inheritance, he longed to find someone to love and be loved.

Nina Poore, fourteen years his junior and a woman of striking good looks, was the belle of the county, an intrepid member of the local hunt and gracious partner on the dance floor. Yet for all her radiant warmth and allure, she was no social butterfly. A woman of independent outlook and deep compassion, the plight of the 13th Duke touched her greatly. Slowly their close friendship turned to something deeper, and in October 1901 they became engaged.

The marriage did not meet with everyone's approval, especially Douglas's sisters who felt jealous of losing their beloved brother to someone else, and this might well explain why two of them absented themselves from the wedding that December.

In contrast to great celebrations in Hamilton, the wedding itself, at Newton Tony, near Salisbury, was surprisingly small and austere, the lack of music a mark of respect for the absence of three of Nina's brothers away fighting in the Boer War. After a reception at the bride's home and a honeymoon at Wilbury House close-by, the young couple set up home in London. There, a little over a year later, on the evening of 3 February 1903, a son, Douglas, was born.

The news of an heir spread rapidly. The Provost of Hamilton and the Duke's Chamberlain were alerted by telegraph in the small hours, and the latter announced the birth to the estate workers the following morning. In celebration, church bells rang out, cannons were fired from the heights of Châtelherault overlooking Hamilton Palace, and flags were paraded all over the town. Similar scenes were played out in the neighbouring town of Motherwell and a congratulatory telegram was sent to the ducal party by the workers at Dungavel, their shooting lodge. A week later three hundred representatives of the Hamilton estates were entertained to lunch by the trustees at the Ducal Riding School where many a toast to the new Marquis of Clydesdale was drunk, along with a rendition of 'For He's a Jolly Good Fellow'.

The town of Hamilton had to wait till 7 August before catching a glimpse of the Marquis in the company of his parents. Rumours of their arrival circulated all day, and when a magnificent landau drew up outside the station at 2.30pm it caused great excitement as thousands converged on Quarry Street. At 4.45pm the ducal train arrived from Glasgow and as the party disembarked the infant Marquis, dressed in a Douglas tartan and carried by his nurse along the platform, became the main focus of attention. On reaching the landau the nurse handed him to his mother, who took him in her arms to show him off to the large crowds that lined the route to the Palace. 'The Duke, Duchess and Marquis, we are glad to be able to state, are all in excellent health,' reported the *Hamilton Herald and Lanarkshire Weekly News*, 'and we express the feeling of the community when we hope that their sojourn here may afford them as much pleasure as it will the people amongst whom they have come to reside.' Not for a long time had the relationship between the House of Hamilton and the town been so cordial, it opined. [2]

The town council unanimously adopted an address of welcome to Nina on her first visit to Hamilton since her marriage some eighteen months earlier, and she in turn reciprocated by inviting them to the Palace for the presentation of the address. The following week she and the Duke received three hundred guests at the Palace's northern entrance and gave them the opportunity to inspect the beautiful suite of rooms inside. After a while the whole company assembled for the presentation by the Town Provost, to which the Duchess replied in suitably gracious tones. A picture post card of the ducal family was released to the public by popular request, selling over three thousand on the first day.

After a couple of weeks in attendance at Hamilton Palace, the Duke left for Dungavel to shoot with Prince Alexander of Teck, the future George V's father-in-law. Nina soon followed but did not linger, deeming that the repair work being carried out there was unsuitable for her baby son. She returned to the Palace and made a private visit to Kinneil House, once the principal seat of the Hamiltons in the East of Scotland, to introduce him to the tenants there.

The decision to enlarge Dungavel, previously known as Grouse Lodge, and situated on the windswept Lanarkshire moors some fifteen miles south of Hamilton, was symptomatic of Nina's reluctance to live at the Palace. Aside from its growing decrepitude, she felt uneasy about the polluted atmosphere of the town, and being a country girl, preferred the wide open spaces of Dungavel. Major extensions had gone on throughout 1903, and for the next forty years it served as the family's main Scottish residence alongside their homes in London, Balcombe in Sussex and Wimborne in Dorset. In addition there was the annual summer holiday at Knoll House, Studland Bay, Dorset, when the family and servants would travel south by rail in their own private carriage to Swanage.

In line with the aristocratic tradition of large families, the Hamiltons had seven children; Douglas - known to the family as Douglo - followed by Jean born in 1904, Geordie in 1906, Margaret in 1907, Malcolm in 1909, David in 1912 and Mairi in 1914. Brought up in a loving secure environment that gave them every opportunity to flourish, the children forged deep bonds with each other that remained throughout their lives.

Because the Duke's infirmity limited his part in their upbringing, although his courage, kindness and love of sporting endeavour all left their mark, the main influence was his young wife. Driven by a burning Christian ethos {she read and meditated on the Bible for an hour each day} the life of this formidable lady, some six feet tall, was spent in the service of others. Aside from her family, Nina was President of the Lanarkshire branch of the Red Cross and active in children's charities, but it was her love of animals that marked her out as a public figure, especially her presidency of the Animal Defence and Anti-Vivisection Society. Seared by her childhood experience of witnessing a pig being cruelly slaughtered, she successfully pressed for more humane methods in slaughterhouses, and as a committed vegetarian she, in time, refused to wear animal furs.

Her passion for animals was passed on to her children, so much so that their various homes abounded with dogs {including strays}, horses and birds. Dr Swanberg, a Swedish doctor who practised a special form of physiotherapy, recalled that the first time he met Clydesdale he was nursing a bird with a broken wing, and when Clydesdale asked him to make it better, he felt woefully inadequate.

They were spectacularly beautiful children as the photographs showed. Clydesdale, Jean, Malcolm and Mairi were very blond. Clydesdale and Jean also inherited their father's dazzling blue eyes, but otherwise took after their mother. The other three were darker especially as they grew older. All had a mixture of both parents' looks.

The children were not only beautiful; there was a vitality and vigour about them which was very striking. Bringing them to heel was a challenging assignment for their young tutor, James Rossie Brown, as they let off steam outdoors, their continuous activity interrupted only for meals.

Possessing a great understanding of the young, Nina encouraged them to be adventurous and self-reliant and to accept misfortune with stoical resilience. She also imbued them with a strong Christian faith - one of the boys read the Bible every morning before breakfast – and to show concern for others. Although gestures of *noblesse d'oblige* did little to obviate the hardships suffered by many who lived on the Hamilton estates, something was better than nothing and there is no doubt that an annual free trip to Edinburgh or a generous Christmas bonus did make a difference. In September 1910 the whole family travelled to the mining village of Quarter where, amid great enthusiasm, the Duchess formally opened a social welfare centre she had given to the local community. The following year she donated a nursing home to Bo'ness, an industrial town on the Firth of Forth, and in 1913 she and her husband inaugurated a gathering for communal games in the gardens of Hamilton Palace. The fact that the children were often present on these occasions helped instil in them the importance of personal etiquette and social responsibility. According to *Strother's Glasgow, Lanarkshire, and Renfrewshire Xmas and New Year Annual*, a Hamilton shopkeeper had commended the Marquis for a deportment that accorded well with his rank. 'The little fellow will order his toy, receive it, pay for it, and will say, "that will be all today, thank you". Then, leaving the premises, he will lift his cap, bow, and say to the humblest assistant, "Good-day."' [3]

To help raise seven children there was 'Old Nan', Catherine Baugh, who had cared for Nina when she was young and was so loved by the children for her warmth and kindness that none of them could ever bear to distress her. There was also the children's tutor, James Rossie Brown, later a Church of Scotland minister, and T.H. Hoste, a former shipmate of the 13th Duke and evangelical missionary who now acted as the Duke's secretary. All formed particularly close attachments to Clydesdale, helping to give him an elevated concept of morality that remained with him throughout his life.

It was through Hoste's close friendship with Roger Casement when serving in Africa together during the late 1890s that the latter became associated with the Hamiltons. Casement, an Ulster Protestant turned Irish nationalist, is chiefly remembered for his failed attempt to win German support for the Irish nationalist revolt in Dublin against British rule which eventuated as the Easter Uprising of 1916, an act that led to his execution for high treason, but prior to the war he had served with distinction in the British consular service. In 1904 he won international recognition for his report uncovering atrocities against the natives in the Belgian Congo, a report that helped bring about drastic reform there. Later, in 1910, following an outcry in Britain over abuses towards the Putumayo Indians of Peru by a British-registered rubber company, Casement, now Consul-General of Brazil, was asked by the British Foreign Office to investigate. His report, submitted in March 1911 and detailing the callous treatment of the Putumayo by the rubber conglomerates, gained him a knighthood.

At precisely what point Casement became acquainted with the Hamiltons is not entirely clear but very probably after the formation of the Congo Reform Association in 1904 - they became patrons of it in 1906. Their friendship certainly blossomed after Casement returned from Peru in 1911 when he stayed with them several times. On 26 June he went to Southampton to meet two indigenous young men, Omarino and Ricudo, whose visit he had arranged in order to draw attention to the plight of the Putumayo. After introducing them to his circle in London he took Ricudo to stay with the Hamiltons for three nights at Knoll House. As Casement looked to raise funds for his Putumayo Mission Fund, he received support from the Duke, who gladly gave him £100, an amount he would have quadrupled, Nina told Casement, had he been raising a punitive expedition to force the Peruvians to behave in a civilised manner.

The Hamiltons also contacted Andrew Carnegie, the Scottish-American billionaire philanthropist, and the Duke of Norfolk to seek their help, and when Casement returned to Peru that August to continue his investigations, Nina urged him to bring all the perpetrators of exploitation to justice.

Following his retirement from the consular service in 1912, Casement turned his attention to supporting Irish independence, but although this placed him at loggerheads with the Hamiltons on this most emotive of issues, it does not appear to have blighted their friendship. The Duke continued to help him with his appeal for the Mission and Nina playfully reproached him for not staying with them in Sussex because he felt underdressed. She invited him to Knoll instead, assuring him that they only wore old clothes there.

Aside from his captivating charm, Casement appealed to Nina as a man of principle who had sacrificed much to champion the helpless. She longed for such a person to influence the boys, Hoste told him, before he went to stay at Knoll in July 1913. A book Casement had sent Clydesdale the previous year had afforded him much pleasure and when they met Clydesdale greatly warmed to him, not least the occasion when in the company of adults Casement was the only one to show any interest in him, an act of kindness he never forgot.

Whether the Hamiltons met Casement again after 1913 and what they made of his subsequent fate is unknown - Hoste contributed £100 towards his defence fund - but their friendship reveals their affinity to people of humanity regardless of their political convictions.

In 1912 Clydesdale was sent to prep school at St Aubyns, Rottingdean, an attractive village near Brighton and home both to Rudyard Kipling, the eminent poet and novelist, and Sir Edward Carson, the leader of the Ulster Unionists. Founded in 1895, St Aubyns, a school for some eighty boys, was run on traditional lines with great emphasis placed on special occasions such as Trafalgar Day and Empire Day when the school song was sung. {Another ritual involved the boys waving Union Jacks and cheering whenever Carson returned home, quite possibly the initiative of a headmaster who was an Ulsterman.} Although Bob

Boothby, later the maverick MP for East Aberdeenshire, hated his time there, the headmaster, C.E.F. Stanford, and his wife were compassionate types and under their aegis the school excelled both academically and athletically. Clydesdale's one surviving report has him bottom of the third form and, more surprisingly, with one of the worst records in the school for discipline, with disobedience and tardiness his particular shortcomings. It was not all bad though. His friend Douglas Simpson, later a Cambridge boxing blue, recalled him as a 'strong, pleasant lad with blond hair and blue eyes. He was a good citizen of the school and worked hard at his studies'. As for his boxing, Simpson rated him the most utterly courageous person he ever encountered in the ring. [4]

In light of his father's infirmity, Clydesdale was very conscious from early on as to the importance of physical fitness, and one of the reasons he took up boxing was to keep himself in proper trim. Although below average height, he was, like his father, exceptionally strong and that allied to his lithe movement and dogged perseverance made him a formidable adversary.

In July 1914 the Hamilton children had their most memorable experience to date when George V and Queen Mary visited Hamilton Palace as part of a tour around Glasgow and its environs. Greeting their Majesties at the foot of the steps, the boys, dressed in kilts, kissed the King's hand and the girls, in white, presented flowers to the Queen. After a few pleasantries the couple made their way up the steps to be met by the Duke and Duchess, who entertained them to tea. It was to be the final stately occasion in the Palace's history, for days later the country was at war with Germany, whereupon it was turned over to the Royal Navy as a convalescent home. By the time it returned to the family in 1919 its fate had been sealed.

- Although most people expected the war to be quickly over the reality was very different. Stalemate quickly developed on the Western Front and soon other alternatives were sought, the most audacious being an Anglo-French-led invasion of Turkey through the Dardanelles masterminded by Winston Churchill, the First Lord of the Admiralty. The landings on the Gallipoli peninsula on 25 April 1915 proved a failure, however, and precipitated the resignation of Admiral Lord Fisher as First Sea Lord, whereupon he headed to Dungavel in a state of near collapse. There he stayed for six weeks, going fishing with the Duke and paying court to all and sundry. Such was the importance that the Hamiltons attached to their guest that Clydesdale and Geordie returned from school to meet him. On one occasion when Fisher wished to confer with Admiral Sir John Jellicoe, Commander-in-Chief of the Grand Fleet, at Scapa Flow, Orkney, he, Nina, Clydesdale and Geordie all drove to Thurso before crossing to Orkney in a destroyer. They had lunch aboard the *Iron Duke* and learned about the mysteries of a 12.5 inch turret. 'For a boy aged nine it was a great adventure,' recalled Geordie, 'even though it was totally irregular.' [5]

It was during his stay at Dungavel that Fisher found in Nina, a friend since 1903, a haven for his wounded pride and deep anxiety over the way the war was being run. Convinced that 'the great Admiral', as she called him, had fallen victim to lesser men wary of his genius, she took umbrage against the Asquith government and prevailed upon leading figures such as Lord Rosebery, the former Prime Minister, to help restore Fisher to prominence.

With their driven, overwrought temperaments, their fund of causes and intense religious convictions, Fisher and Nina formed a bond so deep that they were rarely absent from each other for any length of time thereafter. Yet while Fisher's close attachment to Nina, for all its apparent lack of any impropriety, greatly upset his family, it had the opposite effect on hers. The Duke loved his vivid recollections of life at sea and the children, captivated by his ebullient charm, delighted in calling him 'Uncle Jacky'. He in turn enjoyed being the centre of a lively young family telling the children stories, writing biblical texts in their prayer books and insisting they accompany him to church.

While recovering his health and sanity at Dungavel, Fisher employed his formidable administrative gifts to good effect by restoring a sense of order to the chaotic Hamilton estates. The division of the 12th Duke's estate between his daughter, Lady Mary, Duchess of Montrose, and the Douglas-Hamiltons had created a clear sense of conflict among the trustees, especially since Lady Mary appeared to resent the title passing to a distant cousin. This and family tension caused by the financial mismanagement of various Trust funds by her brothers had driven Nina to distraction. When she poured out her troubles to Fisher he was appalled by her predicament and resolved to help as best he could by becoming a trustee himself. After much opposition from those trustees representing Lady Mary, he helped engineer a private Act through Parliament, the Hamilton Estate Act of 1918, which provided for the division of the 12th Duke's Trust into two separate ones. The first dealt with the Arran and Suffolk estates owned by Lady Mary; the second with the 56,500 acres bequeathed to the 13th Duke and administered by the Hamilton trustees of which Fisher himself was chairman.

In September 1916 Clydesdale followed in the path of a number of his Hamilton ancestors by entering Eton. Founded in 1440 by King Henry VI for poor scholars, Eton had evolved into the nation's foremost school, a nursery for sons of the British establishment. Because of its sheer size, great expectations and competitive edge, it could be an imposing place, but, equally, its emphasis on individual development provided fertile ground for mavericks to flourish. Aside from the seventy King's Scholars housed in College, the remaining nine hundred Etonians were lodged in houses around the town of approximately forty each with each boy allotted his own room.

It was to Clydesdale's good fortune that he had as his housemaster, the much-loved J.H.M.'Bunny' Hare, who had a genius for getting the best out of his charges. It is a measure of the loyalty he engendered that when Cyril Alington, the Head Master, asked him to make way for a younger housemaster in August 1920 Nina instigated a very public show of support among the parents imploring him to reconsider. The gesture appears to have fallen on stony ground because Hare left the house at the end of the next half {term} amidst scenes of great emotion.

Hare's benign leadership helped Clydesdale settle in smoothly, and his surviving letters from that era depict a boy generally happy with his lot. His entry into the college coincided with the bleakest period of the First World War, which helped boost recruitment to its Combined Cadet Force {CCF}. The weekly ritual of the reading out in Chapel of the names of Etonians killed on active service provided a salutary reminder of the war's pitiless legacy, but otherwise college life continued more or less unaffected, albeit in conditions more austere than normal, with sport given pride of place in most boys' priorities.

During the Michaelmas half, Clydesdale was a devotee of the Field Game, one of two codes of football at Eton. Played with a round ball it was a cross between football and rugby with a seven-man scrum known as the bully at its core and scoring that comprised 'rouges' {rather like tries} as well as goals. As one of the three corners in the bully, Clydesdale was soon distinguishing himself by his speed, fitness and capacity to score goals and was central to Hare's winning the Lower Boy Football Cup in 1917.

The following year he had the satisfaction of leading the Juniors to another triumph, this time without conceding a point all half, and was commended for being a 'very excellent captain', in addition to his skills as a dribbler. He was also a valuable member of the House team and awarded his colours. Thereafter he continued to be 'life and soul of the bully', who went very hard in the loose, but much to his disappointment Hare's was not able to repeat its success at lower level.[6]

On 11 November 1918, German resistance in the First World War finally collapsed and the armistice was marked by wild celebrations at Eton as elsewhere. Clydesdale used to recall how the boys walked down the High Street and over the bridge in to Windsor; then eight abreast and with linked arms they walked back towards Eton singing patriotic songs. As they crossed the bridge over the Thames they saw H.K.Marsden, one of the college's most notorious disciplinarians known as 'Bloody Bill', and the cry went up, 'Throw Bill in the river,' whereupon Marsden ran for his life.

Weeks later the State Dining Room at Hamilton Palace was filled to overflowing with the good and the great for an evening of amateur theatrics in aid of merchant seamen internees. In charge of the troupe,

Clydesdale, in company with his siblings, performed sketches from Charles Dickens's *Barnaby Rudge* and from a naval one called *The Nelson Touch*, in which he played 'a typically successful Lieutenant Quilliam, whose gestures and language were redolent of the sea'. [7] The evening ended with Clydesdale reciting extracts from Sir Henry Newbolt's *Admirals All,* a rendition which gave special pleasure to 'Uncle Jacky' who gave a vote of thanks to the cast.

That May Fisher and Nina visited Paris during the negotiations for the Versailles Treaty and lunched with the Prime Minister, David Lloyd George, and his secretary Frances Stevenson. While Fisher entertained the company with his humorous anecdotes Nina sat by his side and prompted him from time to time. 'She does not impress me very much,' Stevenson recorded in her diary. 'I should think she is rather a stupid woman, but evidently he thinks a lot of her.' [8] The feeling remained very much mutual as they wrestled with the future of Hamilton Palace.

Following the extravagance of the 12th Duke and the prohibitive cost of maintaining such a vast establishment, the Palace's days seemed numbered. It is true that by careful husbandry those debts had been paid off by 1908, but the remorseless increase in taxation during the First World War, especially death duties, and the rising cost of labour, had placed many a Scottish estate under strain. This in itself was problematic enough. What finally determined the Palace's fate was its increasing exposure to mining subsidence {coal was mined around it}, a fact that could not be ignored when it was returned to the trustees in 1919. Much as Clydesdale wished to preserve it, Fisher, Hoste and Nina felt they had little alternative but to sanction its demise. Accompanying his father on one final visit to the Palace, the seventeen-year-old Clydesdale was given the opportunity to keep one of the treasures before they were sold. He chose a beautiful mirror inlaid with marble which remains in the family to this day.

The decision to demolish the Palace and sell many of its priceless heirlooms shocked the vicinity and caused rifts within the Douglas-Hamilton family, unhappy already about Fisher's meddling in their affairs. It was a point Helen Acland-Hood, the Duke's sister and no admirer of Nina, put to him, but when she urged him to exercise his rights he told her that all power had been taken out of his hands and asked her to protect his interests. She tried but to no avail.

On 12 June 1919, when the Hamilton trustees presented a petition to the Court of Session in Edinburgh for authority to sell, they had before them a report from Sheriff James Fleming, who wondered whether Clydesdale's interests had been sufficiently represented. One of the judges, Lord Guthrie, declared that it was somewhat unusual for trustees representing one of the great Scottish families to sell old family portraits. Nevertheless, he and his colleagues were unanimous in their ruling that under the 12th Duke's will the trustees had sufficient power of sale which they were entitled to exercise.

At a second great sale that November to dispose of most of the Palace's remaining contents, Clydesdale firmly believed that its black marble staircase should be donated to the people of Hamilton. Instead it was purchased by the contractors, William Lillico of Edinburgh, and the town had to be content with a recreational area within the Palace Gardens. Sold to the contractors in 1921, the demolition of the Palace proved a tortuous business, taking a full eight years. Only the mausoleum, deprived of its bodies, and the hunting lodge, restored in 1987 after falling into disrepair, remain to this day.

Other land sales followed in 1922 with 20,000 acres in Stirlingshire and Linlithgow, including Kinneil House, sold to Bo'ness Town Council. When the council came to demolish it in 1936 it discovered the most extensive and best preserved wall and ceiling paintings in Scotland. Consequently, the demolition was halted, the paintings restored and Kinneil is now under the care of Historic Scotland.

At Eton during the summer half of 1919, Clydesdale's habitual destination was the river. A powerful oar, he was the leading member of his House Four and not only rowed in the Procession of Boats to mark the college's Fourth of June celebrations, but was also semi-finalist in the Junior Sculling. The following half his fortunes turned very much for the worse when he fell prone to a ruptured appendix that the school badly neglected with near fatal consequences. 'We hope to take the young

Marquis in an ambulance to Ferne,' [the family home near Shaftesbury] Fisher wrote to the poet Sir William Watson just before Christmas. 'He has been at death's door, his poor mother also very bad for the strain and mental anxiety bringing on internal haemorrhage, but don't allude to this. She is now better.' [9]

Fisher's dependence on Nina had grown ever greater since the death of his wife in July 1918, and from the proceeds of his memoirs he escorted her and Clydesdale to Monte Carlo in February 1920 to help the latter recuperate. A month at the Hotel Metropole achieved precisely that. 'I'm lying fallow here,' Fisher wrote to the publisher Sir Ernest Hodder-Williams on 26 March. 'The Duchess returning on March 28, and I stay on with the young Marquis, who is recovering his strength as the eagle, and boxes and fences with excellent masters of the art, and plays the big fiddle, and talks French. {All this is my idea of a Gentleman's Education! and I am his Guardian!} His ancestor was Ambassador to Russia, and this will fit him to be the same! And his smile {derived from his Mother} wins every heart!' [10]

As Clydesdale's health recovered, Fisher's went sharply into decline, and he was forced to return early to undergo the first of four operations for cancer. During this period Nina barely left his side, but it was all to no avail as he died on the operating table at her London home on 10 July. His coffin lay in a room there before his grand funeral in Westminster Abbey when Clydesdale, Geordie and Malcolm accompanied their mother in the funeral procession as Londoners turned out in force to pay their final respects.

Fisher's death hit Nina hard. Convinced he was greater than Nelson, she had a memorial slab erected on the wall of her local church at Berwick St John in Dorset, the inscription paying testimony to his greatness. {At its unveiling in January 1923, Clydesdale spoke of the honour and privilege of having known Fisher.} She also lobbied hard for a public memorial in London, but with Fisher remaining a highly divisive figure to many in authority her efforts proved in vain.

Clydesdale's illness had deprived him of much needed practice on the river, but in addition to being semi-finalist in the Junior Pulling he received his Lower Boat colours that summer, 1920, for being a plucky runner-up in the Junior Sculling. During his final half, the Lent one of 1921, he was selected for the Prince of Wales, the third boat, for the First of March Procession. Had he possessed better technical coordination to go with his physical strength and immense stamina he might well have progressed further.

His final half saw him excel with his boxing, winning the middleweight title for Eton in a four-school competition with Dulwich, Haileybury and St Paul's. For the first two rounds he let his opponent, Pettifer of Dulwich, make the running while he contented himself with the occasional blow, but in the third he came out of his shell with a brutal assault that culminated in a knock out with a left hook. According to the *Eton Chronicle*, 'Clydesdale's recovery in this fight was most dramatic and was very loudly applauded'. [11]

He also won further plaudits in the middleweight final of the school boxing competition in one of the most thrilling contests ever seen at Eton. In the opinion of the *Chronicle* there was little to choose between him and his opponent, D.V.Shaw-Kennedy, in physique. 'The Marquis of Clydesdale has not got such a good style as Shaw-Kennedy, and he crouches too much. For pluck and determination, however, he is well up to standard and having all the worst of the two opening rounds he bucked up towards the end of the last round and, going for Shaw-Kennedy, for all he was worth, fought him to a standstill.'[12]

Had there been another round the verdict - a win for Shaw-Kennedy - might well have been different, but in a fight that captured the imagination of the capacity crowd both victor and vanquished were cheered to the echo.

Clydesdale's sporting exploits helped compensate for his travails in the classroom. Only one of his reports survives - that for the Michaelmas half of 1918 - but it rather confirms the subsequent assessment of his contemporary Sir John Maude, later of M15, that 'He was up to normal standard, but I fancy only just - if that'. [13] Out of a maximum of 1,300 marks for the half, he managed only 465 overall with 43/150 for History, 22/170 for French and 56/130 for Science. The Classics brought little joy with 47 per cent for his Latin Translation, 28 per cent for Greek Translation and 11 per cent for Latin Prose. He did, however, show some promise in debating following his election to the House Debating Society in the summer half of 1919. The following October he made a promising debut by speaking cogently for the motion: 'That Ghosts do Exist'.

A year later he strongly opposed the motion: 'That the League of Nations wasn't worth Trying'. Affirming that warfare was wrong for the hardship and sorrow it brought, he lauded the League as an excellent idea which had so far been given little opportunity to shine. All difficulties, however, could be surmounted by the spirit of all nations combining in friendship for one another, sentiments which he continued to hold about the League for some time thereafter.

The Eton CCF was the other activity that absorbed him. Enlisting on the eve of his sixteenth birthday, he served in No 4 Company for three years, rising to the rank of Lance Corporal with qualifications in General Efficiency {'very good'} and Musketry. 'Smart but unintelligent' was the rather unflattering assessment of the CCF on his departure from school in March 1921.[14] Two years earlier he had contemplated joining the Life Guards when old enough; now he was veering towards the Air Corps, a decision that was to have momentous consequences.

As Clydesdale and his siblings grew into adulthood and attained an ever-wider circle of friends, so they opened their doors to many of the bright young things of the 1920s. In 1914 the axis of the family shifted south when they bought Ferne, a large Georgian mansion near Shaftesbury, partly so that Nina could be close to her family and partly to spare the Duke, with his fragile circulation, the harsh Scottish winters. Situated amid meadows and woodlands, Ferne became the family's main residence and a popular destination for their many friends and relations, not to mention a host of stray animals. Waited on by an army of footmen in livery, maids, gardeners, grooms and chauffeurs, guests were treated to lavish hospitality. From early morning prayers, attended by family and staff alike, to the formal dinner for adults, every day would be a ceaseless round of tennis, riding, walking the dogs and indoor games. When the children were older they would attend the formal dinners at which everyone would dress up, and Nina would announce which man would escort which girl in.

At Dungavel, where the family spent the high summer, kilts, bagpipes and reeling very much predominated, alongside walks on the moors, picnics by the loch and rock-climbing for more hardy souls.

For all its privileged lifestyle, Dungavel was not merely a playground for the rich. Clydesdale thought nothing of inviting local boxers there to spar with him and one year played host to a four-man Socialist delegation of miners and schoolmasters from Hamilton. When he and Rossie Brown picked them up on the Saturday morning he found them sullen and antagonistic to everything they stood for. An awkward lunch ensued, but a walk on the moors afterwards and a sumptuous dinner helped break the ice. A game of billiards the next morning and a hearty lunch completed the thaw, and when Clydesdale dropped them back in Hamilton afterwards the parting was most cordial, his guests exceedingly grateful for the excellent hospitality they had received.

While the Duke became increasingly detached in his own private quarters as he battled deteriorating health, Nina became fully absorbed with the Animal Defence and Anti-Vivisection Society following her meeting with its founder, Louise Lind-af-Hageby, in 1920. A self-obsessed Swedish aristocrat of intelligence and drive, Miss Lind's success in extracting large amounts of Hamilton money to finance the animal rights movement won her few friends in the family, but Nina was devoted to her. Together they travelled the country to pronounce on the iniquities of vivisection, and the virtues of spiritualism and reincarnation, fads which she increasingly practised following the death of her daughter Mairi in 1927.

With his parents preoccupied, Clydesdale now played a more active role in family affairs. Although a late developer intellectually, he made up for his lack of scholastic success with his sporting prowess and ability to relate to all types. Twice during 1918 he had donned dungarees and gone to work in the Yarrow shipyards on the River Clyde. Addressed as 'Mr Douglas', he had dutifully joined the relevant trade union, worked regular hours and earned his trade union wage like any other worker, an experience he much enjoyed. Then in August 1921 he attended the first of the Duke of York camps on Romney Marsh in Kent, an imaginative idea of Bertie, Duke of York, the future King George VI, to help break down class barriers by inviting four hundred boys from all backgrounds to a week-long summer camp. Although there was some friction at first it evolved smoothly enough to become an annual event during the wars and Clydesdale attended two more as a helper.

With his well-grounded character and cast-iron principles, he was the talisman his siblings looked up to. All of the brothers took after him in their love of flying, skiing and politics and only Geordie, a godson of George V, refrained from boxing {he was a good enough cricketer to play for Dorset}. He was the intellectual in the family whose intense inhibitions and brusque opinions made him something of a loner at Eton and he leant on his elder brother to see him through the pitfalls of adolescence. Malcolm also disliked Eton, his restless nature rebelling against its rules and regulations. The most ebullient of the four, he would enliven any gathering with his vivacious charm and flair for the bagpipes, but it was his profound love of adventure, be it mountaineering or sailing, interests which he shared with David, his more serious and level-headed younger brother, that afforded him the greatest pleasure.

Although Jean and Margaret emulated their brothers in their talent for sport, most notably tennis and riding, the latter at which they excelled, they were out of a rather different stable. Beautiful, glamorous, artistic and self-indulgent, they fully imbibed the spirit of the 1920s, dancing many a night away to the beat of the Charleston. It was a dazzling lifestyle, and one that did not always please their mother, but in time they settled down and were loyal supporters of their eldest brother as he increasingly took to the public stage.

2. THE BOXING MARQUIS

For a person rarely inspired by academia the choice of Balliol College, Oxford, as the next stage in Clydesdale's education seemed a strange one. For Balliol prided itself on being the most academic and meritocratic of colleges, the legacy of its renowned Master, Benjamin Jowett, one of the greatest teachers of the nineteenth century. It is true that a number of Etonians congregated there, but contemporaries of Clydesdale's such as the literary critic Cyril Connolly and the novelist Anthony Powell were hardly his type.

For all Balliol's intellectual aura, there is little to suggest that Oxford stirred him to academic endeavour any more than Eton had done. After four years of indolence he left without taking a degree, something he later regretted. None of his reports survive, but one incident in September 1924 tells us much. After a fallow year he reluctantly absented himself from the Oban Ball that September, one of the highlights of his year, so he could catch up lost ground with his work, a decision that found more favour with Nina than his sister Jean, who implored him to reconsider.

Although this was the Brideshead era at Oxford when undergraduates from the most privileged of backgrounds indulged in riotous living, there is little evidence to suggest that Clydesdale was part of this world. It was simply not his style. A shy, unassuming type, he preferred the company of a select few, mainly sporting bloods. During his first year he was the stroke of the Balliol VIII, but a broken thumb sustained when boxing and his commitments in that sport, limited his rowing thereafter.

Clydesdale's arrival at Oxford came at a time when boxing's profile was on the rise there. One of the most enthusiastic freshmen, he had the broad shoulders and deft balance of a natural fighter allied to his supreme fitness and courage. Defeated in the final of the middleweight trials because of a tendency to cover up, he won at light heavyweight with his superior punch. Selected for the 1922 Varsity Match at light heavyweight, he lost to his old prep school friend Douglas Simpson in what *The Times* called an unsatisfactory bout. [1] 'Lord Clydesdale {Balliol} reverted to those covering-up tactics which so nearly lost him the preliminary round of the trials here,' commented *Isis*, the Oxford University journal. 'Had he boxed as well as he did in the final round in the gymnasium, his contest with D.A.Simpson might have ended differently.' [2]

Oxford's loss to Cambridge was their fourth defeat in succession, but their prospects for future success were given a substantial boost the following October with the arrival of Eddie Eagan, one of the most charismatic sportsmen to grace the university during the inter-war era.

Born in 1898, Eagan was raised in poverty in Denver, Colorado, his father dying in a railroad accident a year later. While working on a ranch, aged fourteen, he was taught the art of boxing by one of the cowboys so that by the time he had completed school he had won a number of tournaments. After a year's service with the artillery corps in France, he entered Yale becoming the National Amateur Heavyweight Champion in 1919 and winning gold in the light-heavyweight division at the Antwerp Olympics in 1920. By the time he enrolled at Oxford as a Rhodes Scholar in October 1922, his reputation as a formidable boxer with a punch like a mule preceded him.

Out of practice at the time, Eagan was approached by Vivian Bell, the captain, and Clydesdale, attired in blue blazers and grey bags, to join the Boxing Club. Eagan needed little persuasion and soon became Clydesdale's closest friend, constant sparring partner and leading influence on his development as a boxer. Modelling himself on his hero Jack Dempsey, the World Heavyweight Champion, with whom he had previously boxed in an exhibition match in Denver, Eagan taught Clydesdale to be more aggressive. Commending the power of a weighty punch as the key to victory, he also stressed the need to keep moving around the ring, avoid taking a punch whenever possible and the power of positive thinking. Those who thought in terms of victory were more likely to achieve it.

Another important mentor was Sergeant Dick Smith, the former British Amateur Light- Heavyweight Champion, whose engagement as coach in 1922 raised the standard of boxing at Oxford. This became clear a couple of months later when Clydesdale won the university middleweight final. 'Mr Godfrey, the loser, is probably the better boxer,' opined *Isis,* 'but the hard-hitting tactics of Lord Clydesdale and his ability to take punishment brought him through the winner. He has profited exceedingly under Dick Smith's expert tuition.' [3]

For that year's Varsity Match at Oxford, Eagan recalls members of the boxing team marching into Oxford Town Hall on their way to the dressing room and receiving an effusive reception from the undergraduates. As they sat en masse in the bleachers dressed in their black gowns and mortarboards they constituted the most eccentric audience he had ever seen. 'You'll find Simpson a rather stout chap. He can hit hard,' Clydesdale advised Eagan as he checked his gloves before his fight. [4]

With the score at two bouts all in a total of seven, much was expected of Clydesdale in the welterweight, but, according to *Isis,* 'his was perhaps the most disappointing performance of the evening. In the first round he seemed content to take the measure of his man, but he lost the second, too, his opponent, C.A.Nery, evading his blows very skilfully, while scoring a number of points himself. In the third round his strength began to tell, and at one point it seemed as if he might wipe out his arrears, but Nery rallied splendidly and the referee awarded him the verdict, after the judges disagreed.' [5]

Despite Eagan's convincing victory against Simpson, his night was not yet done. He was called upon to fight at light heavyweight, becoming the first undergraduate to win in two classes on the same night as Oxford won 4-3.

After the disappointment of the Varsity Match, Clydesdale turned his attention to the Scottish Amateur Championships, a very different type of environment. For all its aristocratic patronage boxing was predominantly a working-class sport, not least on Clydesdale's home patch of Lanarkshire. With its mining background Hamilton bred stocky little men of powerful physique who shone at boxing. By the 1920s a proud tradition had been established by local trainers such as John Tully and Tommy Murphy, a professional boxer, who trained the likes of Johnny Brown, Tommy Milligan and Jim Higgins. It was the potential of Johnny Brown, Scotland's Amateur Welterweight Champion, which really sparked Clydesdale's interest in boxing in Hamilton. He publicly supported him and enlisted him as a sparring partner and coach, while becoming the best of friends.

On 23 March 1923, Clydesdale became the first Scottish Marquis to appear in a public boxing ring in Scotland when competing in its championship at welterweight. His opponent was Archie Henderson, a sturdily-built miner from Shotts who had been coached by Tom Herbison, brother of Margaret Herbison, later a well-known Labour MP, and himself a Scottish champion. Around the ring at Hengler's Circus in Glasgow there was an air of expectancy as photographers with flashing lights and cameras recorded this historic moment. {The *Daily Record* led with the fight on its front page the next day.}

Having shaken hands, Henderson went after Clydesdale and gave him a pounding, one blow to the body clearly hurting him, but Clydesdale was made of hardy stock and the pain seemed to spur him to greater things. Having sized up his man, he suddenly cut loose and electrified the huge crowd with a straight one-two to the jaw.

He continued his assault in the second round and only Henderson's great strength prevented him from wilting under the endless barrage of blows. He recovered sufficiently to give a good account of himself in the final round, but Clydesdale had the crowd fully behind him, and when he was awarded the match on points they were vociferous in their approval.

Although hailing from extremely different backgrounds, the contest generated a healthy respect between the two competitors and a firm friendship developed that lasted a lifetime, Henderson calling Clydesdale one of the finest men he ever knew. When Henderson founded the first Shotts Amateur Swimming Club shortly afterwards, Clydesdale readily agreed to become its honorary patron and happily presided at galas there, much to the thrill of the boys. He also issued frequent invitations to Henderson and his friend Jim Greenhorn to Dungavel where they would box and wrestle before relaxing over a medley of Scottish songs after dinner.

In the next round Clydesdale faced John Robertson of Leith Victoria and started in ebullient form, sending the hefty Robertson crashing to the floor with a neat short hook to the jaw at the end of the first round. Had the bell not sounded at that point Robertson, the favourite, might well have been counted out, but he recovered and using his longer reach and superior stamina to good effect thereafter he beat the tiring Clydesdale on points.

The following week, at a packed Queen's Hall in Edinburgh, the *Glasgow Herald* reported that the chief attraction was the Boxing Marquis, 'who put up a very fine show in his bout with W.B.Thomson in the light heavyweight'. [6] Accorded a rousing reception when he entered the ring, Clydesdale meted out some early punishment with upper cuts and jabs to the body, but the policeman fought back in the second round. In the opinion of the *Scotsman,* Thomson's reach and experience helped him in the third round, 'his defence easily frustrated the wild blows made by the Marquis'. [7] Defeated but by no means disgraced, Clydesdale gave away the prizes, describing boxing as the finest sport in the world.

Seized with ambition to win the Scottish Championships, Clydesdale asked Eagan, by now the British Amateur Heavyweight Champion, the first American to win the title, to assist him in his preparations for the following March. That summer the two of them went on a cruise boat to Iceland {Eagan was acting as a cruise officer}, boxing daily on board and running when on dry land. Thereafter they repaired to Dungavel where, amid all the comings and goings of the many guests, they continued to train intensively. Joined by Johnny Brown, Tommy Milligan and Jim Higgins, Clydesdale insisted that they did not pull their punches in his desire to become battle-hardened.

Returning to Oxford as captain, Clydesdale kept up his rigorous schedule, helped by his aversion to smoking and drinking, an aversion

Eagan shared. In the university's first match against Woolwich in front of an enthusiastic crowd that included a university professor, a sporting bookmaker and a well-known fish and game purveyor, he so overwhelmed his unfortunate opponent that the referee stopped the fight after half a minute.

In January, at the Hay's Wharf Boxing Club, Bermondsey, he was the toast of the local dockers as he pulverized the club captain, E.R.Lucas, with a series of right hooks to the body. At the end of six two-minute rounds, when Olympic referee Charlie Thompson raised his hand the crowd yelled their approval, despite it being their man he had beaten.

Against the Army, Clydesdale knocked out its welterweight champion, Captain A.J.Jarman, in less than a minute, but in the Varsity middleweight trials he came a poor second to J.A.Buchanan of Balliol and was forced to watch Cambridge win from the sidelines. His luck changed at the Scottish Championships where once again he was the leading attraction.

Fortunate to get a bye in the first round of the middleweight, Clydesdale, urged on by Johnny Brown, cruised to an easy victory in the second against George McKenzie, knocking him down in all three rounds. 'The Marquis is a cool boxer,' reported *Lanarkshire*, 'with a powerful right hand, and a keen sense of sportsmanship. He allows his man time to recover when groggy.' [8] After crushing F.McDermott of Hamilton in the semi-final, he now faced John Robertson, his nemesis at welterweight the previous year, for the crown. 'In these democratic times,' gushed the *Evening Times* {Glasgow}, 'when duke's son and cook's son meet on equal terms, and the former, minus the advantage of mail armour, proves his prowess, he deserves credit, and last night the young Marquis had every reason to be gratified with the result and also with the sustained applause he received.' [9]

Leading with some well-timed left jabs, Clydesdale set off at a furious pace with some telling blows to the body that brought Robertson to his knees on several occasions and pulled ahead in the first two rounds. In the third round Robertson staged a comeback, but Clydesdale held on to his lead to be returned the winner to great acclaim. As friends and well-wishers crowded into his dressing room to offer their congratulations, the critics attributed much of his success to his daily sparring sessions with Johnny Brown. 'His left hand leads were well timed and he has developed a telling body punch which all of his three opponents no doubt remember,' opined the *Evening Times*. [10] 'The Marquis has made all-round improvement since his last appearance in the championship,' commented the *Scotsman*, 'the most notable feature of his display being a good straight left and the power he put into his right-hand punches.' [11]

Weeks later in the British Amateur Championships at Alexandra Palace, Clydesdale, seconded by Dick Smith, was drawn against the Birmingham welterweight, F.Olney. In a furious display of slugging, Clydesdale rushed in with his head down, leaving himself open to a sustained counter-attack. One punch hit him hard on the jaw knocking out his front teeth, but instead of going down as most would, he shook his head and smiled. He continued to absorb the punishment in the second round, and in the third his stamina came into play when he pinned his opponent to the ropes and struck him with several straight lefts.

His late rally, spurred on by the crowd, caused the judges a real dilemma. Unable to agree on the winner, they gave the casting vote to the referee, who promptly awarded the match to Clydesdale. The decision did not meet with universal approval and upset the *Daily Record*. 'It cannot be said that he scored more points or that he showed greater skill. Least of all can it be said that his 'style' was more attractive.— The Marquis is strong, game and rugged, but cannot be described as a great boxer. He rushed repeatedly but rarely successfully.' [12]

In the semi-final against Sgt F.P.Crawley of the Army, Clydesdale was soon into his familiar stride, but his opponent was more than able to withstand his head-down rushes. Side-stepping neatly, he countered with effect and when Clydesdale went for the body he met him with straight jabs, one of which damaged his eye in the second round.

With defeat looming, Clydesdale showed all his legendary resolve by placing his opponent on the ropes and launching a vigorous assault to the head, giving him some anxious moments in the closing minute. Crawley's clear superiority in the opening two rounds won him the verdict, but Clydesdale's pluck once again enthralled the crowd as he left the ring to tumultuous applause. 'He acquitted himself extremely well,' commented the *Scotsman*, 'and though lacking in real science, was as game as any of the many competitors who stepped into the ring.' [13]

On 3 February 1924, Clydesdale had marked his coming of age with a weekend of celebrations at Ferne. Church bells rang out and the family entertained three hundred tenants to supper at which the local agent presented him with a dressing case and the oldest tenant gave him a silver salver handsomely inscribed. The next day he gained Geordie's sympathy for having to address 'thirty odd relations' at lunch. Thereafter the caravan moved on to Hamilton in April, where amidst a week of communal events that included two miners' dances, a historical pageant featuring the Hamilton children and sporting competitions, the highlight was a lunch for three hundred in the former Ducal Riding School. With a feudal touch that fascinated an American such as Eagan, Clydesdale was plied with gifts from mineral tenants, coal tenants and estate workers. On behalf of the former, Hugh Neilson was fully admiring of his willingness to take knocks as well as deliver them. That showed that the aristocracy were not as effete as some had suggested. Embarrassed by all the fuss, Clydesdale, sporting a black eye and swollen nose, raised a laugh by declaring that he had received a few gifts in the ring and those were the ones he recalled the most. He thanked everyone for their generosity before paying a heartfelt tribute to his parents. 'The greatest gift God can give anyone in the world is a good father and mother. Words cannot express what my father and mother have been to me. My poor tongue cannot tell my great love and affection for them. All I am and aspire to be I owe to my darling mother and father.' [14]

Clydesdale's 21st was the occasion for some favourable comment in the Scottish press. The *Weekly Record* praised him for his modesty and concern for others. 'The Marquis has won the hearts of the miners of Lanarkshire, and their sons and daughters as well, because he has shown himself to be an aristocrat who understands democracy.' The journal made much of a recent visit he had made to the Neilsland Colliery and his easy rapport with the miners as 'he wrought like a veritable Trojan'. [15]

The local community had cause to be grateful to him on another matter. Amidst some dissension Hamilton Town Council, at a cost of £20,000, had acquired the site of the old race-course and started restoring it on a site next to Hamilton Golf Club, which still had eleven years of its lease from the Hamilton trustees to run. With no obvious solution in sight the Town Provost travelled to Ferne to see Nina in the hope that she could help by transferring land to the golf club. She was not at home but Clydesdale was and when told the whole story he promised to do what he could. Appreciating that the problem could be solved if a more suitable site for the golf course could be found, he used his good offices with Nina and the Hamilton trustees to facilitate a move to a more attractive site at Riccarton - at a greatly reduced rate.

It was while staying at Dungavel at this time that Eagan had reason to be eternally grateful to Nina for her kindness in helping him cope with a predicament. An accidental pregnancy with a girl he did not love enough to marry had left him feeling desolate, fearful about the future. Nina continued to support him on his return to Oxford by telling him of the reality of God's redeeming love and persuading him to give his life to Christ, so much so that when he returned with Clydesdale to Dungavel that September he happily informed her about their austere routine of study, sport and Bible reading.

While Eagan had worked hard in the Trinity term for his law exams, Clydesdale had spent much of his time down at Eton advising Geordie about entry to Oxford. Thereafter he accompanied Eagan to Paris in July to watch the Olympic Games. On a visit to the headquarters of the American team near Versailles, they were entertained to lunch by the President of its Olympic Committee and Eagan was inveigled into a return to the colours. Any hopes, however, of him emulating his 1920 triumph were scotched by a stomach disorder that restricted his movement. Beaten by Arthur Clifton, his successor as British Heavyweight Champion, in the first round, his defeat killed off any idea of his turning professional.

On returning to London, Eagan met Tommy Gibbons, the renowned American boxer who had taken Jack Dempsey fifteen rounds and was now preparing for his light-heavyweight fight against Britain's Jack Bloomfield. He and Clydesdale trained with him at the London Country Club, and then at Dungavel, preparations which Gibbons considered ideal, especially since he knocked out Bloomfield at the first-ever boxing event at the new Wembley stadium. At a party Clydesdale gave afterwards for the elite of the British boxing establishment and the two competitors, he expressed his sorrow that a good patriot such as Bloomfield had lost, but sought consolation from the fact that his victor had been an American, and a fine one at that.

For his final year at Oxford, an infected eye prevented Eagan from playing an active role as captain. In his absence Cambridge started favourites, but in a night of raw emotion at a packed Oxford Town Hall, Oxford won 5-2, some consolation for Clydesdale after the disappointment of another defeat, his third in the Varsity Match. Pitted against a heavier opponent, S.F.Meikle, at light heavyweight, he found it difficult to land many punches and in his endeavours to breach his opponent's defences he left himself open to a clinically effective counter-attack.

That summer Clydesdale left Oxford without a degree and unclear about his future, but while mulling over his options at Dungavel he put his time to good use. In common with much of industrial Scotland the Hamilton of the 1920s was in many ways an unhappy place. At the Royal Commission on the Mines in 1919, the President of the Miners' Federation of Great Britain, Bob Smillie, a former Lanarkshire miner, claimed that the Duke of Hamilton received £240,000 per year in mining royalties while many who lived on his estates lived in abject poverty. 'Putting it to you as a man and not as the agent of the Duke,' he said to Timothy Warren, 'do you think it is natural or fair that the workmen risking their lives every day in producing the minerals and wealth from which the Duke of Hamilton gets his income should be living under such conditions while the person who does not do anything for that income is living in a palace?' [16]

With unemployment rife, Clydesdale was keen to help the community by establishing a licensed boxing club, strictly on amateur lines, where unemployed men could be trained by professional boxers. With

Johnny Brown fully behind the enterprise, he convened a meeting of the town's leading lights at the Estate Office in October 1925 to sound them out on his proposals. Not only would he place at the disposal of the putative committee the use of the Riding School, he also offered to have the building equipped as a first-class gym with a regulation ring of the highest standard and club changing facilities.

His plan was enthusiastically approved, and accordingly the Douglas and Clydesdale Amateur Boxing Club was formed with ex-Bailie John Graham as president and A.K.Fowlis, the Hamilton Estates' agent, as secretary. The columns of the local press were used to advertise the new club and on the first night sixty signed up to the annual subscription of 2/6 {12 ½ p}. By December a licence to permit boxing matches to be held within the Riding School had been obtained and shortly afterwards two thousand crammed into it for the club's inaugural event. The evening began with a three-bout exhibition between Clydesdale and Harry Mallin, the World Amateur Middleweight Champion, the winner of two Olympic gold medals and a man who remained undefeated in over three hundred fights, a record that has stood the test of time. This may have only been an exhibition, but the pugilism displayed by both boxers immediately brought the crowd to life. According to *Lanarkshire*, all Bob Smillie's strictures on dukes and their progeny were soon forgotten by the miners present when they saw the young Marquis giving his all. [17] Even the town councillors and other local worthies forgot their dignity and let themselves go with cries of 'Into him Dougie', or 'Good old Hamilton'. When asked to speak at the conclusion of hostilities, in which he had matched Mallin blow for blow, Clydesdale received a three-minute ovation even before he recorded his thanks. With Johnny Brown in charge of enrolment and training, the Club was soon a great success, helping to promote an unprecedented boom in amateur boxing the following year during the eight-month-long miners' strike.

During Eagan's final year at Oxford, he had been approached by an American, John Pirie, to take the latter's two sons on a world tour, all expenses paid. When he asked Clydesdale to accompany him, Clydesdale was only too happy to oblige although unable to make the African leg of the trip. After New Year in Switzerland he boarded a boat at Marseilles en route to Bombay, where he met up with the others. On board his boxing exhibitions with various soldiers made for compulsive viewing and word of his talent reached Sir Leslie Wilson, the Governor of Bombay. Invited to lunch at Government House, he and Eagan were urged by Wilson's wife to stage an exhibition for charity. They willingly consented and on 15 February 1926 the Bombay Skating Rink played host to the most eclectic audience that Eagan had ever seen as British Army officers mixed with Maharajahs in their finery along with Hindus and Muslims in loincloths. Both boxers overcame the suffocating heat to give of their best, Clydesdale demolishing Milton Kubes, the most celebrated boxer in Bombay, while Eagan easily saw off Gunner Melvin from Poona. Both pairs of gloves were auctioned off for 330 and 300 rupees respectively, helping the hospital fund to grow by 5,000 rupees, much to the delight of Lady Wilson, who told Eagan that with more visitors such as Clydesdale and himself fundraising would be an easy business.

Once again their exploits went before them so that by the time they took up residence at Government House in Bangalore they were informed that its hospital was also in need of funds. At a hastily-arranged exhibition the following week another large crowd saw Clydesdale beat Lt F.W.J.Mumsford and Eagan make light work of the Army Heavyweight Champion of India. Although the auction of their gloves raised much less than in Bombay, the Honorary Resident seemed well pleased with the overall sum, remarking at the presentation that, as in charity so in boxing, it was more blessed to give than receive.

After tiger hunting with the Maharajah of Mysore, the party travelled to Ceylon where Clydesdale gave a sparkling exhibition to defeat A.K.Marriot, its middleweight champion. Their vintage form continued in Calcutta as both he and Eagan overwhelmed opposition heavier than themselves. Up against Corporal McGuirk of the Prince of Wales's Volunteers, Clydesdale conducted a controlled offensive in the second round before going for the kill in the third. A double right to the jaw had McGuirk in a daze, spitting out blood, and although he gamely stayed the course there was only one winner.

In Delhi they were the guests of the Governor-General, Lord Reading, a boxer in his youth, and the Commander-in-Chief of the British Indian Army, Sir William Birdwood. Thereafter they visited Udaipur and travelled over the Khyber Pass into Afghanistan before heading for Kashmir to spend two weeks on a houseboat in Srinagar, the capital. Their daily workout on board so intrigued the locals that they paddled along in their gondolas to see them, but declined the opportunity to participate, so fearful were they of ruining their handsome features.

After India the party moved on through Burma and Malaya to Singapore, where they gave an interview to the local newspaper, before embarking by boat to Australia, their daily sparring on deck helping to relieve the tedium of the voyage. They arrived in Brisbane in early June and soon repaired to Sydney where they were guests of the Governor-General, Lord Stonehaven, and the Prime Minister, Stanley Bruce. They also met the Governor of New South Wales, Sir Dudley de Chair, and so impressed was he with Clydesdale that he asked him whether he would be at all interested in becoming his aide-de-camp {personal assistant} until after the Duke and Duchess of York's visit the following May.

During a brief stay in New Zealand he and Eagan hoped to box under the auspices of that country's Amateur Association, but with no suitable candidates forthcoming they staged an exhibition match between themselves. Clydesdale also won a ski race for all comers, visited Mount Cook, New Zealand's highest peak, and went down several mines to compare the conditions with those back home.

On returning to Sydney, they prepared for another boxing charity gala that filled the 20,000 Sydney Stadium to capacity. Entering to a chorus of cheers, especially from his many female admirers, Clydesdale immediately set about Tom Dunne, a well-known Sydney heavyweight, knocking him out in the first round. A second fight against R.G. Finlay, the Amateur Middleweight Champion of Australia and some years his senior, proved more formidable with Clydesdale unlucky to lose on points.

Eagan's own fight against the Australian Heavyweight Champion, Jack Brancourt, looked his most challenging yet since Brancourt, at just under seven feet high and weighing 17.6 stone, was a foot taller and five stone heavier than himself, but it proved a disappointing anti-climax. Deterred by some loose talk from Hugh D. McIntosh, the Australian theatrical and sporting entrepreneur, about Eagan knocking out Jack Dempsey in an exhibition match at Brighton the previous summer, Brancourt was unequal to the struggle. Following a pitiful display of boxing he caved in after two rounds much to the disgust of the crowd who jeered him from the ring. The event overall, however, was a considerable success and the Governor-General was greatly indebted to Clydesdale and Eagan for the amount raised for children's charities.

Their tour of Australia concluded with a trip to Canberra, its proposed new capital, and some skiing in the Australian Alps before they set sail for China via Singapore, where they stayed at the famous Raffles Hotel. It was here that they went their separate ways following a request from Clydesdale's mother that he return home to help mind the family estates. The tour had proved an enthralling experience which had helped broaden their minds. It also signalled the end of their active participation in the ring for although Eagan helped Gene Tunney, the new World Heavyweight Champion, prepare for his return match with Jack Dempsey in September 1927, neither he nor Clydesdale boxed competitively again. Despite being the victim of four broken noses and plenty of smashed teeth {although he was never knocked out}, the latter continued to follow the sport with enthusiasm, not least as President of the Scottish Amateur Boxing Association. Not only had it brought him into contact with people from a wide range of backgrounds, his winning of the Scottish Championships {middleweight} at a time when Britain was very strong at this level had also given him star billing north of the Border. Soon his cult status grew ever greater as he performed on a wider stage and in roles more akin to his noble pedigree.

3. THE FLYING MARQUIS

The Hamilton to which Clydesdale returned in November 1926 remained scarred by a year of industrial strife, most notably the General Strike that May. In these circumstances the success of the new boxing club was one bright spark on an otherwise drab landscape. Days after a dinner-dance at Dungavel to celebrate the Duke and Duchess's silver wedding anniversary, at which Nina paid an emotional tribute to her husband and eldest son, the ducal party attended a special exhibition over Hogmanay at the Boxing Club to mark its first anniversary. Illness prevented Clydesdale from actively participating and his place was taken by his brother Malcolm, who regularly helped out at the club, but in his role as Master of Ceremonies he was able to report a very encouraging first year. Men from all types of background could meet on equal terms to engage in recreational activity, something which applied equally to the boys' section that he had subsequently started.

In February Clydesdale was on his travels again, skiing in Switzerland and recuperating in the South of France from an attack of influenza. It was there that word reached him that his sister Jean intended to marry Christopher Mackintosh, an Oxford contemporary of his who happened to be a champion skier, Scottish rugby international, Olympian athlete and scratch golfer. With his parents also in France, it fell to him to arrange the wedding at Dungavel in April, something he rather resented given the amount of work involved.

The day itself passed off without a hitch as the family turned out in force with Clydesdale's youngest sister, Mairi, stealing the show as a radiantly happy bridesmaid. Weeks later this enchanting twelve-year-old in the bloom of health and full of vitality was dead, the victim of a freak accident. While playing in the garden at Ferne with her dog, she stumbled and fell against a garden seat, hurting her nose in the process. At first it seemed nothing more than a trivial mishap, but erysipelas and pneumonia set in and, without access to the proper drugs, she was dead within five days. Bizarrely, three weeks before her death, when out riding with her sister Margaret, she had a premonition that she would not live to be thirteen. She believed she was wanted elsewhere and even earmarked the spot in the garden where she was to be buried.

As the family gathered at Ferne in a state of shock, Geordie experienced the most heart-rending moment of his life as he found his mother overwhelmed by grief and 'Old Nan' bemoaning the fact that she had nothing more to live for. It was only after visiting the peaceful little figure on her bed, surrounded by beautiful white flowers, that the brothers drew some comfort from what had befallen them. 'I stood in the silence of the schoolroom with Douglo,' Geordie recorded in his diary. 'It was a beautiful peaceful feeling and one felt a joyful and happy presence there. Douglo remarked as we turned to go, "I can never now fear Death."' [1]

The next day, in glorious sunshine, Mairi's four brothers gently placed her coffin on a pony chaise drawn by Dauntless, her favourite white pony, to the consecrated ground she had chosen, surrounded by beautiful flowers. There, in a poignant burial, mourners sang her favourite hymns, including 'All things bright and beautiful', before the brothers lowered the coffin into the grave.

Remaining at Ferne with his mother to help her answer the copious letters of commiseration, Clydesdale admitted to feeling rather depressed. It was thus with some relief that he returned to London to concentrate on his flying.

Originally Clydesdale had appeared set on joining the Life Guards. Why he chose the less fashionable RAF over the Army, the traditional preserve of the aristocracy, or indeed the Navy, the service favoured by his father and his ancestors, is interesting. According to James Douglas-Hamilton, Clydesdale experienced a conversion one day during CCF activity at Eton whilst in a trench when he saw the Royal Flying Corps flying overhead and thought the idea of flying an aircraft distinctly preferable to life down below in a trench. Certainly his record there in the CCF had been respectable rather than distinguished and the RAF with its accent on technology, speed and adventure was right up his street. {His propensity for speed gained him more than his fair share of driving offences in his youth.} More important, he told his brother Malcolm that as a career it offered 'better prospects than either the Navy or Army and it is essential for Britain to have a strong fighting force at present and for many years to come'. He added that civil aviation, although still in its infancy, was likely to have a future of far-reaching importance. [2]

In April 1927 Clydesdale experienced his first long-distance flight when he travelled from London to Glasgow with Captain Hubert Broad, the chief test pilot at the de Havilland Aircraft Company, to promote flying in Scotland. Despite inclement weather which forced them to seek refuge in Dumfries overnight, the performance of the Moth light aircraft was such that Clydesdale was persuaded to buy one. Enlisting in 602 {City of Glasgow} Squadron, he began his six-week training with the de Havilland School at Stag Lane aerodrome, North London. Family commitments and adverse weather restricted his lessons to four in May, but June saw him take to the skies thirteen times and on the 22nd of that month he flew solo for the first time. After twenty-one hours flying he took his A Licence on 28 June and passed. Delighted, he hurried north to join his new squadron.

602 Squadron was founded in 1925 as a bomber squadron, the first of twenty-one civilian-manned Auxiliary Forces to support the RAF in peace and war. Based at Renfrew, six miles to the west of Glasgow, and home also to the Scottish Flying Club, the squadron attracted the imagination of enterprising young men driven by a sense of patriotic duty as well as recreational enjoyment. With the squadron's training similar in rigour to the Regular units so as to ensure the highest standards of aviation and safety, the commitment of two evenings per week and three weekends per month was no sinecure, but the *esprit de corps* generated amply compensated.

On 12 July, Clydesdale formed part of the guard of honour by the Auxiliary Air Force when George V and Queen Mary inspected the squadron's new town headquarters at Eglinton Toll. The fact that their Majesties should bestow their favours on an Auxiliary Squadron might have surprised some but not 602's junior ranks. 'It's because we have got the Marquis,' went the rumour. 'They are obviously old friends.' According to the *Glasgow Evening News*, Clydesdale's enlistment in 602 Squadron had given a stimulus to the Auxiliary Air Force.[3] He attended annual camp at RAF Leuchars, near St Andrews, which, aside from the unpopular early starts at 5.30 each morning, was most agreeable. In contrast to the normal practice of living in considerable discomfort under canvas, they stayed in substantial wooden huts and had the evenings to themselves.

It was on camp that Clydesdale first met David McIntyre, who was to become his closest friend and colleague over the next thirty years. Although McIntyre, the son of a Troon shipbuilder, hailed from a different background to himself, their mutual love of flying, their healthy respect for each other's abilities and shared values of trust and responsibility more than compensated. 'David McIntyre was extremely popular, a very good pilot and his outstanding qualities of leadership were beginning to become very marked,' Clydesdale later recalled. [4]

After broadening his experience with 601 Squadron at RAF Lympne in Kent and 605 Squadron at RAF Manston close by, Clydesdale set sail for the US. There he met up with Eddie Eagan in New York, and together they travelled to Chicago to watch Gene Tunney retain his world heavyweight title in a controversial match against Jack Dempsey. Although uncomfortable in the heat, Clydesdale enjoyed the sheer energy and enthusiasm of American life and developed a good rapport with Americans, especially those who he met from the Southern states.

He returned to a spate of invitations, the majority of which he declined, claiming prior commitments, especially his flying, although his schedule then was much less hectic than it was subsequently to become.

His rigorous training focusing on photography, cloud formation and reconnaissance continued the next year under 602 Squadron's adjutant, Flight Lieutenant 'Dan' Martyn, who berated him for not keeping his logbook up to date. Despite his uncompromising demand for high standards, Martyn's top-flight instruction rubbed off on Clydesdale because that year he gained his Wings and in turn became a highly proficient flying instructor himself.

The year 1929 brought more of the same with spins and loops, map reading, camera observance and formation. In May he interrupted his election campaign in Govan to win the Scottish Flying Club's landing competition at Moor Park; in June he made his first overseas flight to Le Bourget and in July he passed his Fighter/Controller Test and his Chief Flying Instructor Test at RAF Cranwell, before delivering the squadron's first Westland Wapiti from Yeovil.

602's morale continued to soar largely through increased contact with the Regulars. That year it won the Esher Trophy, awarded annually to the most efficient squadron of the Auxiliary Air Force, all the more remarkable, according to Dougal McIntyre, the biographer of David McIntyre, since it was the only one still kitted out in the old and cumbersome Fawn bombers prior to flying the Westland Wapiti bombers. In 1930 the squadron took on the Regulars and beat them at the annual RAF bombing camp for the Laurence Minot Trophy, a feat that left the Regulars bemused.

'How on earth did you get so much practice?' they asked.

'Easy,' replied Douglas Farquhar, 602's Commanding Officer at the outbreak of the Second World War. 'We've got our own private range over at the Duke of Hamilton's castle.' [5]

Back in 1927, after obtaining his flying licence, Clydesdale had bought the latest type of D.H.Moth for £730, becoming the first private Moth owner in Scotland with his own airstrip at Dungavel. Two years later he swapped it for a Gypsy Moth and proceeded to give as much pleasure to his passengers as he derived from it himself. According to Princess Sofka Dolgorouky, a friend of the Douglas-Hamiltons and frequent guest at Dungavel, the great delight of that summer was flying with Clydesdale. As he engaged in loops and rolls she found the sensation of being exposed to the open air and breaking up clouds by charging at them in the Moth a profoundly exhilarating one.

In 1930 Clydesdale expanded his horizons by embarking on a lengthy flying trip to Europe during which he chalked up his thousandth hour of flying. After travelling to Geneva for skiing he proceeded on to Hanover via Prague and Berlin, to stay with Prince Ernst August, the grandson of the Kaiser, at his castle Schloss Blankenburg.

In 1931 the squadron developed formation flying with three flights - each with its own aircraft, pilots and fitters. In control of C Flight, Clydesdale developed his own idiosyncratic style with the tendency to lead it down to a low level on cross-country flights in order to establish where he was or to relieve the call of nature.

His foibles were not held against him. That year he took over command of the squadron, becoming the youngest squadron leader in the country. Noted for his calm, methodical temperament, his extreme physical fitness and his sheer love of flying, he was soon to have further honours heaped upon him with his appointment as chief pilot to the Houston-Everest Expedition.

In July 1927 Clydesdale experienced a bolt out of the blue when he was approached by the Govan Conservative and Unionist Association to be its candidate at the next election. [6] The seat had been held by the Independent Labour Party {ILP} since 1918 and with a majority of over 6,000 it would prove a formidable fortress to breach, but internal ILP divisions and a Unionist victory there in the recent municipal elections gave it renewed hope, especially with the right candidate. [7] Clydesdale's aristocratic lineage and boxing prowess which had won him many admirers in Glasgow, gave him a certain cachet to offset his political indifference. 'It is true that the Govan Unionist Association have asked me to stand as their candidate at the next election,' he wrote to Rossie Brown shortly afterwards, 'but I don't think I shall for a political life with all its attractions so often lacks sincerity.' [8]

Although Clydesdale remained elusive to pin down, the Govan Unionists were determined to pursue their quarry. 'Having put those considerations before Your Lordship, may we ask whether it is now convenient to you to communicate your decision to us?' inquired Robin

MacDonald, their secretary that November. 'We need hardly add that we earnestly hope Your Lordship will honour us by coming forward to champion the Unionist cause in Govan.' [9]

Two weeks later their efforts paid off when Clydesdale, after giving the matter much consideration, accepted their offer. 'I know I shall make a damned fool of myself,' he confided to T.H.Hoste, suggesting that part of his reluctance to run was down to a lack of confidence in the public arena, especially his innate shyness and lack of political awareness. [10] {To help address the latter point he attended a political course in London the following year with his sister Margaret.} It is true that his debating at Eton and his international travels had created an interest in current affairs, while through his work in the Glasgow shipyards and his local contacts he had gleaned a few insights into working-class life. It is also true that he had given notice of his political ambitions at his twenty-first birthday celebrations, and weeks later there was talk of him becoming the Unionist candidate for Mid-Lanark, yet he rarely read books or discussed ideas and had shunned political activity at Oxford. What convictions he did have were steeped in the Tory paternalist tradition; defence of the social order; the preservation of national institutions and maintenance of the Empire; combined with a strong Presbyterian ethos of communal responsibility. These convictions placed him firmly within the centre of the Unionist Party of that era and made him a committed supporter of both Stanley Baldwin and his successor Neville Chamberlain, a position from which he rarely deviated.

The 1929 election was the first truly democratic election following the 1928 Equal Franchise Act, which by reducing the age at which women could vote from thirty to twenty-one placed them on an equal footing to men. It was one of several progressive measures passed by the Baldwin 1924-29 government in its efforts to govern in the interests of all. Yet despite the vigorous pursuit of public house-building and lowering the age of the Government-OAP pension from seventy to sixty-five, the Government's record was blighted by its failure to find any panacea to the mass unemployment of the post-war era when industries such as mining and shipbuilding were under intense pressure from foreign competition. The loss of output further exacerbated the traditional bad blood within the mining industry between the owners and men, culminating in the General Strike of 1926. Faced with this trial of industrial strength, the Government felt compelled to stand firm, but its punitive Trade Disputes Act reducing trade union contributions to the Labour Party won it few friends. With unemployment remaining stubbornly high at 1.1 million, some 10.4 per cent of the workforce, at the time of the election, the Unionists were vulnerable on this issue alone provided Labour was deemed credible.

The Govan division was a proud shipbuilding community on the Clyde which had not voted Unionist since 1910 and was the stronghold of the ILP, a radical party affiliated to the Labour Party between 1906 and 1932 with strong roots in Scotland. Yet while Neil Maclean, its MP since 1918, was part of a militant group of Glasgow MPs known as the Red Clydesiders, their colours did not command universal allegiance in a city fiercely divided along class-religious lines. Seven of its fifteen divisions had returned Unionists at the previous election, and despite the challenge of overturning an ILP majority of 6,317, Govan Unionists entered the election in good heart as hundreds of volunteers rallied to the cause.

Part of that optimism was down to a fractious dispute within the Govan ILP. Maclean was a fundamentally decent man, well regarded by his constituents, but in 1927 he had been deselected by his local party in light of a recent investigation into alleged excessive expenditure by members of the executive of the Workers' Union of which Maclean was a member. It was a rejection Maclean refused to take lying down. He claimed that the charges were permissible under the rules governing the executive and even sought a court ruling early in 1929 to overturn his expulsion from the Workers' Union. He lost, but this setback did not deter him from fighting Govan as an Independent Socialist against the ILP's official candidate, Thomas Kerr, the leader of the Socialist group on Glasgow Corporation. It was only half way through the campaign that, following mediation from James Maxton, the ILP's leader, Kerr agreed to withdraw so as not to split the left-wing vote and let Clydesdale in, although even then the ILP still refused to endorse Maclean.

At his adoption meeting, Clydesdale made clear he would be making no reference to these divisions during the campaign. He was out to fight Socialism with all the vigour he could muster but not any particular Socialist. He professed that the main difference between the parties was nationalisation. He condemned it for its waste and inefficiency, citing his experiences on the nationalised Indian and Australian railways, the former the dirtiest he had ever known. To nationalise the mines would cost £300,000, while doing the same to the banks would lead to the printing of paper money and soaring inflation of the type that had ravaged Weimar Germany in the mid-1920s.

After a hectic opening to his campaign during which he addressed large crowds, Clydesdale's courteous style of electioneering, his ready grasp of all the issues that affected the local community and, above all, his sincere desire to improve the standard of living of the workers gave rise to general satisfaction. 'The position in Govan is now a decidedly open one,' commented the *Evening Times*. 'The young sporting Marquis has captured the fancy of many electors in Govan, and his sunny personality has made him many friends. At the same time Neil Maclean is just about the best candidate for such a constituency as Govan. If he cannot hold the seat no other man in Glasgow could.'[11]

Clydesdale's engaging personality also won support from an unlikely source, Maclean admitting to having the greatest respect for his Unionist opponent. The Marquis was just the sort of young man that every mother would like to have as their son. He could offer no higher praise than that. But the fact that they would like to have him as their son did not mean they should elect him as their representative to Parliament. Well aware that the newly-enfranchised flapper vote was drifting Clydesdale's way, he advised female electors not to be carried away by a handsome face.

The cordiality remained throughout the campaign. On one occasion when both Clydesdale and Maclean arrived simultaneously at the gate of the Fairfield shipyard to speak to the workers during their lunch break, they agreed to toss and Clydesdale won.

Part of his allure was his glamorous following. According to the *Evening Times*, 'It must be a long time since the good people of Govan had the pleasure of so many aristocratic young ladies working among them as at the present time.' [12] Every morning a party of helpers from Dungavel under Margaret Douglas-Hamilton would arrive at his campaign headquarters in chauffeured-driven cars to canvass. Foremost amongst them was Sofka Dolgorouky, a beautiful, vivacious Russian princess forced into exile by the Revolution of 1917. Speaking in flaw-less English, she regaled audiences with her family's plight in Russia to warn about the perils of Socialism. Yet the experience of encountering hundreds of unemployed lining the streets in enforced idleness and visiting rancid, overcrowded tenements opened her eyes to a form of primary poverty she did not believe could exist. Later, when she came to write her memoirs, by which time she was a committed Socialist, she recalled that her experiences in Govan had convinced her that a very different system was needed to bring about a fairer distribution of wealth.

The politics of inequality inevitably surfaced during the campaign as opponents of Unionism slated it for low wages, inadequate pensions and high rents. At a crowded meeting at Broomloan Road School, later the first school of Sir Alex Ferguson, the renowned football manager, Clydesdale was asked whether he thought 32 shillings {£1.60} per week was sufficient to keep a wife and family of four. 'No,' he answered, 'but that gentleman's wages will go up immediately the de-rating scheme comes into operation.'

He also saw de-rating, the reduction of the rates on agriculture and industry, along with import tariffs as the panacea for reducing unemploy-ment. It could not be solved by social upheaval, a message which often grated with Socialists in the audience as they subjected him to rowdy interruptions, but Clydesdale won friends for the engaging way in which he dealt with them. An editorial in the *Govan Press* congratulated both candidates on living up to their wish for a clean fight. 'The Marquis was essentially a different candidate. His evident love of fair play, unfailing courtesy and lack of 'side' all made him popular. He never taunted, or twitted, or tried to score points, but reasoned matters out calmly and sincerely. These qualities won the regard and respect of Govan's hardy sons of toil and made the tussle good-humoured and fine to behold. — It was a quiet fight, but a great one, and the winner is worthy of everybody's congratulations.' [13]

On the day of the election, Clydesdale, in relaxed mood, toured all the polling stations, shaking hands with friend and foe alike. A large crowd of women and children waited outside his campaign headquarters in Govan Cross and the way the children flocked after him resembled the Pied-Piper of Hamelyn. The local pundits declared the contest wide open with Maclean marginal favourite. In the event they underestimated the solidity of the Labour vote.

With the country swinging Labour's way, a swing large enough to enable Ramsay MacDonald to form another minority government, Clydesdale did well to reduce Maclean's majority by 2,000. Sir John Gilmour, the outgoing Secretary of State for Scotland, congratulated him on 'the very good fight you made in Govan. I know your supporters were delighted'. [14] The Govan Unionists passed a resolution at their next meeting warmly commending him on his performance and urging him to be their candidate at the forthcoming election.

It was an invitation that left Clydesdale stumped for an answer. He said nothing for nearly a year until politely declining. Whether he was keeping his options open in the hope of securing a safer seat is unknown, but while nothing concrete appears to have materialised it is possible that something more alluring had been hinted at. Whatever the case, an unexpected opportunity came his way at a by-election in East Renfrewshire caused by the death of Alexander MacRobert, its respected Unionist MP who had been Solicitor General for Scotland in the Baldwin 1924-29 government.

With his aristocratic pedigree, local connections and creditable performance at Govan, it is not entirely surprising that Clydesdale should be the sole nomination of the selection committee and unanimously adopted at a large meeting of the Unionist association on 4 November.

The East Renfrewshire division, straddling both banks of the Clyde, was not only the largest in Scotland, it was also one of the most varied, its affluent Glasgow suburbs contrasting with more industrial areas such as Renfrew and Barrhead, and its rural hinterland. Since its inception in 1885, its loyalties had been mainly Unionist, but the election of a Liberal MP in 1910, and a Labour one in both 1922 and 1923, showed that with a 1,500 majority to defend it could not be taken for granted.

The by-election came at a time when the minority MacDonald government was battling with the devastating effects of the worldwide Great Depression. The scale of the challenge would have taxed any government, but for a relatively new party desperate to prove its credentials in office it fell some way short of expectation. With industrial activity stagnant, the public finances fast deteriorating and unemployment rising to unprecedented levels, disillusion soon set in, not least within the Labour Party, which was to have a significant bearing in East Renfrewshire. The ILP candidate there, Thomas Irwin, an unemployed riveter and Glasgow councillor, stood very much in the radical Clydeside tradition. His refusal to offer unconditional support to official Labour Party policy meant that its National Executive Committee {NEC} felt unable to endorse him, and despite efforts by the Scottish ILP to effect a compromise, nothing proved forthcoming, much to the consternation of James Maxton, its leader. If the Labour government preferred a Tory marquis to a left-wing Clydeside worker, he opined, he hoped that the electors of the division would not let it have that choice. His comments brought tumultuous applause from his partisan audience, but it remained a minority view as Irwin's red-blooded Socialism rattled even some Labour voters, let alone floating ones.

Divisions also afflicted the Unionists following their unexpected general election defeat in 1929. As antipathy towards Baldwin gained currency, a populist campaign for Empire Free Trade was launched by the press barons Beaverbrook and Rothermere which commanded support on the right of the Unionist Party. On 31 October 1930, the Empire Crusade won a spectacular by-election in South Paddington, but Beaverbrook's hopes of recruiting Clydesdale to his cause came to nothing. Although an advocate of closer trading links with the Empire, he questioned the practicality of such a scheme, given the unwillingness of the Dominions to countenance free access to British goods.

He was also reluctant to support taxes on food, knowing how the issue of protectionism had blighted the Unionists in both the 1906 and 1923 elections. When challenged directly on the issue he tried to evade it by saying it was a matter for negotiation between Britain and her Dominions. His stance, and professions of loyalty to Baldwin, upset the Empire Crusade enough to consider running a candidate against him, but although its threat came to nothing the ramifications resurfaced a decade later at the time of the Hess affair.

With no Liberal standing following their recent drubbings there, much attention focused on the recently-formed National Party of Scotland {NPS} and its candidate, Oliver Brown. Invariably attired in his kilt, the charismatic Brown injected much colour into the campaign with his eloquent demands for Scottish independence and social upheaval. Although warming to Clydesdale on a personal level, he was not averse to lampooning him, describing him as a mere demi semi-quaver of a Scotsman. 'To the Marquis of Douglas and Clydesdale, and all other of the candidates who represent the power of English domination in Scotland, who supported the system under which Scotland is swindled, plundered and neglected, I say what Wallace said to the friars of Edward 1, "Go back to your English masters and tell them that we have come here not to treat with them, but to fight and to set Scotland free."' [15]

In response to Brown's jibe, Clydesdale raised a laugh from his supporters by observing it was better to be a quaver than a haver. As a lifelong anti-centralist who agreed with the nationalist view that too much power was concentrated in London, he saw the case for a Scottish parliament, but only when the time was right. He rejected Brown's challenge of a debate, declaring it would serve no useful purpose, prompting Brown to accuse him of moral cowardice.

With the NPS lacking finance and a sophisticated organisation, the election was a straight fight between Unionist and ILP. With the political breeze behind him and a dynamic local association to support him, Clydesdale remained very much the favourite but took nothing for granted. He visited every corner of the constituency and sometimes spoke as much as eight times a day. The response was overwhelming with vast crowds flocking to the main centres and good ones to the rural ones. Even unseasonably early snow failed to deter them. When Clydesdale's appearance at Eaglesham was delayed because of the state of the roads, a hastily-arranged concert featuring the naval chairman of the Unionist association singing sea shanties entertained the capacity audience until his arrival at 10pm.

Although a rather diffident speaker with little original material, Clydesdale's sincerely-held views and unflustered temperament won him many friends. That is not to say he always avoided controversy as evident at one rowdy meeting at Renfrew Town Hall during the course of a lively exchange about unemployment. The trouble began when Clydesdale was asked what qualifications he possessed to represent the working class since he knew nothing about its lot in life, and what he hoped to do if elected. He responded that he would transfer the working class from the dole to wages. Amid the general tumult he was heard to say, 'If you want a fight, come up here and you will get it.' When a member of the audience expressed surprise that an educated gentleman should challenge a working man to a fight, Clydesdale insisted that it had nothing to do with the man's background. The man had been very discourteous to a lady in the hall and that alone explained his remarks, but his answer was lost in the growing pandemonium.

Opening his campaign at Cardonald, Clydesdale warned of the grave crisis confronting the country with both industry and agriculture mired in depression. He panned the Labour government for its broken promises and for presiding over record unemployment. Offering emergency tariffs as the remedy for ailing industries, he continued to beat the protectionist drum throughout the campaign and while there was little variety in his repertoire, it was a sound that resonated with a manufacturing constituency especially susceptible to the world slump. When questioned why tariff countries such as the US and Germany suffered from even higher unemployment, Clydesdale retorted that the depression had been caused in the former by speculation. Prior to that, it had enjoyed ten years of growth.

Aside from rebutting a Socialist allegation that he had once retired from a fight against a working-class opponent - he had never retired from any fight - there were other questions of a personal nature to respond to. When quizzed about mining royalties, as he repeatedly was, he refused to disclose the amount his father received, stating it was a personal matter, but won loud cheers for supporting their nationalisation- as proposed by the 1926 Samuel Commission.

'Have you ever done a hard day's work in your life?' he was asked.

'Yes, I fought seven men in one day,' he replied, to howls of indignation from a group who claimed he had insulted the workers.

His stature continued to grow throughout the three-week campaign. Seven hundred turned up to listen to Sir John Gilmour speak for him at Barrhead, a second meeting at Cardonald drew so many people that Clydesdale had to address two audiences instead of one, and when some opponents deigned to jeer him at Thornliebank they were drowned out by the cheers of the majority.

He wound up his campaign at Yoker asking whether the people of East Renfrewshire wanted an unofficial representative of a divided, discredited party with no solution to the country's problems, or one belonging to the only important party with a credible policy to help alleviate unemployment. He raised a laugh with his observation that the fight had been hard and it had been well fought. As a matter of fact he was sorry it was so nearly over because he loved a fight. He concluded with a rousing rallying call. 'The last three weeks have been mine; tomorrow is yours; Saturday and the future, I hope, will be ours.' [16]

That was certainly the hope of the media. 'The Marquis of Douglas and Clydesdale, the Unionist candidate, has addressed numerous meetings,' declared the *Renfrew Press*, 'his appearances at Renfrew, Yoker, Barrhead, etc., arousing considerable enthusiasm among Mr Baldwin's supporters of whom there must be many in East Renfrewshire.' He had stated his views directly and convincingly. [17] The *Glasgow Herald*, while slating Labour for its economic ineptitude, commended Clydesdale as 'an excellent fighting candidate, and at every meeting he plants a well-timed blow through the crumpling Labour defence'. [18]

With polling day shrouded in thick fog, Clydesdale was unable to use his aircraft to tour the constituency, but compensated by visiting many a polling station by car accompanied by a black cat mascot given to him by the daughter of the previous MP. Despite the atrocious weather, a large crowd gathered outside Paisley Town Hall the following afternoon to await the result. When Clydesdale's success was announced a huge cheer erupted, mingled with a few boos, his majority of 6,498 on a 69 per cent turnout rather better than his supporters had anticipated. Half a dozen of them hoisted him on their shoulders as many surged around him to shake his hand, singing 'For He's a Jolly Good Fellow'. According to his chairman, Clydesdale's candidacy had greatly boosted the size of the Unionist majority. When he later attended a victory celebration with his mother and brothers they sent a note to Baldwin reaffirming unbounded confidence in his leadership.

Clydesdale's arrival in the House of Commons gave rise to much fascination and curiosity. As he waited for the ceremonial parade with his two sponsors, Sir John Gilmour and Sir Frederick Thomson, he betrayed more signs of nerves than prior to a boxing match. He entered to hearty cheers from the Unionist benches and when Ramsay MacDonald offered him a quiet word of encouragement, it prompted a left-wing Glaswegian MP to shout out, 'Congratulations, Ramsay. You did your best for him.'

From the moment he was elected to Parliament, Clydesdale was committed to East Renfrewshire. At weekends he would fly back to Dungavel, spending much time in his constituency, attending many functions and lending a sympathetic ear to those in trouble. How much he cared for the former is open to doubt as later on he asked his agent to cut down on the whist drives and dinner dances, insisting that the best way he could serve his constituents was by attending Parliament itself, something he did assiduously. He rarely spoke but when he did it was with sincerity on subjects about which he cared deeply, most notably on RAF matters and hydro-electric schemes in Scotland.

On 17 March 1931, in a debate on the Air Estimates, he made his maiden speech. While expressing disappointment about the lack of increase in the number of flying boats as they helped solidify links with the Empire and promote better relations with other countries, his main reservation concerned the absence of any increase in the non-Regular units of the Air Force.

He also voiced concern about the backward state of Scottish aviation. It lagged behind not for lack of enthusiasm - the Scottish Flying Club was one of the most popular flying clubs in the country - but owing to ignorance about the potential of the aircraft. No RAF machine had ever graced an air meeting in Scotland, despite crowds of over 50,000 at Renfrew the previous year. In order to rectify this oversight could the Air Ministry not help out by sending representatives of a regimental squadron and machines to a Scottish air meeting?

The speech generated much interest and won him many a commendation, not least from the Under-Secretary of State for Air, Sir Philip Sassoon.

Following Clydesdale's election things went from bad to worse for the Labour government with unemployment rocketing to 2.5 million by December 1930. The expense of paying out unemployment benefit to so many in turn helped create a gaping hole in the public finances, all the more serious following the European banking crisis of July 1931. With money draining out of London as foreign investors lost faith in the Government, the Chancellor of the Exchequer, Philip Snowden, adhering rigidly to the axioms of free trade and financial orthodoxy, felt compelled to introduce a programme of stringent cuts. The fact that these cuts included the highly emotive one of a 10 per cent reduction in unemployment benefit proved all too traumatic for many in the Cabinet. Faced with this impasse, MacDonald resigned on 24 August only to be asked by the King to stay on to form a National Government. Although the majority of Labour rejected the deal, the Unionists and Liberals supported it, enabling MacDonald to remain as Prime Minister, and Snowden as Chancellor. In September Snowden introduced an austere budget which raised taxes and cut public expenditure, and this formed the backdrop to an October election on a 'doctor's mandate' to restore the economy to health.

With Labour divided and demoralised, the only real question was the size of the National Government's majority. These divisions were again on show in East Renfrewshire where James Strain, a Glasgow councillor, was eventually selected as a compromise ILP candidate following the rejection of James Maxton's sister, Annie. Like his predecessor, Strain invoked the rhetoric of the class war, imploring his fellow workers to vote for one of their own rather than the son of a duke who lived off the royalties of the miners, a rather stilted form of attack that failed to draw blood.

To Clydesdale the ineptitude of Labour in contrast with the National Government's steady start was to be his recurring theme throughout the campaign. He admitted that the cuts would hurt, but deemed them essential to Britain's recovery, as were the tariffs, not least on agriculture. Applied wisely to struggling industries, these tariffs would increase jobs and reduce prices. He also advocated greater trade with the Empire since it offered vast markets for British goods.

As pertinent as the message was, the messenger mattered even more, especially since Clydesdale's rapport with East Renfrewshire grew ever closer. 'He has the added strength of an attractive personality,' commented the *Scotsman,* 'he is a cool-tempered fighter, and a tolerant antagonist.' Having paid dues to his assiduous work on behalf of his constituents, it concluded. 'His popularity, always high, has steadily mounted since his first triumph, and he should be able to assure himself that his is one of the safest seats in Scotland.' [19]

Following on from the by-election, Renfrew Town Hall was once again the main location for raw political combat. The trouble began even before the meeting when a capacity crowd led to the gates being closed, much to the annoyance of late-comers and only the substantial police presence kept the situation under control. As Clydesdale expounded his remedy for national recovery, he was frequently interrupted and his remarks were drowned out in the melee.

A further meeting in the town hall during the closing days of the campaign proved to be equally disruptive, but despite the passion of many a Socialist their party was struggling against the current. Even in working-class strongholds such as Yoker and Barrhead there was a general disgruntlement over Labour's inability to bring them greater prosperity, a mood that played to Clydesdale's advantage.

In an election which saw the Labour Party decimated in Scotland, as elsewhere, and the return of 50 Unionist MPs in Scotland, their highest-ever tally of seats there, Clydesdale was returned with a greatly increased majority of 15,263, polling 27,740 votes compared to Labour's 12,263 and the NPS's 6,498. He professed himself delighted with the result and attributed it to his superb organisation as once again he received a rousing reception from his supporters.

Clydesdale returned to Parliament assured of a safe seat for as long as he remained in the Commons, since on the death of his father he would automatically succeed him in the Lords. There were those who predicted great things for him politically, but in truth that was never a realistic prospect. Aside from his reluctance to spread his wings over wide swathes of political territory, his limitations as a speaker and general lack of driving ambition meant that he was content to lurk in the shallows. In any case his attention had been drawn to more immediate matters.

4. On top of the world

In April 1933 Clydesdale, along with David McIntyre, won lasting fame by becoming the first men to fly over Mount Everest, and while the motives behind the expedition have recently been the cause of some controversy, no one has ever doubted the skill, courage and endurance of the leading participants.

The flight took place against a background of spectacular advances in aviation that saw two Englishmen, John Alcock and Arthur Whitten Brown, become the first men to fly over the Atlantic in 1919. With such feats adding greatly to Britain's prestige, it is perhaps not surprising that the conquest of Everest should so excite the imagination. Any assault of the world's highest peak, situated deep in the Himalayas at just over 29,000 feet, was a hazardous undertaking, for despite three climbing expeditions to date and the loss of thirteen men, including George Mallory and Andrew Irvine on the ill-fated 1924 expedition, scaling its summit remained as elusive as ever.

Attempts from the air had fared no better. Sir Alan Cobham, the eminent British aviator, had fallen way short in 1924 owing to a dearth of oxygen, a similar fate that befell the Americans Richard Halliburton and Meyro Stevens early in 1932. Yet as another expedition under Sir Hugh Ruttledge was preparing to climb Everest, the creation of the Pegasus supercharger engine, capable of reaching unprecedented heights in the air, opened up new possibilities.

It was this development that prompted Colonel Stewart Blacker, the grandson of Valentine Blacker, a former Surveyor-General of India, and an intrepid Indian Army officer with wartime aviation experience, to dream of making history over Everest. His idea of flying over its summit, conceived early in 1932 just when the French and Germans were contemplating something similar, drew a positive response from his friend and fellow officer P.T.Etherton, a former Consul General in Chinese Turkestan, and an explorer *par excellence* with an intimate knowledge of the Himalayas. They established a Mount Everest Flight Committee that March and by emphasising the geographical and scientific benefits of such a flight, as well as the kudos that would accrue to British aviation, they won the backing of both the Air Ministry and the Royal Geographical Society. While the former gave them access to its facilities for flight testing, the latter contacted the Secretary of State for India to advise him of its support for the expedition. The India Office and the Viceroy, Lord Willingdon, were equally helpful. Not only did they loan them RAF personnel in India, they opened negotiations with Nepal, a remote mountain kingdom that bordered Everest from the south-east, to use its airspace. Given its hostility to European exploration its consent could not be taken for granted, but in August its government responded favourably subject to certain conditions such as no practice flights over its territory.

The Committee was further bolstered by the admission of Earl Peel, a former Secretary of State for India and Blacker's father-in-law, and John Buchan, the celebrated novelist and MP for the Scottish Universities, to its ranks. An accomplished mountaineer in his youth and an avid explorer with a lifetime's fascination by Everest, Buchan fathomed that the success of such an expedition could help restore Britain's primacy in aviation in face of recent advances by the US, which had seen it become the first country to fly across both the North and South Pole. In awe of Clydesdale's prowess as an aviator and his physical fitness, Buchan sounded him out early in June 1932 about his availability for the expedition.

Aside from the aviation challenge, Clydesdale needed no second persuasion, especially since he had been contemplating taking a sabbatical in India to learn more about its troubled relationship with the mother country. He met Etherton soon afterwards and not only joined the Committee but was appointed its chief pilot. Later that year it was primarily on his recommendation that David McIntyre, an outstanding flight commander in 602 Squadron, was chosen as the second pilot. 'That the Committee elected to put their trust in two relatively unknown Auxiliary Air Force pilots rather than more experienced RAF officers is remarkable and provided the two Scots pilots with a determination to prove the Committee's choice to have been a sound one,' remarked Dougal McIntyre. [1]

Throughout the summer preparations continued apace with the appointment of lawyers, travel agents and accountants. Shell Oil Company granted free fuel; Peninsular and Oriental Steam Navigation Company offered to ship two large aircraft to Karachi and back free of charge; and Messrs Fry, the chocolate manufacturers, loaned one of their aircraft. Others obliged with free clothing, cameras and camping equipment. By September two of the three leading obstacles to the expedition - official approval for the technical planning and permission to fly across Nepal - had been overcome. There remained, though, the small matter of the finance, a problem exacerbated by the dearth of anticipated donations from firms and individuals adversely affected by the economic depression of the early 1930s. With negotiations having begun with an open air company that seemed intent on exacting the most stringent of terms, they still had one card left to play.

Lucy, Lady Houston was a true British eccentric who had travelled a long way from her humble origins as a Cockney chorus girl to become the nation's second richest woman by virtue of three well-endowed marriages, most notably to Sir Robert Houston, a ruthless shipping magnate and Conservative MP who died in 1926 leaving her £6 million.

An avid suffragette in her youth, Lady Houston won the DBE for war services during the First World War, most notably for establishing a rest home for overworked nurses, and continued to be generous towards worthy causes. Yet her philanthropy could not conceal a mercurial character with autocratic tendencies and outlandish political views, most notably in her hatred of Bolshevism and admiration of the Italian dictator, Benito Mussolini, whom she ranked the greatest statesman of his era.

In 1933 she purchased the *Saturday Review*, a patriotic weekly, and turned it into something more sinister as a mouthpiece for the far right. A withering critic of the National Government, not least for its apparent neglect of the nation's defences, she had won the gratitude of many for her gift of £100,000 that enabled Britain to win the Schneider Trophy, the blue ribbon prize in European aviation, for the third successive time in 1931. It was this largesse that Etherton recalled and he asked Clydesdale whether he could approach her about playing Mother Bountiful once again. Fund-raising was not something that came naturally to Clydesdale, but because Lady Houston was an acquaintance of his mother he realised he stood as good a chance as anyone of persuading her to give generously.

On meeting her at her home in Hampstead, he struck up an immediate rapport as one patriot to another, but while warming to his modest charm and expressing her staunch support for British aviation Lady Houston remained unconvinced about the viability of such an expedition. Until such time as she felt sufficiently reassured she would not commit herself financially.

It was shortly after this encounter that word broke in the Scottish press about the proposed Everest flight, much to Clydesdale's dismay, especially since he had yet to broach the matter with his constituents. He was tracked down to the home of the Secretary of State for Air, Lord Londonderry, where he was a guest for the weekend, and asked for a comment. He admitted his interest, but otherwise gave little away.

The news caused consternation in East Renfrewshire, not least with Clydesdale's party chairman, Provost Michie. Their concern about his safety had been compounded by his fortunate escape days earlier when poor visibility had forced him to make an emergency landing in his constituency. The resulting publicity was not lost upon Lady Houston. Accentuating her interest in the whole expedition, she summoned Clydesdale to her home in the Highlands and agreed to back it to the sum of £10,000 with a further £5,000 as a loan. According to her secretary James Wentworth-Day, what eventually swayed her was the support given to the expedition by her close friend the Master of

Sempill, a pioneer of British aviation who had recently joined the Everest Committee, and while this was undoubtedly true another reason beckoned.

With her firm belief in Britain's imperial destiny, Lady Houston had been horrified by the growing popular unrest in India, cleverly orchestrated by Mahatma Gandhi, the great resistance leader, and the National Government's 'pusillanimous' response as it contemplated granting provincial self-government. In these circumstances a renewed demonstration of British imperial power would not only enhance national morale but would also deter indigenous races from challenging the status quo.

Anxious to quell local fears about his impetuosity, Clydesdale arranged a meeting with leading figures in his constituency at Paisley Town Hall on 5 October- only then to fall victim to a serious bout of influenza sustained after a day's shooting at Lady Houston's. Compelled to miss the occasion, he deputed his secretary to read out a letter requesting temporary leave of absence from his constituency, although there was no law that made it obligatory for MPs to attend Parliament. Beginning with a word about safety, he assured them that he had no wish to subject them to the inconvenience of a by-election. Next he went on to explain the purpose behind the expedition, placing it very much in an imperial context, somewhat at variance with its previously stated objectives, presumably as a sop to Lady Houston, and figuring it would play well with his patriotic audience.

'The success of the flight will have a great psychological effect in India. It will do much to dispel the fallacy that this country is undergoing a phase of degeneration, but rather instil the truth that Britain is ready to pass through a process of regeneration. It will show India that we are still a virile and active race, and can overcome difficulties with energy and vigour, both for ourselves and for India.'

Accepting that he would be absent for several months, he tried to sweeten the pill by referring to the amount of time he devoted to his constituency duties and his lack of business interests compared to many of his parliamentary colleagues. 'I feel that this is an opportunity in which I can really be of some service to my country. It is something big, and well worth doing, and doing properly, even at the expense of having to be away for some time from East Renfrewshire and the House of Commons.' [2]

Clydesdale's overtures had their desired effect. One old soldier reminded the gathering of the Douglas reputation for gallantry, the kind of spirit that had made the British Empire. Others spoke in similar vein, and the decision to grant him leave of absence was taken unanimously.

Now that the expedition had been placed on a sound financial footing it could finalise the logistical planning. With Clydesdale in agreement with Blacker about the virtues of the Pegasus engine and its flying speed of 140mph at 35,000 feet, selecting it became a formality. Less obvious was the choice of aircraft, since few were capable of carrying the requisite load of observer, cameras and other equipment to such heights. Following a recommendation from Cyril Uwins, a pioneer test pilot of British aviation and the new holder of the world altitude record, Clydesdale visited the Westland aircraft manufacturers in Yeovil to look at their PV3, the fastest two-seater the RAF had ever tested, and the likeminded PV6, later known as the Westland Wallace. With their good climbing capacity and ability to function at high altitudes, Clydesdale liked what he saw and the Committee went ahead with an order. Both the PV3, to be christened the Houston Westland, and the Wallace would be modified with the installation of heating and oxygen equipment, rear cockpits and the Pegasus IS3 engines, while to lighten their load, all military equipment would be removed, the wheel brakes discarded and parachutes dispensed with.

The expedition so far had owed much to Blacker's drive and enterprise, but within the Air Ministry doubts persisted about his technical expertise, sentiments that Clydesdale appears to have shared. Taking his lead from the Chief of the Air Staff, Sir John Salmond, he thought that the time was now ripe for the appointment of an executive leader with complete control of the technical and logistical side. His choice lay with Air Commodore Pitcher but the vote went to Air Commodore Peregrine Fellowes, a highly decorated pilot in the First World War whose administrative efficiency was matched by an equable temperament. 'No better choice could have been made,'

Clydesdale later recalled. 'The Air Commodore was not only an able officer and a good organizer but an enthusiast in the cause of flying.' [3] A firm believer in forward planning, Fellowes was aware of all the hazards posed by high-altitude flying, especially given their decision not to take parachutes. Stringent medical and oxygen equipment tests would be critical. Having passed the former with flying colours, Clydesdale accompanied Blacker to the Royal Aircraft Establishment at Farnborough in December to test their physical capabilities in the pressure chamber.

Exposed to the atmosphere of high altitudes as air was withdrawn from the chamber, Clydesdale decided to experiment so that he could discover the consequences of a dearth of oxygen should it occur in full flight. Removing his mask at 25,000 feet, he discovered he could survive for about four minutes whereas at 35,000 feet he only had thirty-five seconds before his sight became affected and he began to lose consciousness. 'The sensation was rather that of taking gas without the unpleasantness,' Clydesdale later reflected. 'Putting on the mask I soon had my supply of oxygen flowing again and was surprised once more at the rapidity of my recovery. I took no more liberties at greater heights.' [4] He thought that the experience in the use of oxygen had proved advantageous for two reasons. First, it had taught him that losing consciousness still gave him enough time to put the aircraft into its gliding angle; second, even if a pilot lapsed into a semi-consciousness a few deep breaths from an oxygen mask could help effect recovery once the emergency supply had been turned on.

While Clydesdale conditioned himself to the curious swirling disturbances in the air over the Swiss Alps, so very different from the Grampians, and McIntyre underwent a course in aerial photography at Farnborough, Westland worked all hours to get the machines ready. A leading priority was to protect both pilot and observer from the extreme cold at high altitude by establishing a large windscreen in front of the pilot's open cockpit and constructing an entirely closed one for the observer. Every effort was also made to facilitate the taking of photographs from all angles and at frequent intervals.

On 25 January 1933, Harald Penrose, Westland's chief test pilot, flew the aircraft PV3 to 35,000 feet at 140 mph in temperatures of -60 centigrade and found the electricity and oxygen to be working perfectly. The next day Clydesdale and Blacker, both suitably attired in their high altitude suits of waterproof khaki, heated gloves, rubber-soled sheepskin boots and helmets, complete with electric wires, climbed to 30,000 feet. Everything from engines and heating to oxygen and cameras functioned perfectly, much to Clydesdale's satisfaction.

The following week it was the turn of the PV6, otherwise the Wallace, to undergo similar testing and it too emerged unscathed apart from the failure of the shaft of the petrol pump, precipitating an unscheduled landing at Hamble on the Solent, the only significant mechanical failure to either Everest aircraft throughout the whole trip.

Once the tests were complete and the Wallace was deemed to be airworthy, the two aircraft were dismantled, packed in special crates, along with tons of support equipment, and transported to Tilbury to await their journey to India on board the *SS Dalgoma*. Realising that Lady Houston's largesse would not cover the whole cost of the expedition, Etherton had aimed to recoup some of that cost by selling the film and newspaper rights to the Gaumont-British Film Corporation and *The Times* respectively. The former organised two experienced cameramen to go, Sidney Bonnett and Arthur Fisher, while the latter deputed its aeronautical correspondent, E.C.Shepherd, to provide its readers with exclusive despatches.

While the film crew travelled by boat with Etherton, the remainder flew out in three small aircraft that would be used for reconnaissance, flying practice and transport work. Leading the party in Clydesdale's Gypsy III Moth was McIntyre, the chief navigator, followed by Fellowes with his wife in the Puss Moth and Clydesdale, accompanied by Shepherd of *The Times* and Hughes, the mechanic, in the Fox Moth loaned by Fry's. Their route was the longer, more challenging one via Italy, the coast of North Africa to Cairo and across Persia, a move dictated to by their insurers who shied away from insuring small aircraft through the Balkans in winter because of the waterlogged-snowbound state of their aerodromes.

On 16 February 1933, a large crowd of family and well-wishers braved the early-morning cold at Heston aerodrome in West London to see them off. As Clydesdale said farewell to his mother she handed him a mascot in a brown package, the contents of which she refused to divulge. Then having posed for the cameras in front of their aircraft it was a relief for the party to be on their way. With a roar of engines the three pilots moved into position and with a final wave they ascended into the clear blue sky. After a chilly crossing of the Channel an excellent lunch at Le Bourget revived them before continuing on to Lyons. They made good progress the next day crossing the Alps and hoped to make it to Rome that evening, but bureaucratic delays when refuelling at Sarzana, a small military aerodrome near Pisa, forced them to stay the night at a primitive local inn. It was the beginning of an intensely frustrating week in Italy, plagued by dire weather and excessive meddling by the Fascist authorities wary of foreign aviators, legitimate or otherwise. At Naples they had their cameras impounded for photographing Mount Vesuvius and faced further extensive interrogation by the authorities at Catania, Eastern Sicily, for innocently flying over prohibited parts of the island. Delayed overnight, they were then subjected to ferocious storms the next morning and obliged to spend four days of inactivity there. Having gained special permission from Rome to refuel at Trapani military base on the western side of the island, the elements were still against them once they had made it back into the air.

Landing in driving rain at Trapani, one of the wheels of the Fox Moth sank into the saturated ground, necessitating a frantic dash by the handling party over the aerodrome while Clydesdale opened up his engine to lift the wheel out of the morass. Obliged to seek refuge in the austere surroundings of the town's one hotel which was full of seamen and dockers, they were indebted to McIntyre for the rum punch that came their way.

Their departure from Trapani in a gale proved challenging, but conditions improved markedly over the Mediterranean as the North African coast came into view. Their time in Tunis was notable for the sumptuous hospitality showered upon them by genial French officers at their Mess, and having veered east along the North African coast they enjoyed something similar from Italian officers in El Sirte. From there they faced a hazardous time negotiating cross winds in the desert before arriving at the Egyptian coastal town of Mersa Matruh just before nightfall. Revived by a good night's sleep, they flew on to Cairo the next morning.

In Cairo there was a welcome respite while the aircraft underwent an extensive service, giving the party an opportunity to see the Pyramids. A stiff tailwind took them to Amman in Transjordan, the first British-controlled aerodrome since their departure, where Clydesdale and McIntyre managed a game of squash before dinner at the Group Captain's house. With dust storms forecast the next day, the party heeded the advice of their hosts and kept close to the oil pipeline, but deteriorating visibility caused Fellowes to become separated from the others and they were not reunited until Rutbah Wells, an isolated fort in the Iraqi desert. After an uncomfortable night at the local rest house they were up early and rediscovering the pipeline they made it to Baghdad by breakfast. Here they were guests of the British Ambassador, Sir Francis Humphrys, and Clydesdale was granted an audience with King Feisal, whose brother, the Emir Deid, had been a friend of his at Oxford.

Delayed in Baghdad because of the non-arrival of their permits to fly across Persia, they were once again subjected to ferocious sandstorms and minimum visibility as they followed the railway line south. Becoming separated from Fellowes, Clydesdale and McIntyre sought refuge at Batha station. Heeding the advice of the station master they headed to Ur, some twenty miles up the line, where they spent the night in a railway rest house washing the sand out of their throats with expensive Japanese beer.

The next morning they met up with Fellowes at Shaiba, the RAF base north of Basra, and flying over the Tigris estuary they journeyed on to Bushire, a port at the northern end of the Persian Gulf. A relaxing stay there provided the prelude to the longest and most gruelling day of the whole trip during which they travelled some 850 miles in over eight hours' flying time. When they stopped at Bandar Abbas for refuelling the heat was such that the pilots climbed on the wings of the aircraft to pour in the fuel through their handkerchiefs so as to avoid dust infiltrating the fuel tanks. It was after taking off that Clydesdale was forced back down again after his handkerchief became enmeshed in the control cables near the tail. What with that, and trouble from overbearing customs officials on the look-out for illegal contraband, the party were all intent on avoiding a further stop in Persia, opting instead for Gwadar, just over the Baluchistan border.

Arriving there in the gathering gloom and on an empty stomach, they were bemused to find an aerodrome consisting of a small dilapidated hut, but at least it had a telephone which connected them to the local post office some eight miles away. An order for food and bedding was taken on trust by the official there, and some four hours later a generous proportion of both arrived on camels, complete with a cook and butler. After a sumptuous five-course meal the reinvigorated party chose to resist the lure of the rest house with its rancid odour and sleep under the stars, or in the case of the Air Commodore and his wife in their aircraft. It was a romantic setting, but Clydesdale's failure to anticipate the heavy dew meant that his jacket and trousers, exposed to the elements overnight, were saturated by the morning. While waiting for his clothes to dry, he stood on the upper wing of the Fox Moth in his pyjamas pouring tin after tin of oil into the tank.

From Gwadar it was a mere three hundred miles to Karachi and the end of the first leg of their expedition. Looking back on eighteen days of rather hazardous travel, Shepherd confessed 'that on the evidence of this flight an air journey from England to India is not to be undertaken lightly in winter by the amateur pilot'. [5].

Their arrival, accompanied by much publicity, coincided with that of the *Dalgoma*. Transporting the crates to the RAF depot some nine miles away was a painstaking business, but the RAF Officers were nothing if not the height of professionalism. Within four days they had carefully erected the aircraft and slightly modified the engines in light of the trial flights at Yeovil.

After a brief respite at the exclusive Sind Club, Clydesdale, in his Gypsy Moth, and McIntyre, in the Fox Moth, set off on a 1,500 mile reconnaissance flight across India to Lalbalu, their landing base some three hundred miles north of Calcutta. The first night was notable for the exquisite hospitality they received from the Maharajah of Jodhpur at his medieval desert fort. Then having met up with Blacker in Delhi they were briefly reunited with Etherton at Bhagalpur before his mission to Nepal to allay any fears that its government might have harboured about the Everest flight.

From Bhagalpur it was but a short distance to Lalbalu airfield, 160 miles south-east of Everest, where they found the landing strip and large hangars in good working order, and to Forbesganj, fifty miles north of Lalbalu, which they designated as an emergency landing site for the Everest flight. Their return to Karachi was marred by a serious mishap at Allahabad, where the Fox Moth was destroyed by a ferocious storm at night, consigning the three of them to an uncomfortable rail ride to Delhi. There Clydesdale and Blacker managed to hitch a lift with a local pilot the rest of the way, but McIntyre was not so fortunate having to pay 80 rupees for the dubious privilege of a seat on the Royal Indian Air Mail aircraft among the mail bags.

Back in Karachi the Westland aircraft had been assembled and were now ready for test flights at high altitude. McIntyre's performed without a hitch, but Clydesdale discovered a minor fault with the heating when cruising at 4,000 feet. He returned to base to have it fixed, and by early afternoon he and Blacker were back in the air, climbing to 35,000 feet. With the two aircraft passing their fuel test the next day, it was time now for the whole expedition to move on to Purnea.

While the film crew and mechanics travelled there by train, and Dick Ellison, the reserve pilot, flew the aircraft lent to the expedition by the Karachi Flying Club, Clydesdale and McIntyre followed in the two Westland aircraft. Once again they were entertained in style at Jodhpur and in Delhi they were able to thank the Viceroy, Lord Willingdon, for all his support. By the time they landed at Lalbalu, nine miles from Purnea, they were the talk of the locality as thousands, alerted by Ellison's earlier arrival, converged on the village to witness the sight of an aircraft for the first time. It needed the full force of the local police to hold back the surging masses while Clydesdale and McIntyre landed, and thereafter they were never able to shake off the great Indian obsession with their venture.

Purnea was a remote town of some 20,000 inhabitants situated in the Bihar province of North-East India some fifty miles from the Nepalese border, and surrounded by jute and sugar cane plantations. It was there that the main party settled into a bungalow equipped with cool, comfortable rooms and a spacious veranda overlooking an enclosed garden, the gift of the Maharajah of Darbhanga. The Raja of Banaili loaned them a fleet of cars to ferry them to and from Lalbalu, where the rest of the party were stationed close to three canvas hangars for the aircraft.

From the outset the official expedition and ground crew followed a strict daily routine. Up at 5.15 each morning, they received a daily weather bulletin from S.N Gupta, the Indian meteorologist, complete with his theodolite and balloon equipment to trace wind speeds at high altitude, and, if conditions allowed, a reconnaissance flight report on the cloud formation from Fellowes.

After breakfast the morning would be given over to working on the aircraft, while Clydesdale and McIntyre analysed weather reports and discussed navigational routes. The afternoon permitted time for tennis or swimming in the crocodile-infested pool when they were not performing shots for the cameras of Gaumont. At 6pm they would receive an up-to-date weather report from Gupta, the prelude to further deliberations before dinner at the Planters' Club.

Despite the mood of collective endeavour and dedicated professionalism which permeated the party, their morale was inevitably undermined by the deterioration in the weather. Ten days of constant rising winds interspersed with several tropical downpours wreaking havoc in the hangars {although no damage was done to the aircraft} reduced them to relative inactivity.

By 31 March the winds began to abate, but Fellowes and Clydesdale observed clouds gathering on Everest on reconnaissance flights to the

Nepalese border. It was the same story on the morning of 2 April when the promise of better conditions brought many locals to Lalbalu in a state of high excitement. With the cloud still too thick, plans were aborted for that day, but that evening Gupta was able to report something better for the next day with the winds dropping to a velocity of 57 mph at 33,000 feet and the sky almost clear. The crew took heart from his forecast and in conference after dinner they resolved to make history in the morning, subject to final checks. It was while rummaging through his belongings that Clydesdale came across his mother's parting gift. Opening the mysterious package he found it to be a blue enamel depicting St Christopher, the patron saint of all travellers in dangerous places, battling his way through floods. He placed it in his flying suit.

The next morning the pilots went at once to the observatory where Gupta, having lost one balloon in the dust haze, was working on a second one. They left him and travelled in some anxiety to Lalbalu, the bumpy roads doing the cameras no favours. There the mechanics were hard at work moving the aircraft on to the landing strip to carry out the final checks. As the bottles of oxygen were carefully placed in the storage, the pilots and observers, Blacker travelling with Clydesdale and Bonnett with McIntyre, climbed into their flying suits. Never comfortable at the best of times they had to proceed carefully in order to avoid perspiring which would have added to their cold and discomfort at high altitude.

It was while they were loading the survey cameras that Gupta arrived with news of a wind speed of 67 mph at 28,000 feet and 58 mph at 30,000 feet. Official estimates had revealed that a wind velocity of over 40 mph would deem an Everest flight unsafe as the aircraft would drift sideways off course and consume much fuel, but this was the first time that the wind velocity had fallen below 100 mph. Some quick calculations by the pilots informed them that a wind speed of 67 mph would give the aircraft fifteen minutes over the summit of Everest without running out of fuel.

Gupta's latest bulletin coincided with Fellowes' return from a reconnaissance flight up to the Nepalese border in the Puss Moth. He reported that while the higher mountains were obscured in haze there were no clouds visible at 17,000 feet and the wind strength was reasonable. Well aware that they might not stand a better chance, he ordered the engines to be started up. With the waiting almost over, the pilots and observers pulled on their boots {heated to the knees} and donned their cumbersome head gear; the leather helmet with many leads and connections, electrically heated goggles and oxygen mask. Then lowering themselves into their aircraft and receiving a final few words from Fellowes, they opened up the throttles and taxied off at 8.25am amid heartfelt cheers from the ground crew.

On a still morning they climbed slowly over the arid plains in order to save the engines as much as possible until such time as they had tested all the essentials. At a height of 10,000 feet, as they passed over Forbesganj in a great dust haze, Clydesdale and McIntyre signalled to each other that everything was in good working order. {The one exception was Clydesdale and Blacker's phone, forcing them to communicate by paper.} Thereafter they crossed the Nepalese border and jungle gave way to the foothills of the Himalayas. When they emerged from the haze at 19,000 feet, an awe-inspiring vista of 'startling white beauty' opened up before them as the snow-capped peaks of Everest, Kanchenjunga and Makalu glistened in the clear blue sky. According to Blacker, not only was the light on the snow a wonderful thing in itself, the sheer size of the mountains stunned the senses and the clear air upset estimations of size and distance.

At 30,000 feet, both Clydesdale and Blacker were laid low by a dearth of oxygen, the former suffering from blurred eyesight and chronic cramp. He immediately turned on both the main and reserve supplies of oxygen to the full and began to breathe deeply. It was now that his extensive training prior to the expedition came to his aid since his physical defects soon disappeared. He turned off the reserve oxygen but kept his main supply on.

At 9am they passed over Chamlang at the southern end of the Everest range at 31,000 feet, but it was at a height somewhat lower than intended. Owing to the haze and poor visibility, Clydesdale had flown at a lower altitude than planned in his doomed attempt to locate the village of Komaltar, the start of the survey for the vertical photography. Now in a strong westerly and blown off course well to the leeward side of the mountain, both aircraft confronted a violent downdraught much fiercer than anything they had anticipated as fragments of ice showered the cockpit. Despite their 120 miles of speed they scarcely made headway and within a few seconds the Westland PV3 lost 2,000 feet in what Clydesdale later described as the most unpleasant experience of his life. Neither able to veer left since it would expose them once again to the downdraught on to the peaks below nor right since they would crash into Makalu, Everest's deadly neighbour twelve miles to the south-east, Clydesdale's only option was to climb straight ahead and cross the lowest point of the adjoining range between these two great peaks. Despite his engine throttle wide open and at maximum climbing angle as they crabbed sideways towards the ridge, he was unable to determine if they were level with it or below. Eventually they skimmed over Lhotse, the southern peak of Everest, by 'a smaller margin than I cared then or later to think about—'.[6] With great skill Clydesdale fought his way through the Everest plume of ice particles and felt an upward momentum on the windward side of the mountain which he compared with being swept up into heaven. Gaining height quickly, he and Blacker surged over the summit of Everest at 10.05am, clearing it by some 500 feet, lower than they had intended but quite sufficient. Looking down, Clydesdale hoped he might catch a glimpse of the human remains of Mallory and Irvine last seen attempting the final 2,000 feet to the summit in 1924, but nothing was forthcoming.

Turning into the wind on the western side of Everest to enable Blacker to photograph its unknown secrets, Clydesdale decided that the risk of flying relatively low was too great given the likelihood of a downdraught. It was while flying over the summit for the second time that he espied McIntyre as the two aircraft passed each other on the north-eastern side. With Blacker's oxygen flow-meter moving downwards, indicating that their time on Everest was running out, Clydesdale turned right over the Rongbuk Glacier and moved slowly down the valley between Everest and Makalu en route for home. Their fifteen minutes circling the summit had seemed to Blacker a lifetime of 'amazing experiences', not least the vastness of the ice precipices, and yet all too short.

For McIntyre, on Clydesdale's right and carrying a heavier load in a less powerful aircraft, the ordeal had been even greater as he lost 3,000 feet in the downdraught. Blown towards Makalu and hemmed in by gigantic fortresses on all sides, he realised that their only option was to climb straight ahead and hope to clear the lowest point in the range. A fortunate up-current of air came to their aid at the right time, enabling them to cross their first hurdle. Everest, however, still towered above them and three times he had to circle, risking a turn towards the downdraught before he had sufficient height to circle round the north side of the mountain and over the top.

It was while crouching in the cockpit in order to have a full camera for the summit that Bonnett had trodden on his oxygen supply pipe and broken it. Maintaining his composure he managed to repair the leak with his handkerchief, but on attempting to stand up again he lapsed into unconsciousness. As McIntyre swivelled to look at him he suddenly experienced great cold as his oxygen mask fell off and lay on his knee. With great alacrity he managed to wrench it back, but was forced to hold it there with one hand while operating the controls with the other. Not knowing whether Bonnett was alive or not, he lost height as safely as possible until at 8,000 feet he observed him struggle up from the floor and tear off his mask.

The return journey passed surprisingly quickly. Flying over the plains in the mid-morning heat, the pilots sweltered in their suits. At 11.25am, after three hours in the air, the two of them taxied down in perfect formation, Clydesdale first, McIntyre second. Crawling out of their cockpits they cheerfully announced their triumph, then turning over their machines to the mechanics they stripped off and headed for the pool. A post-flight medical revealed Bonnett to be shaking, Blacker tired and McIntyre suffering from slight frostbite, but Clydesdale appeared both fit and happy. Shrugging off their narrow escape, he referred to their sense of awesome wonder that they had been where no man had been before. ' Days must pass before we can appreciate what we have seen in those few sublime crowded minutes looking down on the world's last penetralia,' commented Blacker in his report. 'Overriding the winds, man's art has torn the veil from another of Nature's secrets. The uttermost peak is no longer inviolate.' [7]

The conquest of Everest, 'nature's final frontier', caught the imagination of the world gasping for good news in the middle of a depression. Congratulations poured in from the King, the Prime Minister Ramsay MacDonald and Lady Houston, and when Clydesdale's mother opened the Wide World Missionary Exhibition in Glasgow the next day, she was cheered ecstatically by a large crowd.

The Times devoted vast coverage to Shepherd's copy, one of the longest ever published by the paper, and was unstinting in admiration in its editorial. 'When every tribute has been paid to the wise care lavished upon organisation, the last and warmest praise of all must be for the pilots, LORD CLYDESDALE and FLIGHT LIEUTENANT MCINTYRE, whose cool and skilful control of all the complexities of high altitude flying yesterday converted a well-studied hypothesis into a glorious fact.' [8]

The *Daily Telegraph* was similarly effusive, commenting that to fly over the top of a mountain 29,000 feet high in the midst of a vast range of lesser peaks 'required courage no less than technical airmanship'. [9] {Ironically, on the same day of the Everest triumph the largest airship in the world, the Akron, crashed into the sea in the US, killing seventy-three, showing the dangers of aviation in its infancy.} As to its significance, *The Times of India* called it 'as important a landmark as any in the short history of aviation', while the *Central European Times* placed its daring and technical skill on a par with the American Charles Lindbergh's crossing of the Atlantic in 1927, the first man to do this solo and non-stop, especially in overcoming the treacherous down-currents and lack of oxygen. [10/11] Aside from enhancing the prestige of British aviation, Clydesdale and McIntyre had proved there was no part of the world over which aircraft could not fly. Only Hamilton Fyfe, the veteran radical journalist, in *Reynold's Illustrated News*, dissented from the general euphoria. Under the headline 'These Useless Stunts', he questioned the value of such an expedition and wondered why a man elected to Parliament to help manage the nation's affairs should be allowed to go off for several months on a joyride.

Amid the celebrations, doubts persisted as to whether the vertical survey cameras had functioned properly throughout the flight, and a visit by McIntyre to the India Air Survey Company in Calcutta the next day duly confirmed the worst. Owing to the intensity of the dust haze, very little appeared on the survey films and what little there was proved of scant value. It was partially to test the vertical cameras before the possibility of another Everest flight that Fellowes decided that he and Ellison, accompanied by Fisher, the Gaumont photographer, and Bonnett as observers, would fly over Kanchenjunga, the world's third highest peak, the next day. It was an assignment fraught with risk since neither pilot had flown their aircraft before nor had they experienced flying suits and oxygen equipment.

Exposed to thick cloud and severe turbulence, the two became separated after nearly colliding over the mountain. Fellowes in the Westland gave up any hope of reaching the summit, but troubled by his badly-fitted oxygen mask, his memory became suspect and he lost his bearings on descent. Touching down at Shampur, sixty miles to the east of Purnea, he headed off in a westerly direction only to discover that he was running short of petrol. Forced to seek refuge at Dinajpur, they received a rousing welcome from a town fascinated by the novelty of an aircraft.

Fellowes' disappearance, conveyed to the others by Ellison on his return, was the cause of much anxiety {although his wife remained composed} until he cabled to announce his location. Later that afternoon, Clydesdale flew over to Dinajpur in the Puss Moth with pickets and covers, his landing even more fraught than that endured by Fellowes as thousands congregated at the landing site. Entertained that night by the local Methodist Mission, they returned to Purnea the next morning after Ellison had flown over with more fuel.

The bad weather that confined the pilots to base gave Geoffrey Barkas, the director of the flight documentary, ample opportunity to film. Determined to get his pound of flesh, he proved a hard taskmaster, demanding a plethora of shots of the pilots climbing in and out of the aircraft in their suits, as well as taking off and landing. He also wanted Clydesdale to release a smoke bomb from his machine on conquering Everest, something Clydesdale had dismissed as 'an objectionable piece of theatricality' that detracted from his other duties.

His lukewarm attitude to the filming was not appreciated by Barkas and caused some dissension with his colleagues, who sensitive to the hefty fee Gaumont had paid for the film rights, felt they should try to accommodate them. Consequently, Clydesdale acceded to Barkas's idea of his trailing a smoke bomb at 3 to 4,000 feet, an image that inadvertently upset local sensitivities.

To a deeply religious people who revered the sacred nature of their mountains, the failure of past expeditions to climb Everest had been attributed to the gods wreaking vengeance upon them. Now that they saw the white man emerge unscathed from its summit, they were awe-struck by his temerity with some even falling to their knees in adulation as they flew overhead. It was the same when Clydesdale had dropped a message of greetings over an orphanage situated in the hill station of Kalimpong, run by Dr John Graham, the ex-Moderator to the General Assembly of the Church of Scotland. Such was the sensation caused that some even considered him a god. Yet alongside this sense of admiration went an inbuilt suspicion of foreigners so that when rumours circulated they were engaged in bombing practice to help the warring factions in China, the prevailing mood quickly turned hostile. It needed an aerial display by the pilots at the Raja of Banaili's Easter race meeting and a football match between an Everest Expedition XI and an Indian XI - Clydesdale scoring his team's only goal in a 3-1 defeat - to help restore goodwill.

The misadventure over Dinajpur was a cause of some alarm back home. The insurers regarded it as a second flight over Everest and decreed that any further attempt would cost an additional £600. Their attitude unnerved Lady Houston who convinced herself that she would be responsible for many lives and dependants now that they were uninsured. Always apprehensive {and with good reason} about the risks of such a venture, she conveyed her fears to Clydesdale by telegram. 'The good spirit of the mountain has been kind to you and brought you success. Be content. Do not tempt the evil spirits of the mountain to bring disaster. Intuition tells me to warn you that there is danger if you linger.' [12]

Once Nepal accepted a second flight against her wishes, Lady Houston's tone became ever more hectoring as the London Committee set its face against a second flight. At first Fellowes and his colleagues were inclined to ignore its instructions, believing they had full power to act independently on the spot, but confronted with a barrage of telegrams, Fellowes eventually succumbed. Reluctantly he gave the order to pack up and return home.

It was at this stage that fate intervened as the Air Commodore was confined to bed for several days with a serious bout of influenza. While he was laid up his troops began to mutiny. Not only did they feel honour-bound to provide the Royal Geographical Society, the Nepalese government and the India Office with the scientific surveys they had promised them, they also felt that to give up now would discredit them. There could be no moral justification for abandoning the expedition on grounds of personal risk. Aware that their defiance could be construed as insubordination, they calculated that a safe return home would protect them from an official backlash. They were supported by Barkas, who clamoured for more film footage of the mountains, and Shepherd, sensing a good story provided it remained a *Times* exclusive. Pleading the case for more scenic photography, they managed to win Fellowes' consent for one final high-altitude flight provided they kept in gliding distance of the plains.

To add to their woes the weather had remained unsuitable for high-altitude flying and they had been deprived of the services of Gupta after an accident with one of the hydrogen balloons. On 18 April, with the monsoon season fast approaching and Fellowes showing signs of recovery, the conspirators - Fisher had replaced Bonnett as McIntyre's observer - decided that only one day remained. In desperation they had the machines loaded up in great secrecy and hinted to the doctor that evening to keep Fellowes in bed for another day.

The next morning at first light they crept out of the bungalow while Fellowes was still asleep, feeling rather ashamed. With wind speeds of 80 mph predicted and ominous clouds rolling in from the west, a forecast confirmed by Ellison's scouting survey, they resolved to follow McIntyre's ingenious plan of approaching Everest this time from the west downwind to preserve fuel and oxygen at a time when the latter was running short.

Having installed the cameras with great precision so as to avoid a repetition of their previous failure, they set off at 7.50am heading in a north-westerly direction, the first fifty miles at 2,000 feet. The cloud proved much deeper than expected, but when they emerged from it at 18,000 feet they were rewarded with the finest views of the trip as a range of majestic peaks extending for several hundred miles came into view. 'Cloud and mountain cast back the glare of the sun towards the sky,' Clydesdale later recounted, 'and we found ourselves in a world not only of brilliant reflections and high lights but of marvellously clear visibility.' [13]

Climbing more rapidly, they changed course to fly direct towards Everest and then at 21,000 feet Clydesdale turned on the oxygen. It was shortly afterwards that he suddenly noticed that the electric plug of his oxygen heater had fallen out of its socket and begun to vibrate. Unable to fix it, he telephoned Blacker to ask for his screwdriver. This did the trick, but in the meantime a mighty downdraught, twice as powerful as anything experienced on the first flight, had swept him off course. He flew to within three and a half miles of the summit of Everest, but well aware of the dangers awaiting them he chose not to call on undue reserves of good fortune. Veering east towards Makalu, he gave Blacker every opportunity to photograph the ranges and ridges running south-west towards it from Everest; then having flown over Makalu he returned via Chamlang and Forbesganj, landing at 11.25am.

Fifteen miles behind Clydesdale, McIntyre remained in formation till 32,000 feet, at which point Clydesdale branched east. Unsure what to do, McIntyre chose to stay on course towards the summit of Everest, enabling Fisher to capture some classic photographs, the finest mountain scenery this experienced cameraman had ever recorded. It proved to be a tense fifteen minutes as they battled through the currents, but thanks to the strength of the aircraft and the power of the Pegasus engine, they continued on upwards, a ferocious bump signalling they had crossed the summit. Casting an anxious glance round to check there was no structural damage, McIntyre turned to the right in a homeward direction, but confronted by thick cloud and featureless landscape he was not entirely sure of his bearings. With his fuel running short this posed obvious problems, until emerging from the cloud he recognised Darara, a small hamlet he had flown over a few days before. Arriving back fifteen minutes later than Clydesdale and with his fuel tank nearly empty, he found his fellow pilot in the company of a worried-looking Fellowes.

On reaching the aerodrome ninety minutes after they had left, the Air Commodore was clearly surprised to find they were not back. After a nerve-wracking half hour he started making some inquiries and on discovering that all the cameras and oxygen were missing, he soon learned the real purpose behind their trip. Naturally aggrieved by this flouting of his authority, any resentment he felt was almost outweighed by the sense of relief to see everyone back unscathed. When Clydesdale sought to make amends by indicating their willingness to forego publicity, Fellowes would not hear of it. The most to which he agreed was a postponement of his report until the next day by which time the result of the aerial survey would be known. With so much riding on the survey it proved to be a tense afternoon as Blacker and Aircraftsman Fraser worked in the darkroom developing the films. The results were everything they could have hoped for with excellent survey photographs of the south face of Everest that helped Sir Edmund Hillary and Sherpa Tenzing Norgay become the first men to reach its summit in 1953.

The relief was palpable. 'For the first time since landing with the whole caravan at Purnea,' McIntyre later wrote, 'the weight of anxiety was lifted and we could take the modest pleasures which the place offered with easy minds.' [14] Having been feted by the local planters and treated to a Victory Dinner at the Golf Clubhouse, they happily reciprocated the hospitality shown them by hosting a garden party in the grounds of their bungalow. It was to be their swansong before the Everest party went their separate ways.

With no Fox Moth to fly home, Clydesdale opted to return by boat from Karachi, leaving McIntyre to fly his Puss Moth home in company with Fellowes, his wife and Ellison, but before that he and Ellison would be responsible for flying the two Westland aircraft to Karachi. They set off on 24 April, catching a final glimpse of Everest, en route to Delhi. When they stopped at Jodhpur the next day to refuel, they learned that the aircraft carrying the mail from Delhi to Karachi had been forced out of action after being struck by a vulture. Clydesdale's offer to transport the mail himself was gratefully accepted. It was to be his final contribution to an expedition that cemented his name in history. '— I can assure you that Clydesdale himself, with his wonderful thoroughness and care for detail, has been an inspiration to the whole expedition,' Fellowes wrote to Nina.

Nothing is too much trouble for him when it comes to getting down to actual preparations, and his determination to succeed in whatever he attempts is outstanding. There is no doubt about it he has got a great career in front of him. He seems to like the Indians very much, and they appear to reciprocate. Who knows; perhaps this may be the forerunner of his holding some great post out here. He certainly has that very necessary gift of charm, which perhaps misleads some people as to the determination of purpose lying behind it, which is perhaps just as well. [15]

The Times was equally complimentary. It called the second flight 'one of those acts of constructive insubordination which cannot be justified until they have succeeded, and which, when they have succeeded, need no justification'. The flight was the more forgiving because it was carried out not for the glory of the pilots and observers but as a debt to science. 'Seldom, if ever, has an expedition fulfilled its undertakings as completely. To have completed them, perilous as they were, without a casualty of any kind says all that volumes could say about the quality of the personnel, the machines, and the organisation. AIR COMMODORE FELLOWES and his party— have a perfect accomplishment to look back upon. Everest stands high among mountains, higher yet in the records of British adventure.' [16]

Following a leisurely journey home on the *SS Mooltan,* Clydesdale disembarked at Marseilles where he met his mother and travelled home overland. Arriving in London almost unrecognised, he spent a few hours with friends before heading north since he and McIntyre were due to participate in the Scottish Flying Club's air pageant at Renfrew. Although the occasion was marred by some minor disturbances in an anti-war march organised by local agitators, Clydesdale was mobbed by cheering crowds, as he and McIntyre were presented with silver plaques bearing an engraving of their aircraft by the President of the Scottish Flying Club, Sir Harold Yarrow. There were emotional scenes at Renfrew Town Hall, when entering to the sounds of 'See the Conquering Hero Comes', they were given a standing ovation by six hundred members of the East Renfrewshire Unionist Association. Presented with watches by Provost Michie, who told them that their courage had won the admiration of the world, Clydesdale in reply thanked his constituents for granting him leave and won loud applause for his encomium to British engineering. Their aircraft and engines had shown they could fly over the highest peak in the world.

The plaudits did not end there. The following weekend he won great acclaim at St Giles' Cathedral in Edinburgh during the General Assembly of the Church of Scotland where he was acting as aide-de-camp to John Buchan, the Lord High Commissioner. 'He looked so fit and brown and charmingly diffident in spite of being the hero of the hour, fresh from the fields of achievements,' declared the *Scots Observer.* [17] Days later he interrupted his duties to attend a lunch in London given by *The Times* in honour of the Everest Expedition at which the Duke of York presented him, Fellowes, Blacker and Ellison with silver medals struck at the Royal Mint. He returned to Edinburgh that evening by aircraft for the final session of the General Assembly, becoming the first person to land in Holyrood Park.

Next it was the turn of 602 Squadron to honour two of their fellow officers at a big dinner in Glasgow, and then the Parliamentary Air Committee entertained the leading members of the Expedition to dinner in the House of Commons Dining Room. Over fifty MPs attended, including Winston Churchill who sat next to Clydesdale, and Ramsay MacDonald sent warm words of appreciation for their triumph.

Clydesdale's achievements were also the cause of local celebration. At a reception at Dungavel he was presented with a silver cake stand by the estate workers, and on 5 July he received the Freedom of Hamilton. The previous day he had been mobbed by autograph-hunters at a lunch hosted by the Empire Union and although tiring of all the attention the invitations continued to flood in. A number he felt obliged to accept, and there was talk of a lucrative three-month tour to the US, but after expressing an initial interest he turned it down because of constituency commitments.

Behind the scenes all was not sweetness and light. Infuriated by the defiance shown her by the second Everest flight, Lady Houston was in no mood to welcome back the expedition. A bad-tempered fracas between her secretary Wentworth-Day and Blacker, during which the former was struck in the face by the latter, only compounded her sense of indignation. Instructing the Master of Sempill to freeze the Committee's funds and erase Blacker and Etherton from the film, she warned Clydesdale off having anything to do with them.

Clydesdale wrote her a soothing reply. 'We have all had a strenuous time on the Expedition, and it is not altogether surprising if Blacker's nerves were somewhat overwrought.' He assured her that Blacker was willing to fall in with the wishes of the Committee - he was a man of the highest honour - and having complimented her on her generosity towards the expedition, asked her to show restraint so as not to mar its achievements. [18]

Lady Houston's peremptory action in treating the Committee as her personal fiefdom was met with a united front from those on the expedition. 'It is, of course, very difficult dealing with someone who is not quite normal,' Clydesdale confided to Blacker. [19] Fortunately, Blacker was able to persuade Lady Houston's personable solicitor Willie Graham that Field Service Regulations of the Army permitted the recipient of a formal order to depart from the letter in the absence of those giving it when circumstances changed, an argument which enabled him to make his peace with Lady Houston.

Never comfortable with the filming, Clydesdale had spent some time at the Gaumont film studios on return all in the cause of aviation, but repelled by what he saw as its money-grubbing ethos, he consulted his solicitors about the contract to see whether he could eliminate from the film any pictures of him that could be considered offensive. They advised him to abide by the agreement, although he could object to any material introduced in the documentary that appeared detrimental to his position as an MP or squadron leader.

When the documentary *Wings Over Everest* appeared in June 1934, Clydesdale was very critical of its editorial deficiencies that saw the two Everest flights mixed up. Aside from the absence of any explanation at the beginning, and the omission of any reference to leading Indians such as the Maharajah of Darbhanga and Gupta, he regretted the lack of emphasis placed on the geographical-scientific survey.

He and McIntyre also took exception to Blacker and Fellowes' account of the expedition in their book *First over Everest,* which said little about the actual flights. Consequently, they employed Shepherd of *The Times* to help them write their own account, *The Pilots' Book of Everest*, published in 1936, and which is much more adept at conveying the drama of the occasion.

In a recently-acclaimed account the historian Patrick G. Zander has argued that the Everest Expedition was part of a far-right programme to regenerate Britain at a time of economic and political decline. Not only could technological modernisation and heroic endeavour impress less industrial peoples, it would raise imperial prestige, not least in India where British rule was becoming ever more precarious. [20] If that was the case, and it is certainly true that leading advocates of the expedition such as Lady Houston and the Master of Sempill perceived an opportunity to stem the tide of Indian independence, then it clearly failed as that movement continued to gain momentum. The Government of India Act of 1935 granting a large measure of provincial autonomy aroused implacable opposition from Tory diehards such as Winston Churchill, but not Clydesdale who disappointed both Churchill and Lady Houston by supporting it, thus belying his reputation as a reactionary imperialist. That is not to say that national-imperial prestige played no part in the motives behind the Everest flight; it did, as it did for the US when it put the first men on the moon, but it was very much secondary to the cause of aviation and science. A greater knowledge of flying at extreme altitudes and a greater understanding of Everest's south-east ridge were no mean achievements, and in that capacity Clydesdale and McIntyre's legacy lives on.

5. TROUBLED DECADE

After all the euphoria of his Everest homecoming, Clydesdale found there was plenty to occupy him. Aside from the thousands of letters to answer, there were his duties as an aide-de-camp to the Lord High Commissioner to the General Assembly of the Church of Scotland. It was a role he had first performed in 1924 for James Brown, an Ayrshire miner and Labour MP. Despite their different backgrounds and political allegiances the two of them struck up an instant rapport so that when they were both guests of honour at a church fete in Ayr a few years later, Brown referred to their good friendship; he just wished Clydesdale would join another party. In his reply Clydesdale won applause for his comment that the Church of Scotland meant more to Mr Brown and himself than any political party.

One of Clydesdale's greatest assets was his ability to relate to all types, a quality on view at the 1933 General Assembly, for while John Buchan proved to be a distinguished Lord High Commissioner, his daughter Alice encountered Captain Brian Fairfax-Lucy, one of the other aides-de-camp. After a whirlwind romance they were engaged and at their wedding that July Clydesdale was best man.

In addition to his duties with 602 Squadron and participating in various air displays, twice with the Londonderrys in Northern Ireland, he gave many lectures on Everest including one to the Royal Geographical Society and another at the Duke of York's Camp at Southwold. Indeed his commitments would have been even greater were it not for a dangerous attack of peritonitis that befell Geordie. By the time he had recovered it was Clydesdale himself who was laid low by a virulent bout of influenza, complicated by a slight congestion of the lungs. An eagerness to return to work as soon as possible only exacerbated his condition, and on the orders of Sir John Weir, Physician Royal to George V, he cancelled all engagements to the following March.

Advised that residing at high altitude would aid his recovery, Clydesdale spent most of the time convalescing at a hotel in the Swiss resort of Arosa, going for daily walks in the mountains, the prelude to a month in Egypt in February 1934. On 12 March, he flew to Haifa to return home on board the Glasgow liner *Letitia*, the same day that the *Greenock Telegraph* ran a story that he was to retire from Parliament. Sensitive to the charge that he had been largely an absentee MP for the previous year, Clydesdale was incensed by the article. Issuing a furious denial through his private secretary from the ship he called it a 'contemptible series of mean, personal lies, aimed at stealing a few votes in what is no doubt considered to be an impossible Labour seat. These methods of hitting below the belt may be typical of Socialism, but such tactics do not pay in the long run'.

'In denying these deliberate lies I would assure my constituents that I have completely recovered from the severe attack of influenza I unfortunately contracted in September last and I shall be resuming my Parliamentary duties very shortly.' [1]

He did, after a short skiing holiday with McIntyre in Austria, and on his return announced that he felt fit enough to box ten rounds. In June he hosted two thousand Unionists to a fete at Dungavel at which the guest speaker, Lord Londonderry, lambasted Sir Oswald Mosley's British Union of Fascists; then in July he attended camp with 602 Squadron followed by a fortnight's Air Publications course at Andover, activities he found preferable to his sedentary life in Parliament.

In 1931 Clydesdale had been promoted to Squadron Leader and for the next five years 602 Squadron thrived under his leadership. That year the *Aeroplane*, the leading aviation journal, had compared its mechanical expertise with the best squadron in the RAF, and its professionalism continued to grow as a result of greater contact with the Regulars. A further boost came when the squadron moved to Abbotsinch {now Glasgow

International airport} in January 1933, giving it its own purpose-airfield, and becoming, along with 603 {City of Edinburgh} Squadron, the first squadrons in the RAF to form their own pipe bands, both wearing the Duke of Hamilton's Grey Douglas tartan. According to Hector MacLean, a 602 Battle of Britain pilot, Clydesdale's courteous and charming manner concealed the heart of a lion, an assessment borne out by a hazardous day's flying at camp at Hawkinge, Kent.

One afternoon when the squadron were up in the air they were quickly enveloped by a thick coastal fog. On the ground the fitters and riggers were anxiously listening for the sound of aircraft circulating above the mist, and then landing 'blind'. Eventually all landed except for one pilot who tried several times, but was unable at the last moment to judge accurately his height, and was forced to head off again into the ether.

At this point Clydesdale strode purposefully to his aircraft, started up and took off in search of his colleague. Minutes later he led the pilot in, the aircraft almost nose to tail, and both landed safely, an act of selfless leadership which further raised his stature within the squadron. [2]

Another with fond memories of the Commanding Officer {CO} was William Matheson, the assistant adjutant, who recalled the direct look and friendly smile on first acquaintance that convinced him he would enjoy serving under him. On one occasion Clydesdale asked him if he would bring his private aircraft from Abbotsinch to Dungavel. Although Matheson had not flown the aircraft before he thought he could handle this short flight, but when he saw Dungavel surrounded by fir trees with a nasty cross wind blowing he realised he was in trouble. He came in diagonally to offset the cross wind and clear the trees but landed too fast. Unfortunately there was a deep gully near the boundary into which the aircraft went on its nose; soon afterwards Clydesdale appeared dressed in a smart suit already to go. 'Matheson must have been in despair,' recalled Hector Maclean, 'but the CO just said, "Hard luck, I nearly did it myself once. I shall have to get that ditch marked".' Matheson had liked his Commanding Officer very much before this incident, but from that moment he loved him. [3]

Clydesdale's charisma was immediately evident to Sandy Johnstone, 602's commanding officer during the Battle of Britain, when he applied to join the squadron in 1934. 'Although not particularly tall, one could not but be impressed by his fine physique and bearing—. His searching blue eyes were sizing me up.' When Johnstone admitted that he had never flown before, Clydesdale gave him an immediate opportunity to rectify that. It proved to be a rather frightening experience and it was not till sometime later that Johnstone learned that the seemingly harsh treatment had been nothing more than a ploy to find out whether he was squadron material. [4]

When Clydesdale was indisposed during the winter of 1933-34 he handed over command of the squadron to McIntyre, giving him considerable leeway to run things according to his lights. One minor conundrum he left him was how to respond to the proposal of John Fullerton, his predecessor as Squadron Leader, for a Flying Competition between 602 and the Scottish Flying Club. He was loath to support it, fearing that it might encourage ill-discipline in the air, thereby jeopardising his intention of making the squadron as professional as the Regulars, a view shared by McIntyre.

In 1934 602 took possession of the Hawker Hart, the RAF standard light bomber with a top speed of 170 mph, and the following year it became the first Auxiliary Squadron to participate in an Armaments and Gunnery Course, winning a prize for its bombing, a feat that gave Clydesdale much satisfaction. When he handed over to McIntyre in September 1936 he could rest content that 602's reputation remained in the top flight, a precursor to the renown it achieved during the Second World War.

The year 1935 had begun with the news that Clydesdale, along with McIntyre, had been awarded the Air Force Cross, a military decoration for RAF personnel for acts of courage outside active engagement with the enemy. He celebrated with a month's skiing at St Moritz, Klosters and St Anton in the company of family and friends before returning for his investiture at Buckingham Palace. In March he twice acted as best man, first for Vivan Bell, his Oxford and 602 contemporary, and then for McIntyre; then at Easter he was back skiing in Switzerland before joining a group of MPs as guests of the Archduke Albrecht of Hungary, one of the richest landowners in Central Europe. They had not met before, but the Archduke, an enthusiastic aviator, was keen to make his acquaintance and having arranged the visit through an intermediary, proved to be the most genial of hosts.

May saw Clydesdale once again as aide-de-camp to the new Lord High Commissioner, the Duke of Kent, and Reviewing Officer of the Silver Jubilee Review of the Glasgow Battalion of the Boys' Brigade, a Christian youth organisation to which he was much attached. Ten thousand marched past him in Queen's Park and when he called for three cheers for the King, George V, they cheered themselves hoarse.

During the summer Clydesdale was approached by a student delegation from Edinburgh University to stand as their Rector, an elected high-ranking official in Scottish universities. Previous holders had included such eminent names as Gladstone, Lloyd George and Baldwin, and with Lord Allenby, the conqueror of Palestine, the leading contender, he decided to allow his name to go forward on the grounds that the holder should be a Scot. 'Supported by such an imposing family record, Lord Clydesdale's personal merits must make a great appeal in this Rectorial Election,' commented *The Student,* the Edinburgh University journal. Complimenting him on a life of achievement, not least as an MP, it reckoned that he would not only make a decorative Rector but also an active one. [5]

Despite an energetic campaign that played on his youth and sporting prowess, Clydesdale made little impression against the established candidates, Allenby and Douglas Chalmers Watson, an eminent Edinburgh physician, finishing a poor third above the radical Scottish poet C.M.Grieve, better known as Hugh MacDiarmid. He was to fare rather better at his next election.

The general election of November 1935 took place against a background of international tension caused by the Italian invasion of Abyssinia the previous month. The crisis had placed the Government in something of a quandary because Italy was a traditional ally out to expand in a region peripheral to British interests, and reluctant perennially to play the role of the world's policeman, its natural instinct was to turn a blind eye. In normal circumstances this might just have worked, but given the overwhelming public support for the League and with electoral considerations in mind, the Government felt compelled to support it by imposing economic sanctions on Italy.

In an election fought as much over foreign policy as economic recovery, Labour's divisions came back to haunt it as pacifists clashed with pragmatists over the need to confront Fascist bellicosity. As a staunch upholder of the League of Nations and international cooperation, views strengthened by a recent visit to its home in Geneva, Clydesdale fully supported the imposition of economic sanctions. In a speech at Renfrew at the start of the campaign, he was fiercely critical of Labour's reckless approach to Abyssinia, especially since it had toyed with disarmament for so long. Had Britain's defences been stronger, he argued, war in Abyssinia might not have started.

His attempt to sound the tocsin on foreign policy was not entirely successful, since a section of his capacity audience was more interested in eliciting his views on the Means Test, the investigation into a person's financial circumstances to determine whether that person qualified for government assistance. Following constant interruptions the chairman threatened twice to call the police as amidst further uproar Clydesdale's words were increasingly drowned out.

The disturbances at least brought the election locally to life, which up to then had been a sedate affair. In a constituency that had grown by another 28,000 since the previous election to 84,000, making it the largest in Scotland, Clydesdale started overwhelming favourite against his Labour opponent, James Barr, a Greenock councillor and pacifist, and the Scottish National Party's Oliver Brown.[6] 'Few of our young Parliamentarians have come on so well in the art of public speaking as the Marquis of Douglas and Clydesdale, who is again offering his services in East Renfrewshire,' commented the *Glasgow Evening News* correspondent. 'I have heard him in three campaigns, and yesterday at the Conservative Club he showed no trace of the natural and youthful hesitancy of his early and ineffective struggle to woo the electorate in Govan.' [7]

In contrast to Clydesdale's call for greater aircraft manufacturing facilities in the West of Scotland, Barr's pacifism did him no favours in an area where rearmament helped bolster jobs on the Clyde. Yet national trends aside, it was hard to counter the right-wing bias of the local media in thrall to the chivalric tendencies of an attractive young aristocrat. 'In the main the campaign has been conducted with good feeling,' reported the *Scotsman's* special correspondent, 'but it is to be regretted that in certain industrial centres such as Barrhead and Renfrew there have been numerous manifestations of Socialist rowdyism.' [8]

The relief was palpable when Clydesdale was re-elected with a majority of 13,646 on the back of another sweeping majority for the National Government. '— East Renfrewshire have acted wisely in returning the Marquis of Clydesdale, whose distinctions in many directions have made him a member of whom any constituency might well be proud,' declared the *Paisley and Renfrewshire Gazette*. [9]

With the election safely over, the Government's ambivalence towards Italy was revealed in a secret pact between the British Foreign Secretary, Sam Hoare, and his French counterpart, Pierre Laval, which ceded much of Abyssinia to Italy. When news of the deal leaked out there was outrage at such a blatant betrayal of the League and Clydesdale added his name to a parliamentary resolution opposing any concession to Italy after its unprovoked aggression.

The uproar was enough to bring about Hoare's resignation and restore the status quo, but with League sanctions omitting the vital one of oil Italy was not deterred from pursuing its path of conquest. By May 1936 Abyssinia had fallen and confronted with this *fait accompli* the Government, bowing to the inevitable, abandoned sanctions, a decision which Clydesdale reluctantly supported. 'Appalling and dastardly as the war has been,' he wrote to a constituent, 'the continuation and intensification of Sanctions would now face this country with the risk of war as well as creating even more unsettled trade conditions than exist at the present time.' Only military sanctions accompanied by war, he added, could put an end to such aggression as Italy had waged against Abyssinia. [10]

He continued to support closer relations with Italy as Mussolini proved resistant to British advances, but rejected an invitation to join the Anglo-Italian Cultural Association in July 1938 on the suspicion that the organisation was a veneer for political propaganda. These suspicions had been heightened by a recent visit to Rome for an international conference on leisure time and recreation, which had brought him face to face with totalitarianism.

Clydesdale was resolutely behind the Government's policy of non-intervention in the Spanish Civil War {1936-39}, fearing that it could have developed into a general European conflagration with the most devastating effects for both Britain and the rest of Europe. Yet for all his declarations of neutrality, his sympathies, like the majority of his party, lay firmly with the rebel Nationalists under General Franco, convinced that the left-wing Republican government was but a shield for the Communists. {His brother Malcolm helped transport arms to the Nationalists in August 1936.} The onset of Communist rule was conducive to a Fascist backlash, he warned, and both were enemies of democracy. When the Nationalists emerged victorious, he advocated a quick recognition of Franco's government if only to put an end to the suffering and restore British influence in the Western Mediterranean.

On the leading constitutional issue of the time - the Abdication of King Edward VIII in December 1936 - Clydesdale was fully in accord with the Government's position, namely that the King could not marry Mrs Wallis Simpson, a twice-divorced woman, and remain on the throne. The fact that it had come to this he viewed as tragic, but derived comfort from his successor, George VI, whom he considered to be thoroughly reliable and probably better able to cope with his responsibilities than his predecessor.

By far Clydesdale's biggest political priority was the future of the aviation industry, which he pursued both inside Parliament and outside. Back in 1932 he had locked horns with Sir Christopher Bullock, the

Permanent Under-Secretary at the Air Ministry, over his concern that all flying instructors at RAF Cranwell should be specially selected officers holding commissioned rank. He viewed with the greatest apprehension the Air Ministry's policy of posting more non-commissioned ones to all training establishments, believing it eroded the standards of flying efficiency, a view that Bullock thought fundamentally mistaken.

In October 1934 Clydesdale, following in Churchill's footsteps, used speeches in Glasgow and Aberdeen to highlight the neglect of Britain's air defences, the result of massive cutbacks in the armed services since 1919. With the rise of the dictators, the failure of the Geneva Disarmament Conference and the very real threat to British cities from aerial bombardment, he advocated an expansion of the RAF, especially its bomber force.

It was a message the Government seemed finally to have grasped, although Hitler's announcement in March 1935 that Germany had achieved air parity with Britain gave fresh ammunition to its critics.

In March 1936, in a debate on the Air Estimates, Clydesdale regretted the fact that expansion had not come three years earlier, but complimented the Air Ministry on the way in which it had dealt with the difficulties. He hoped it would enable a greater number of short term officers to be selected for permanent commissions as this would boost recruitment. He also welcomed the news that liaison officers appointed to the public schools would in future be high-ranking Air Force officers, a move which would help these schools overcome their prejudice about flying and encourage their pupils to join the RAF.

He continued to press for better aerodromes, meteorological facilities and training establishments for pilots in Scotland, which lagged well behind those in England, partly due to a lack of interest there, as well as the development of aircraft works. Given the vulnerability of London and the South to bombing attacks, he thought it of immense importance that manufacturing industries were scattered around the country.

His resentment over the bad hand dealt to civil aviation came to a head over the treatment of Renfrew aerodrome, the home of the Scottish Flying Club and once of 602 Squadron. Back in 1932 Clydesdale had been assured by Lord Londonderry when Air Minister that Renfrew would be kept in operation for civilian purposes; later in 1936 he had urged Sir Philip Sassoon to give the aerodrome civilian status, something Sassoon was reluctant to do, thereby placing its future in jeopardy. Disillusioned by the Air Ministry's attitude and unable to sustain annual losses of £300 to £500, Renfrew Town Council voted in April 1938 to close down the aerodrome unless it was recognised as the civilian one for South-West Scotland. 'Certainly I think that the Town Council have been shockingly treated and have a definite grievance,' Clydesdale wrote in the *Daily Record*. 'It all seems indicative of the haphazard manner in which the Air Ministry is being run.' [11]

Under pressure from the town council, the Scottish press and many of its MPs led by Clydesdale and James Maxton, the Air Ministry changed tack and grudgingly designated Renfrew as a civilian airport for South-West Scotland for the next three years. 'For sheer consistency Lord Clydesdale's record as a supporter of local authorities in general and Renfrew in particular would be very hard to beat,' declared the *Paisley and Renfrewshire Gazette*. [12]

Clydesdale had already won much gratitude locally for his part in founding Scottish Aviation Ltd in 1935. Dismayed that Scotland was lagging behind other countries in aviation, he and McIntyre returned from Everest with high hopes of rectifying this by establishing an RAF Reserve Training School there. The kudos generated by their triumphant expedition undoubtedly helped their cause, but what really brought it to fruition was the deteriorating international situation and the expansion of the RAF. This required a substantial increase in aircraft production and the training of more crews, but with government capital investment at a premium the Air Ministry looked to private companies such as de Havilland to put up the capital in return for RAF training contracts.

Given Clydesdale's association with de Havilland it is perhaps not surprising that he and McIntyre should entice it into collaboration with their proposed new venture. Not only did it become an important shareholder and the supplier of sixteen Tiger Moths, soon to be twenty, two of its leading employers, W.E.Nixon, its financial director, and T.P.Mills, its acting chairman, joined the board, along with R.L.Angus, a local industrialist, McIntyre, who became managing director, and Geordie Douglas-Hamilton to represent the Hamilton interest since Clydesdale's role as an MP precluded him from participating in a company that handled government contracts. On 9 August 1935, the Scottish College of Aviation Ltd, soon to become Scottish Aviation Ltd {SAL}, was registered as a self-managing company with the nominal value of £26,000. With their experience of flying in the West of Scotland, Clydesdale and McIntyre had earmarked the coastal town of Prestwick, some thirty miles south-west of Glasgow, as an ideal location given its exceptional visibility. Once Clydesdale had persuaded the Hamilton trustees to become the leading shareholder, they bought some 350 acres of farmland to accommodate a hangar, offices and a control tower. Construction of the aerodrome began that September and was completed the following February, days before Number 12 Elementary Flying Training School was due to open under the terms of a contract the company had signed with the Air Ministry the previous October.

On 16 February 1936, thirty-four pupils and eight instructors, all experienced pilots, reported for duty at Prestwick and from the outset the school's commitment to the highest of standards reaped dividends, as did its excellent fog-free location which enabled it to complete instruction much quicker than in other schools. With an expansion of training contracts, the training of the Air Force Reserve from 1937, the establishment of the Air Observation Navigation School from 1938, and an engineering workshop, SAL soon exceeded all expectations. One idea never realised, however, was a major international airport in Scotland serving both Edinburgh and Glasgow.

It had always been Clydesdale and McIntyre's ambition to involve SAL in airport operation, and the expansion of the RAF's training scheme, especially the formation of a Voluntary Reserve, appeared to make this possible. They began to seek out potential aerodrome sites, and their plans were given impetus when the Air Ministry decided to set up a training centre in Edinburgh. Edinburgh Town Council was happy for SAL to develop aerodrome facilities on its behalf and when

Macmerry in East Lothian was deemed unsuitable by the Air Ministry, it accepted the company's alternative at Grangemouth, near Falkirk, which it envisaged as a joint airport for both Edinburgh and Glasgow.

The site was developed in record time and was in operation for two months before the official opening on 1 July 1939 by Lord Trenchard. The coming of war, however, had an adverse effect on SAL as enemy raids on the Forth and Clyde put paid to the flying training programme and led to it selling Grangemouth to the Air Ministry at a loss of £10,000. The Ministry used it as a base for Fighter Squadrons throughout the war, but let it lapse thereafter so that the dream of a Central Scotland airport remained precisely that.

As Europe began rapidly to rearm and war once again beckoned, the Government oversaw a national health campaign. In February 1937 Clydesdale had been invited by Baldwin to join the National Council for Physical Fitness (Scotland}. It was a cause close to his heart. 'Healthy bodies, healthy minds' was a message he was always propounding to the Boys' Brigade, and in order to encourage more popular exercise he publicly proposed that employers should start and finish work one hour earlier each day, a proposal that won only lukewarm support.

In June 1938 Clydesdale, along with Wavell Wakefield, the former England rugby captain, and Sir Noel Curtis-Bennett, a leading pioneer in youth welfare, attended the Third World Congress on Leisure Time and Recreation in Rome. He abhorred the Nazi-Fascist emphasis on regimentation in physical training, but noted the failure of the democracies to keep pace with the dictatorships in the provision of health and recreational facilities. It was imperative that Britain took immediate steps to inform the world it was serious about providing such facilities for its people.

It was a message he reiterated at Renfrew that October in reaction to the notorious Munich Agreement, which saw the Sudetenland returned to Germany under threat of war. Enhancing the nation's strength meant a great national effort: contrary to his previous philosophy he thought it the duty of the state to provide work for everyone, as well as the right kind of nutrition and exercise, and when someone suggested housing as well he agreed.

Throughout 1939 the main focus of Clydesdale's work was directed towards Germany {see below}, and following its annexation of Czechoslovakia in March 1939 he pinned his hopes for peace on the British government's diplomatic mission to the Soviet Union. Although resolutely opposed to Communism, a visit to an air force display in Moscow in August 1937 gave him an opportunity to see for himself the strength of the Russian Air Force, which might help explain his desire for an alliance. He bitterly denounced those who questioned the Government's motives in looking eastwards, but in the end the sceptics were proved right as neither country was able to shed its misgivings about the other, leaving the way clear for the notorious Molotov-Ribbentrop Pact that made war a near certainty.

Although scattered far and wide by the 1930s, the Douglas-Hamiltons continued to congregate at Ferne and Dungavel for special occasions, their close family bonds strengthened by their mutual flair for adventure and love of flying. They also helped Clydesdale out on the campaign trail with Nina proving one of his most loyal supporters, even speaking for him during his illness in 1933-34. She did, however, cause ructions within her family by her increasing stridency against animal cruelty. On one occasion she had cause to berate Clydesdale for organising a shoot at Dungavel in her absence, professing that it contravened everything she had instilled into them as children. On another occasion she made him fire a humane killer in her drawing room to show off its safety when, much to his consternation, the bullet went through the table and out the other side and into the floor.

More controversial was the large amount of Hamilton money Nina ploughed into the animal rights movement. So serious did the situation become that Clydesdale and Geordie incurred her wrath by threatening legal action if she continued to act accordingly. Reluctantly she acceded to their demands but ultimately she was to have the last laugh by leaving Ferne to the Animal Defence and Anti-Vivisection Society to run an animal sanctuary there.

At the heart of these disputes was the rather sinister figure of Miss Lind-af-Hageby and the baleful influence she exerted over Nina. While Clydesdale could fully support the campaign for slaughter-reform, he could not stomach their strictures on the eating of meat, the banning of medicines discovered through vivisection and their psychic activity in battling human diseases. Whether his young sister Mairi could have been saved with the correct treatment remains a moot point - Dr Swanberg, an old family friend and one of their doctors, certainly believed it quite possible. What is incontrovertible is that Geordie's near-fatal experience in August 1933 set Clydesdale permanently against Miss Lind and ruptured his relationship with his mother.

After playing cricket at Ferne Geordie developed an acute pain in his side, but when appendicitis was suspected Miss Lind casually dismissed such a prognosis, pronouncing it merely a strain. By the time a doctor was called he was desperately ill with peritonitis and when Clydesdale brought in the distinguished surgeon Sir Alfred Webb-Johnson from London, it was just in time to save his life. It took six months of convalescence for him to recover, not that his illness impeded his career. Soon to become a QC, Geordie was also an Edinburgh town councillor, a Commissioner for Special Areas in Scotland 1937-1939 and Commanding Officer of 603 {City of Edinburgh} Squadron.

After the marriage of Margaret Douglas-Hamilton to Major James Drummond-Hay in 1929, Malcolm had married Pamela Bowes-Lyon, a cousin of the Duchess of York, later Queen Elizabeth, in 1931, and then in 1937-38 two more of his brothers were to follow suit.

Despite no shortage of female admirers, Clydesdale quietly kept his distance from them, appearing embarrassed by the flattering profiles he attracted in the gossip columns. 'I should have no hesitation in awarding a prize for good looks in the House to this tall, fair and handsome bachelor,' commented *Home Journal* in July 1935, 'definitely one of today's eligibles.' [13]

The following month Angus Quell of *Pearson's Weekly* described him as just on the right side of thirty {despite being well over thirty-two} with looks, money, a nice disposition and all the other qualities that any sensible girl would like. 'Why doesn't he marry? I can't tell you. Probably he is too much interested in other things. The air, for example. When I dined with him the other evening, he couldn't keep off the subject. There were several women present who were anything but air minded. The Marquis of Clydesdale tried to convert them all.'

Having spoken with great relish about the future of civil aviation, he looked at his watch and asked to be excused, as he had an appointment at the Commons. 'The women looked sadly disappointed.' [14]

That was all to change in the autumn of 1936 when Clydesdale met Lady Elizabeth Percy, the eldest daughter of Alan Percy, 8th Duke of Northumberland, a man of extreme right-wing views, and his wife Helen, daughter of the 7th Duke of Richmond and Gordon. The Percys were one of the oldest and richest families in England with great estates at Alnwick in Northumberland, the family seat, Syon House in Middlesex and Albury Park in Surrey. It was here amid the splendour of the latter that Elizabeth, born in 1916, spent much of her formative years educated by a formidable governess.

Only fourteen when her father died, Elizabeth was presented at court in 1934 and three years later she was to act as a train bearer to Queen Elizabeth at the coronation, her mother having been appointed Mistress of the Robes to the Queen on the accession of George VI. Tall, attractive, intelligent and public-spirited, she made a great impression on Clydesdale and he wooed her at Alnwick and Dungavel, where she was a frequent guest with her younger sister Diana. Elizabeth later recalled that she had never met a family with such charm. 'They had wonderful looks, but it was more than that. They radiated vitality. All were physically very athletic. They were also gifted, especially Jean, Margaret and Malcolm who were very musical.' [15] When she accepted Clydesdale's proposal in marriage in October 1937, he remarked that it was the most successful raid ever carried out over the Border by a Douglas, referring to the historical enmity between his family and the Percys.

After a London reception for six hundred at Claridge's given by Nina, the wedding on 2 December was the most dazzling seen in Edinburgh for years. Despite the intense cold, crowds lined the route ten deep to watch the bride leave Holyrood Palace, the first bride since Mary, Queen of Scots to dress there, to make her stately way up the Royal Mile to St Giles' Cathedral. She arrived to great cheers and looked every inch a princess as she proceeded serenely up the aisle with her seventeen-strong bridal train. In a service that combined the liturgy of the Church of Scotland with the rites of the Church of England, the groom, attired in full Highland dress, looked nervous and stammered his response to the marriage vows. Later it was the turn of his bride to appear nervous as they were piped out of the cathedral and through a guard of honour from 602 Squadron to face the battery of press photographers. Thereafter they drove through crowded streets to the Assembly Rooms in George Street, arriving to a tumultuous welcome from excited onlookers who broke through the police cordon to surround the bridal car. At the champagne reception for nearly two thousand, fashionable society mingled with farmers in hard-white collars and bowler hats and estate workers in tweed to watch Clydesdale cut the eight-foot wedding cake with his skean-dhu.

After the honeymoon at Kielder Castle in Northumberland and Albury Park, they were welcomed home to Dungavel on a wintry evening by cheering estate workers as they proceeded up the drive in an old-fashioned sledge. In the New Year they moved into their new London home, 107, Eaton Square, Belgravia, and it was there that September that their first child, Angus, was born. Four other children, James, Hugh, Patrick and David, were to follow over the next fourteen years.

It was through Clydesdale that his brother David met Prunella Stack, the glamorous head of the Women's League of Health and Beauty, a mass fitness movement founded by her mother, when she opened a swimming pool in Dorset in May 1937. Three weeks later they met again at the Festival of Youth at Wembley and David invited Prunella for a sailing weekend with him and Malcolm on the Solent. She went and was captivated by the charm and vitality of the two brothers. A climbing holiday with David in the Alps followed, and by May 1938 they were engaged amid much publicity since Prunella had become one of the most famous women in the country, christened 'Perfect Girl' by the press. The wedding took place in Glasgow Cathedral that October with a reception for 1,500 in St Andrew's Halls. They spent their honeymoon in Skye and Austria, where they were guests of the Duke and Duchess of Brunswick, the parents of David's great friend from Oxford, Prince Ernst August. In the aftermath of Munich, Prunella observed how opinions were hardening on both sides as they debated the morality of Germany's expansionist foreign policy.

They met again briefly the following April when skiing in Switzerland and stayed up all night discussing the escalating crisis in Europe with a real sense of anxiety. The next morning Ernst August returned to Germany. He was never to see David again.

6. THE GERMAN CONNECTION

When Rudolf Hess landed on a lonely Scottish moor on 10 May 1941 with a view to meeting the Duke of Hamilton he touched off one of history's great mysteries. Why had Hess, Hitler's Deputy, risked everything with such a reckless mission, and why had he come to visit Hamilton? Seventy-two years on, the reasons are still not entirely clear as conspiracy theories continue to abound, the more extreme of which incriminate Hamilton in a devious plot to make peace with Nazi Germany as Britain fought for its very existence. This is a grave charge and one that needs to be fully answered.

For a quiet unassuming type who cultivated good relations with his political opponents, there was nothing about extremist politics which appealed to Clydesdale, not least the cult of the leader, crude displays of mass demagoguery and, most reprehensible of all, campaigns of orchestrated hate against vulnerable minorities. As a parliamentary candidate in the volatile West of Scotland during the depressed 1930s he was not immune from outbursts of raw populism on the streets, but instead of resorting to something similar he remained calm and reasoned throughout, sensitive to the plight of those less fortunate than himself. Although Conservatives of the post-1945 generation tended to depict the party of the inter-war years as unduly laissez-faire, it tried under Baldwin's leadership to act as a moderating force in a divided society and was by no means entirely unsuccessful. This was especially the case in Scotland. According to the historian I.G.C.Hutchison, the Unionists there were more liberal than the party nationally and that during these years there were only three MPs on the right; F.A.MacQuisten, Sir Thomas Moore and Captain Archibald Ramsay, who founded the notoriously anti-Semitic Right Club in 1939.[1] Were Clydesdale really an extremist then Ramsay, an Old Etonian, would surely have been the type of person with whom he would have consorted, yet in Richard Griffiths's study of Ramsay and his activities during 1939-40 he does not rate a mention. [2]

Clydesdale does not feature in three other major studies of Fascism: Griffiths's *Fellow Travellers of the Right: British Enthusiasts for Nazi Germany 1933-1939*; Richard Thurlow's *Fascism in Britain: A History 1918-1985*, and Stephen Dorril's *Blackshirts: Sir Oswald Mosley and British Fascism*. In Martin Pugh's *Hurrah for the Blackshirts: Fascists and Fascism in Britain during the Wars*, the author describes Clydesdale as a loyal mainstream Conservative MP who shunned the diehard opposition to the Government of India Act, only then to call him 'an apologist for Hitler', apparently on account of his lukewarm support for war in 1939. This was an unfortunate choice of words since Clydesdale's letter to *The Times* of October 1939 {see below} differentiates quite clearly between the need for all-out war against Nazism and his desire for a just settlement with a putative democratic German government.[3]

A similar line was pursued by Gavin Bowd in his recently-published *Fascism in Scotland*. A photo of Clydesdale in the book asserts that he had been a prominent friend of Nazi Germany because he had favoured 'peaceful arrangements' with Hitler before 1939, as well as his letter to *The Times*. Yet in a book that exposes greater support for the far right in Scotland during that era than previously acknowledged, there is absolutely no suggestion that Clydesdale was in any way associated with these various groups.[4]

On the surface it is easy to see how the allegations against Clydesdale gained currency, especially given the floundering response of the British government to misinformation about him and Hess following Hess's arrival in Britain. During the mid-1930s, Clydesdale had come into contact with leading representatives of the German government, especially Joachim von Ribbentrop. He also was a good friend of Prince Ernst August whose parents, the Duke and Duchess of Brunswick, were avowed Nazis. Whether he was a member of the Anglo-German Fellowship, an elitist group established in 1935 to foster closer relations between the two countries and containing a number of people sympathetic to the Nazi regime, remains a matter of some conjecture. {His brothers Malcolm and David were.} [5] Later, in 1939, his mother appears to have joined the Nordic League, a far-right, anti-Semitic organisation, quite possibly the result of her fierce opposition to Jewish practices of slaughtering animals. [6]

Nazi apologists were also prominent in the world of aviation, not least the Master of Sempill, who passed military secrets to the Japanese, Lord Londonderry and Charles Grey, the editor of the *Aeroplane,* but though Grey was close to Clydesdale, his anti-Semitic prejudices repelled him. Two of Clydesdale's German friends were of Jewish origin or part-Jewish origin in the cases of Dr Kurt Hahn and Dr Albrecht Haushofer respectively, and in his letter to *The Times* Clydesdale made peace with Germany conditional on justice for all races, as well as the removal of Hitler and Nazism.

Even before *Kristallnacht,* a series of government-inspired attacks against Jewish homes, synagogues and businesses on 9-10 November 1938, Clydesdale had shown his disapproval of Nazi excesses. At a lecture on physical fitness in Glasgow in November 1937, he denounced them for substituting a compulsive form of violent physical training for the voluntary one that previously existed. The next year he refused an invitation from Hitler - conveyed through the Anglo-German Fellowship - to attend the Nuremberg rally, and in the spring of 1939 he cancelled a series of aviation lectures he was due to have given in Germany. That May, addressing the annual rally of the Boys' Brigade at the Royal Albert Hall, he told them that they were the antidote to the godless authoritarianism of paramilitary groups such as the Hitler Youth. 'What appals me is that these gigantic national organisations, embracing all the youth in their countries, are to some extent compelled to adopt methods and regimes which are not merely anti-Christian, but vilely Satanic, and cruel deeds in which godless doctrines are rampant.' [7]

Separated from his disdain for Nazism was Clydesdale's admiration for the German nation, a view not uncommon among many of the British establishment at that time. Its people had amazing qualities, he told a meeting at Renfrew in October 1936; they were energetic, efficient, patriotic and pro-British. The more contact the two countries had with each other the better, a view he continued to espouse right up to the forcible German *Anschluss* with Austria of March 1938.

Taking their lead from the British monarchy with its blood ties with its Prussian/German counterparts over the previous two hundred years, the Hamiltons had links with the Baden family dating back to 1843 when the 11th Duke had married Princess Marie Amelie of Baden. One of her friends was the Duchess of Teck, whose daughter Mary later became Queen Consort of Britain as wife of George V. Although Clydesdale did not speak German, his three brothers did: Geordie had been educated at the University of Bonn, while Malcolm and David's interest in youth work, mountaineering and skiing had drawn them back to Germany time after time. What is interesting is that many of their closest German friends, for all their patriotism, were avowed opponents of the Nazis. Aside from Albert Haushofer who tried unavailingly to moderate Nazism from within, there was Kurt Hahn, the exiled headmaster of Salem who founded Gordonstoun, the school which educated Prince Philip, and Professor Eduard Reut-Nicolussi, the inspirational leader of the South Tyrol Germans, whose aspirations to return to Austria as opposed to becoming absorbed into Italy, had been disowned by Hitler.

Clydesdale's support for an accord with Germany was also born of a general sympathy towards its treatment at the Treaty of Versailles. Although less critical about the reparations settlement than many given Britain's need to repay all her war debts to the US, he thought that the break-up of the Austrian-Hungarian Empire and the subjection of German-speaking peoples to the rule of other countries a recipe for future trouble. As those troubles fermented and Hitler spoiled for a fight, Clydesdale firmly supported the appeasement policies of the Baldwin-Chamberlain governments. These policies were not simply a reaction to the terrible slaughter of the trenches or a reluctance to become embroiled in European disputes that were peripheral to British interests; they were the reservations of an overstretched imperial power living beyond its means. The Great War had deprived the country of much of its overseas wealth and accelerated the decline of its export trade as cheaper competitors successfully exploited a gap in the market. Not only would another war further erode Britain's economic reserves, it threatened to undermine its social-political structure- people remembered how the Communists seized power in the Soviet Union in 1917, massacring the Czar and his family in the process. Finally, it would expose all too clearly gaps in its defences and the vulnerability of an Empire under threat from rising nationalist sentiment in Egypt, Palestine and India.

That said, once the policy had failed and the country was at war again, Hamilton {as he was known from March 1940} was resolute in his determination to eradicate the threat from Nazi Germany. The idea that a serving officer such as himself with an unblemished record of personal integrity should conspire with Hitler's Deputy to bring about the downfall of Churchill, his leader and friend, and make peace with a regime he despised was absurd. An example of the flawed thinking that has coloured many an account of Hamilton's role comes in *Double Standards: The Rudolf Hess Cover-up* by Lynn Picknett, Clive Prince and Stephen Prior when describing his movements in the couple of weeks after Hess's arrival. Hamilton's entry in his diary for 18 May 1941 reads Leigh Hill, Malcolm Douglas-Hamilton's home in Wiltshire, but these authors have misinterpreted Leigh Hill as Leigh Mall, Air Marshal Sir Trafford Leigh-Mallory, the Commander of 11 Fighter Group, who, they allege, was aware of a plan by two German secret agents to assassinate Hess. [8] {On 19 May 1941, the plot was foiled after two parachutists were captured by the British Secret Service near Luton Hoo, interrogated and shot without trial.}

They also interpret Hamilton's itinerary between 18 and 30 May 1941 - Albury, home of the Duke of Northumberland, Leigh Hill, London to see Churchill and eight days at Lesbury, a house lived in by his mother-in-law Helen, Duchess of Northumberland - as making contact with members of the aristocracy who were implicit in the peace plan. [9] Aside from the bizarre claim that Churchill was somehow embroiled in covert peace negotiations with the Nazis, which went against all his basic instincts and his existence as Premier, there were valid reasons why Hamilton was absent from his fighter base, RAF Turnhouse, Edinburgh. James Douglas-Hamilton recalls that after his father had interviewed Hess for the second time he had been asked by Churchill to return once more to London for further consultations, but soon became an appendage as the Prime Minister turned his attention to the invasion of Crete and the sinking of the *Bismarck*. Hamilton's friend Sandy Johnstone, then stationed at Turnhouse, offers another reason. His diary for 17 May 1941 stated that Hamilton had been ordered to stay away from the base until such time as the allegations about his connections with Hess had been fully investigated. If this is the case - and Johnstone himself thought the allegations to be worthless - then it soon became clear that ministers and the RAF had reached a similar conclusion, as evident by Hamilton's promotion to Group Captain on returning to duty on 30 May. [10]

Although Germany and its future had been a perennial problem throughout the inter-war period, it seems to have played little part in Clydesdale's career until the general election of November 1935, by which time the threat from Nazi militarism had become more readily apparent. That year Germany had started large-scale rearmament and announced the existence of the Luftwaffe, both in clear contravention of the Versailles Treaty, but had cleverly softened the blow with pro-fessed overtures of peace to Britain, leading to a naval disarmament pact between the two countries that June.

While the focus was on Italy and Abyssinia during the 1935 election, Churchill had deigned to attack Germany for rearming in a speech that had upset Clydesdale. It was unfortunate, he said, to equate Germany with Italian aggression. Her case should be considered on its own merit. It was tragic that she had such a troubled relationship with France, implying that the intransigence of the latter had caused much of this mutual mistrust.

Clydesdale's dealings with Germany became more pronounced the next year mainly through the determination of his good friend Lord Londonderry, now out of office, to develop closer relations with her. On 4 April he was present at a dinner hosted by the Londonderrys for Germany's roving envoy in Britain, Joachim von Ribbentrop, weeks after the German reoccupation of the Rhineland, causing a major setback to French security. Although Clydesdale, like most of his countrymen, sympathised with Germany's desire to reclaim her former territory, the peremptory manner in which Hitler had gone about it had disturbed him. He raised the matter with Ribbentrop, but Ribbentrop stood his ground, arguing that his country had the right to station her troops up to the border with France.

They met again weeks later at the Londonderry home, Mount Stewart, in Northern Ireland, where the Ribbentrops were honoured guests and Clydesdale's 602 Squadron was part of a special aerial display specifically designed to show off British air power. No record of their conversation survives, but it is likely to have been fairly genial given the excellent impression that the display left with Ribbentrop.

A further encounter occurred in July when the Anglo-German Fellowship hosted a lavish dinner at the Dorchester for the Duke and Duchess of Brunswick. The following month Clydesdale flew over to Berlin with his brother Geordie and Jim Wedderburn, the MP for West Renfrewshire, to meet up with a delegation of MPs who had been invited to the Olympics. The rationale behind his invitation was probably down to his fame as an aviator-sportsman and possibly to his desire for closer Anglo-German relations, an invitation he was only too happy to accept. Not only would it enable him to watch some top-flight boxing, he could see something of the German Luftwaffe, his curiosity aroused by an incident the previous year. Flying home from a skiing holiday in Switzerland in February, he had been interrogated by the German authorities when bad weather had forced him to land at Mannheim because the aerodrome there happened to be a secret flying training school for the Luftwaffe.

Throughout his six-day stay in Berlin, Clydesdale, his brothers Geordie and David, and sister Jean were each provided with a personal car and chauffeur by the German government, part of the fulsome hospitality meted out to them. {'Between them the brothers know more about modern Germany than most of the experts put together,' noted Pamela Murray in the *Glasgow Herald*.} [11] At a glittering dinner dance for six hundred hosted by the Ribbentrops, the Douglas-Hamiltons were seated at a table with Robert Ley, the head of the German Labour Front, the Brunswicks and 'Chips' Channon, the diarist and Conservative MP, and his wife; then the following evening Clydesdale was guest at a large dinner party given by Hitler in honour of Sir Robert Vansittart, the head of the Foreign Office. Clydesdale did not actually converse with Hitler, especially as neither spoke the other's language, but when encountering him in the receiving line he found him distinctly unprepossessing. More to his liking was Albrecht Haushofer, a part-Jewish academic, introduced to him by his brother David at a party at the British Embassy.

Haushofer's father was Karl Haushofer, a well-connected major-general who had served in the German Imperial Army during the First World War. Disillusioned with his country's defeat and seeing no future for himself in the military, especially given the massive restrictions placed upon it by the Treaty of Versailles, he put the cultivated atmosphere of his childhood to good use by becoming Professor of Geopolitics at Munich University. There, his theories of autarky and expansionism, later known as *Lebensraum*, found a ready audience with his students including Rudolf Hess, one of his foremost disciples.

Hess, the son of a prosperous businessman, was brought up in some style in Egypt, then under British rule, before attending school in Germany from the age of sixteen. A promising academic career was interrupted when war broke out in 1914. Wounded twice on the Western Front, he transferred to the Flying Corps and trained as an officer pilot. Returning to Munich post-war, he joined the right-wing *Freikorps* and helped overthrow the Soviet-backed republic in Bavaria. Captivated by the charisma of Adolf Hitler, the leader of the newly-formed Nazi Party, Hess became his most ardent supporter, taking part in the failed Munich putsch of 1923 and helping him write *Mein Kampf,* his political testament, in captivity afterwards.

Hess's continuing unfailing loyalty to Hitler was rewarded with his appointment as his Deputy in 1933, with responsibility for the internal development of the party. His ideological fanaticism distanced him somewhat from Karl Haushofer, but they remained close, and when Nazi anti-Semitic legislation threatened to remove Albrecht Haushofer from public office - Karl Haushofer's wife was part-Jewish - Hess ensured that they were granted special non-Aryan status.

According to James Douglas-Hamilton, Albrecht Haushofer was one of the most fascinating and mysterious characters who lurked in the undergrowth of the Third Reich. Scholar, poet and musician, Haushofer was a man of great erudition whose intellectual self-confidence was such that it did not make him the easiest of companions and his journey through life was a rather solitary one, which perhaps helps explain why he was so drawn to Hess, his fellow student at university, and later to Clydesdale.

After graduating in History and Geography at Munich University, Haushofer went to Berlin in 1924, becoming Secretary-General of the world-renowned German Geographical Society the following year and editor of its periodical. In 1931 he was appointed Hess's personal adviser and later, through his good offices, he taught Political Geography at Berlin's prestigious German Institute for Politics.

Although different in character from his hard-headed father, Albrecht Haushofer held a similar political outlook, his belief in German expansion tempered by his disdain for Nazi brutality and its ideas of military expansion and racial supremacy. The fact that he was swimming against the tide as Hitler's grip tightened engulfed him in ever deeper water. Rejecting the opportunity to go into exile, he tried to extricate himself by concealing his true views and working as a moderating force in international relations as Hess's foreign policy adviser. A convinced Anglophile who spoke excellent English, he travelled to Britain frequently between 1934 and 1938, forming a wealth of contacts in high society. Over dinner with Clydesdale and his colleagues during the Olympics, he disassociated himself from the Nazi Party and caused some merriment by mimicking Ribbentrop. He also referred to Goebbels as 'a poisonous little man, who will give you dinner one night and sign your death warrant the next morning', a probable allusion to Goebbels's attempt to categorise him a Jew before Hess's protection. [12] Taxed with British concerns about German expansion, Haushofer reassured them that further concessions over Versailles would blow the wind out of Hitler's sails. 'Haushofer proved to be a man of remarkable knowledge in many fields, and unusually well-versed in the history of Britain,' Clydesdale later recalled. 'In conversation the brilliance and power of his intellect became strikingly apparent and exercised a fascinating effect on those who met him. Combined with a rather surprising sense of fun and a sincere enjoyment of simple things, the depth and subtlety of his mind gave to his personality an unusual quality of charm. While not without his limitations in that gathering of prominent Germans assembled in Berlin for the Olympic Games Albrecht Haushofer stood out as a man of undoubtedly superior calibre.' [13]

It was through Albrecht Haushofer that Clydesdale met Hermann Goering, the Commander-in-Chief of the Luftwaffe, at a glittering reception Goering hosted at his official residence in Berlin. With his Nordic looks, aristocratic lineage and feats as an aviator, Clydesdale cut a fine dash, and when he asked the ebullient Goering if he could see the Luftwaffe, Goering was most obliging. He called over his deputy, Erhard Milch, who willingly arranged for him to be showed units at Staaken and Doberitz the next day, remarking that their two countries shared a common enemy in Bolshevism, a sentiment which Clydesdale fully acknowledged. Questioning Milch closely, Clydesdale discovered that rapid rearmament had caused problems in training and recruitment, but noted the privileges granted even to non-commissioned officers, information that he passed on to the British military attaché in Berlin.

After a week in Berlin, Clydesdale flew his brother David down to Innsbruck in Southern Austria, where he met Eduard Reut-Nicolussi and German-speaking Tyrol patriots opposed to their continued subjection to Italian rule, a cause to which he vigorously lent his support thereafter. On his way back via Munich, Clydesdale inspected the Luftwaffe station at Lechfeld, but was denied access to one of its bombing units. A subsequent visit to lecture to the Lilienthal Society, a German aviation association, courtesy of Goering, that October, gave him further opportunities to survey aircraft factories as German rearmament forged ahead. He returned enthused by the hospitality accorded him, but ever more convinced that Britain must have air parity with Germany and the Soviet Union.

In order to keep abreast of events in Germany, Clydesdale wrote to Albrecht Haushofer while skiing in Austria in January 1937 and proposed a meeting. Haushofer's reply was most positive. Two weeks later they met in Munich, and Haushofer drove him to the family estate at Hartschimmelhof to pay a courtesy call on his parents. They discussed aviation and afterwards Clydesdale sent Karl Haushofer a copy of his book on Everest which intrigued Hess, an accomplished aviator himself, when he happened to visit the Haushofers days afterwards.

Having resumed contact Clydesdale was keen to keep in touch and invited Albrecht Haushofer to stay when he travelled to London that March to rescue Ribbentrop from his own blunders, as he told his host. Although rather stiff and formal in his demeanour, Haushofer clearly felt much at home in Clydesdale's company and soon referred to him as Douglo. Having thanked him for giving him such a splendid time in London, he expressed the hope that their friendship could continue to flourish.

At Clydesdale's instigation, Haushofer was invited to give a lecture to the Royal Institute of International Affairs, Chatham House, in April. 'I strongly feel that the German case should be properly explained, as very unfortunate impressions have been created by past speakers,' he wrote to him. [14] When Haushofer spoke, his blunt explanation of German hatred for the Versailles Treaty and the loss of the German colonies won him few admirers, but staying with Clydesdale afterwards he told him of Ribbentrop's increasing intransigence, a state of affairs he again expressed at their meeting in June.

Throughout this time Clydesdale had kept in touch with Ribbentrop, by now the German Ambassador in London. In November 1936 they had met at a house party given by the Londonderrys at their stately home, Wynyard Park, County Durham, and then on successive nights in May 1937 during the coronation celebrations when both the German Embassy and the Anglo-German Fellowship played host to Field Marshal

Werner von Blomberg, the German Minister of War, representing his country at the coronation.

Clydesdale also invited the Ribbentrops to his wedding in December 1937 - they were unable to attend - and he, his wife and his mother, along with most of the Cabinet, were guests at the German Embassy the following March to mark Ribbentrop's departure as Ambassador. By then a heavy chill had descended on Anglo-German relations. Ribbentrop's conceit and ideological posturing had not endeared him to British society, and as he returned home to become German Foreign Minister the prospects for better times ahead seemed remote, especially given Hitler's forcible *Anschluss* with Austria.

This new stridency in German foreign policy was the cause of much concern when Albrecht Haushofer stayed with Clydesdale at Dungavel in April 1938. He caused some consternation by drawing an ethnological boundary on his host's atlas, denoting those parts of Czechoslovakia that should be ceded to Germany, while accepting the dangerous consequences of such a move. His own relationship with Ribbentrop had always been difficult and with Hitler more firmly ensconced in the saddle than ever, the Führer's words about further territorial revision in Central/Eastern Europe appeared no idle threat.

Perturbed by Haushofer's prognosis, Clydesdale wrote to Lord Halifax, the Foreign Secretary, informing him of his friend's visit to London that May in case he should care to meet him. Halifax replied that demands on his time made this impossible, but reassured him that Haushofer was in touch with the Foreign Office.

As the tension between Germany and Czechoslovakia escalated over the three million Sudeten Germans, Haushofer asked Clydesdale if he could come again in June for a week or so. He arrived looking tense and haggard, his contempt for Ribbentrop ever more pronounced. Anglo-German contacts seemed more necessary than ever if they were to avoid developments of great danger, sentiments which Clydesdale fully shared. 'I am rather gloomy about the future unless the Czechoslovakia problem can be settled by common-sense,' he informed him. 'Anglo-German contacts are indeed at this time very necessary and important.' [15]

Following his stay, the last time that the two were to meet, Haushofer informed Ribbentrop that Britain still hoped to reach an understanding with Germany, but such hopes were dwindling as the latter appeared resolved on European hegemony. The Runciman mission to Czechoslovakia that August to bring Czechs and Sudeten Germans together made little headway, and with Hitler threatening war unless Czechoslovakia acceded to his demands, Neville Chamberlain, the British Prime Minister, took up the baton himself. Intent on avoiding an all-out war, which he saw as fatal to his country's interests, he flew to Germany on 15 September to begin an agonising fortnight of negotiations with Hitler. Just when it appeared that war was a near certainty, Chamberlain electrified the House of Commons with the news that Hitler wished to settle the Sudeten crisis by peaceful means. Prunella Stack recalls visiting the Commons to discuss with Clydesdale the possibility of bringing forward the date of her wedding to David. 'He greeted us with tears in his eyes. "Chamberlain has just announced that he's flying to Munich," he said. "He may avoid war. But at what price?"' [16]

The next day Chamberlain duly flew to Munich and with the French oversaw the transfer of the Sudetenland to Germany. He returned to a hero's welcome as the man who had preserved peace, but the price indeed was a heavy one.

As far as Clydesdale was concerned, his earlier reservations about Munich seem to have receded for when asked at a meeting in Renfrew in late October if Czechoslovakia had been sold, he firmly denied this. 'It was not sold it was saved.' [17] The Sudeten Germans had legitimate grievances that warranted recognition, Czech defences were weak and Britain had no commitments in Central Europe. It was thanks to Chamberlain that disaster had been averted. That said, he expressed his concern that the crisis had exposed the vulnerability of Britain's defences, and in order to counter this weakness he was advocating a large national organisation with every able-bodied man and woman earmarked for a special job in the event of an emergency.

He continued to place his trust in Chamberlain as the hopes of permanent peace began to fade, not least the shocking events of *Kristallnacht* when Nazi thugs went on the rampage killing Jews, destroying their synagogues and looting their property.

As Hitler stepped up his anti-British tirades and Mussolini humiliated Chamberlain on a visit to Rome in January 1939, there seemed little justification for Clydesdale's upbeat assessment that the international situation appeared much brighter now that the Nazi hawks were in retreat. Days later, on 15 March, he was forced to eat his words following Hitler's conquest of the rump of Czechoslovakia. The annexation marked a sea-change in British attitudes towards Germany with the scales falling from the eyes of many an appeaser. In a speech at Salisbury two weeks later, Clydesdale called Hitler a blatant liar and a 'double-crossing racketeer'. The march into Czechoslovakia had been 'unpardonable' and they should be under no illusion as to the type of man they were dealing with. He believed it only now that the true value of Munich could be seen. It had preserved peace at a time when the country was not prepared for war. Neville Chamberlain had done everything possible to extend the hand of friendship. 'He went to the furthest extreme that he could, and this is the way he has been treated. It is a shocking affair that an unscrupulous gunman should be at the head of such a powerful race as the Germans.' Stressing the Government's policy of additional rearmament since Munich, he reiterated his call for a really strong bomber force so that the country could be in a position 'to hit hard, hit often and keep on hitting'. [18]

During that same week Clydesdale was given an ecstatic reception from the Liverpool Battalion of the Boys' Brigade when he stressed the importance of its religious principles. 'In some foreign countries in Europe boys in national organisations are trained to conform to the creeds of certain regimes, and we must face the fact that these regimes often embrace Satanic methods.' [19] It was important to make Christian principles supreme, and he would like to think that members of the Boys' Brigade felt that the country's welfare depended on them.

Clydesdale's growing antipathy towards Nazi Germany in public, manifested in his cancellation of a projected visit there to give some aviation lectures to its branch of the Anglo-German Fellowship, a visit which had been approved by the Air Ministry, was asserted by similar reservations in private. Writing to his friend Douglas Simpson in America on 1 June, he admitted that 'Europe is indeed in a ghastly mess'.

— I have travelled in Germany a good deal during the past few years, and I have many German friends; but I have reluctantly become convinced that Nazism is out for nothing short of world domination and in its endeavours to achieve this will go to any extreme. This regime has indeed a stranglehold on the people of Germany, and only something very drastic can remove it.

I believe that firmness is the only thing that may prevent war, and it seems the only possible way to deal with a nation whose leaders base their diplomacy entirely on military strength and at the same time have no regard for international law or treaties. The one good thing is that the free countries of the world still possess a vast preponderance of power which if compelled can be used as a military force. [20]

Clydesdale continued to work discreetly for peace, participating in a high-level summit at the Foreign Office on 9 June, attended by Lord Halifax and Walter von Reichenau, a leading figure in Hess's diplomatic intelligence, and was kept informed of developments in Germany by various friends there.

In July 1939 he returned to a subject that had previously vexed him; Hitler's removal of thousands of Germans from the South Tyrol to accommodate Mussolini's intensification there, thereby ensuring him of Italian support for his expansionist designs elsewhere. Given Hitler's attitude towards frontier revision in the South Tyrol, Clydesdale called on him in the Commons to do something similar to the Germans in Danzig in order to diminish the likelihood of war.

His comments so unnerved Albrecht Haushofer that he felt compelled to write at length, and at great risk to himself, about current events from neutral Norway where he was on holiday. It was, according to James Douglas-Hamilton, a remarkable letter from a leading German adviser to an officer of another country with which Germany would soon be at war. Having explained why he had kept silent for so long - the need to shore up his position at home as his moderate line in foreign affairs had become less acceptable - Haushofer conveyed to him his fear about Hitler's growing aggression.

I just want to give you a sign of personal friendship - I do hope you will survive whatever may happen in Europe - and I want to send you a word of warning. To the best of my knowledge there is not yet a definite time-table for the actual explosion, but any date after the middle of August may prove to be the fatal one. So far they want to avoid the 'big war'. But the one man on whom everything depends is still hoping that he may be able to get away with an isolated 'local war'. He still thinks in terms of British bluff, although the Prime Minister's and Lord H's [Halifax's] last speeches have made him doubt- at least temporarily; the most dangerous thing is that he is racing against time: in more than one sense.

Economic difficulties are growing, and his own feeling {a very curious and remarkable one} that he has not a very long time of life ahead of him, is a most important factor. I could never adapt myself to the idea that any war might be inevitable; but one would have to be blind not to realise that war may be very near.

So the question: what *can* be done? gets all the more important. But perhaps I should have added a few things about the psychological position in the mind of the German people before trying to answer that question. On the merits of their present government, the Germans are less united than at any date since 1934. But if war breaks out on the Corridor question, they will be more solidly behind their present leader than over any case that might have led to war in these last years. The territorial solutions in the East {Corridor and Upper Silesia} have never been accepted by the German nation, and you will find many and most important Englishmen, who never thought them to be acceptable - and said so! A war against Poland would be not unpopular.

World war of course is quite another thing: but few people in Germany realise that they would be up against a world war. [21]

Haushofer appealed to Britain to come up with a plan that accepted peaceful change in Eastern Europe. He ended with a request that the letter be destroyed {although he gave Clydesdale permission to show it to either Chamberlain or Halifax} and to send him a simple post card to confirm its arrival.

Clydesdale's first port of call, however, was Churchill. Approaching him one evening in the Commons, he requested a private audience and Churchill invited him round to his flat that evening. On Clydesdale's arrival, he emerged from the bath in a large towel and was handed the letter. Taking his time to read it and digest its significance, he returned it explaining that there was going to be a war very soon, to which Clydesdale replied, 'In that case I very much hope that you will be Prime Minister,' reflecting his long-held belief that if war came Churchill should lead the nation. [22]

Having then shown the letter to Halifax and Chamberlain via Lord Dunglass, later Lord Home, his private secretary, Clydesdale sent, as requested, a non-committal reply about his family to Haushofer.

As the spectre of war loomed over Europe, Clydesdale and Elizabeth retreated to Dungavel to join the rest of the family. Prunella Stack recalls them dining there in style, all four brothers in Highland dress, each dish served by footmen amid gleaming silver and sparkling glass. As conversation and laughter abounded, she wondered whether this civilised enjoyment was the last vestige of a vanishing world.

The next morning when they congregated at breakfast they learned that Germany had formed a security pact with the Soviet Union. With war a near certainty, everyone beat a hasty exit as Swedish friends of Malcolm's returned home and all four brothers were called-up by the RAF.

Although the British declaration of war on Germany was in one sense a momentous decision with Churchill returning to the Admiralty, little actually changed during those first few months as ministers pondered the wisdom of going to war over Poland, a country in which few

British interests were at stake. Their ambivalence was echoed by many Conservative MPs and other establishment figures, especially since Germany appeared to present a lesser threat than the Soviet Union. 'I do hope that we can do all we can to impress the fact that our war aims are to crush Hitlerism and not Germany,' Malcolm Douglas-Hamilton wrote to Clydesdale. 'I feel sure that if only we could get this across to Germany the moderates would then do the rest.'[23]

His sentiments were similar to his younger brother's. Of all the Douglas-Hamiltons, David was the one who knew Germany the best having worked in one of its labour camps one university vacation and also down a coal mine. Well aware of the alien conditions under which the working class laboured and the brutal treatment meted out to his friend Reut-Nicolussi in the South Tyrol, he was under no illusion about the realities of the totalitarian state. {He once irked Ribbentrop by telling him that Hitler lacked the support of the working class.} Yet for all his loathing of the Nazi regime, David found the prospect of war against the German people a depressing prospect. 'It's so utterly mad when you think of Ernst and all other friends fighting on the other side,' he intimated to Malcolm. 'How utterly wicked to plunge the world into war like that.' [24]

David derived some comfort from Kurt Hahn's assessment that the opposition in Germany would act against Hitler if Britain was prepared to offer it a fair deal and if influential members of the younger generation such as Clydesdale spoke out to that effect. Hahn's assessment mirrored David's in that Britain needed to make clear that her quarrel was against Nazism and its unwarranted aggression as opposed to the German people. A week later he presented his eldest brother with a draft statement drawn up by Hahn and urged him to get five or six MPs who were serving officers to sign it. He did, only for Chamberlain to get cold feet, thinking it undesirable for serving officers to be associated with pronouncements of that kind. His intervention disconcerted Clydesdale who told Halifax that 'now all the impression of unity is knocked out of the statement at a time when it seems urgent that all efforts should be made to influence the moderates in Germany.' [25] Not to be outdone, he sent the letter to *The Times* under his own name. It appeared on 6 October and was broadcast on German radio later that day. The formula was one which was invariably employed by the US - to state any war it undertook was against an enemy government, not its people.

Sir, Many like yourself, have had the opportunity of hearing a good deal of what the men and women of my generation are thinking. There is no doubt in any quarter, irrespective of party, that this country had no choice but to accept the challenge of Hitler's aggression against one country in Europe after another. If Hitler is right when he claims that the whole of the German nation is with him in his cruelties and treacheries, both within Germany and without, then this war must be fought to the bitter end. It may well last for many years, but the people of the British Empire will not falter in their determination to see it through.

But I believe that the moment the menace of aggression and bad faith has been removed, war against Germany becomes wrong and meaningless. This generation is conscious that injustices were done to the German people in the era after the last War. There must be no repetition of that. To seek anything but a just and comprehensive peace to lay at rest the fears and discords in Europe would be a betrayal of our fallen.

I look forward to the day when a trusted Germany will again come into her own, and believe that there is such a Germany, which would be loth to inflict wrongs other nations such as she would not like to suffer herself. That day may be far off, but when it comes, then hostilities could and should cease, and all efforts be concentrated on righting the wrongs in Europe by free negotiations between the disputing parties, all parties binding themselves to submit their disputes to an impartial equity tribunal in case they cannot reach agreement.

We do not grudge Germany *Lebensraum,* provided that *Lebensraum* is not made the grave of other nations. We should be ready to search for and find a just colonial settlement, just to all peoples concerned, as soon as there exist effective guarantees that no race will be exposed to being treated as Hitler treated the Jews on November 9th last year. We shall, I trust, live to see the day when such a healing peace is negotiated between honourable men, and the bitter memories of twenty-five years of unhappy tension between Germany and the Western democracies are wiped away in their responsible co-operation for building a better Europe.

Yours truly,

Clydesdale

House of Commons. [26]

Clydesdale's letter, while well-intentioned, was injudicious, prone to misunderstanding to friend and foe alike. In Germany its effect appears to have been quite considerable. According to James Douglas-Hamilton: 'It is very likely that one of the Haushofers or Hess learnt about it, and that a sentence in the letter appealed to Hess, namely "We shall I trust live to see the day when such a healing peace is negotiated between honourable men". To the Nazis honour implied loyalty. It was not for nothing that the motto of the S.S. was "Our honour is our loyalty" and Hess's loyalty to Hitler was beyond doubt. Hess would have been the first to have considered himself an "honourable man", and would not have paid attention to the rest of Clydesdale's letter, which he would not have liked.' [27]

Never keen on war against Britain, Hess remained committed to peace with her, even during the summer of 1940 when she lay at the mercy of Germany, and once Hitler announced his intention to invade the Soviet Union, the Deputy Führer began formulating plans of his own.

7. THE UNIVITED EMISSARY

On the immediate declaration of war Clydesdale headed to Uxbridge as a controller to 11 Fighter Group with its responsibility for the defence of London and the South-East. As a controller he would have to deal with all interceptions with enemy aircraft, and ensure that RAF Fighter Aircraft were scrambled when required, making certain that they were sent to the places of highest priority. The controllers, like the senior commanders, were also very anxious to keep all RAF stations operational and Clydesdale's log book for that period shows him visiting stations such as Tangmere, Biggin Hill, Manston and Heston on a frequent basis.

In March 1940 his duties were briefly interrupted by the death of his father. Although increasingly infirm in his later years, the 13th Duke bore his afflictions with heroic fortitude, not least the terrible burns he suffered when he accidentally set fire to his bed. His love of his family remained constant, as did his interest in the world around him so that even in his twilight years life never lost its meaning or purpose. Having celebrated his 78th birthday on 6 March, he contracted a serious form of bronchitis and died ten days later at Ferne surrounded by his wife, his two eldest sons and his valet of twenty years.

At his funeral at St Columba's Church of Scotland, Pont Street, his four sons, dressed in RAF uniform, acted as pallbearers, and again at Hamilton Old Parish Church the next day when family and friends gathered to celebrate a life well lived. In a highly personal eulogy his blind friend Godfrey Mowat, a lay reader and faith healer, spoke of his courage in adversity and the agony of longing for freedom. 'To use his own words, "A free world is all the world to me," and yet he never complained—. There was no greater gentleman than Douglas Hamilton.'[1]

After the service the Duke's cortege wended its way through Hamilton's crowded streets to Dungavel, where amidst the sounds of 'Lochaber No More' from his faithful piper, he was lovingly laid to rest.

Hamilton's elevation to the dukedom meant his automatic transition from one House of Parliament to the other, thus ending a decade in the Commons. 'We thank you for the years you have given us as the representative of this constituency,' wrote J.S.M.Jack, the Chairman of East Renfrewshire Unionists, 'and for the kindness and courtesy you have always shown in your work amongst us; and your splendid record of public service.' [2] Another to rue his departure from the Commons was the Socialist firebrand James Maxton, who lived in his constituency at Barrhead. 'I know that when we met my conversation was mostly chaff and badinage, but I hope that did not hide the real liking that I had for you.'[3] Probably no tribute gave him greater pleasure since to Hamilton the intensity of the party battle had always been devoid of personal rancour, a quality he bequeathed to his son James in his lengthy career as an MP and MSP.

Hamilton's most important mission during the opening year of the war took place in May 1940 when he was sent to France by Air Chief Marshal Sir Hugh Dowding, Commander-in-Chief of Fighter Command, to report on the deteriorating situation there. His mission came at a time when Dowding was fiercely resisting pressure from the new Prime Minister, Winston Churchill, and the French to send more British aircraft there, given the unsustainable losses already in what looked increasingly like a forlorn cause.

On Friday 17 May, Hamilton set out from Northolt in a two-seater Miles Magister trainer for Arras, then on the front line against the northern flank of the expanding German salient. The next day he flew west to Abbeville at the mouth of the River Somme, the Germans' prime target in their attempt to cut off the British Expeditionary Force and the French elite forces in the Pas de Calais and Belgium. He returned to Arras and proceeded north to Bethune and Merville.

On Sunday he flew home as Abbeville was falling, only to return to France that same day. It was while spending the night in Calais that he was nearly killed by a flying bomb. On Monday he flew again to Merville, the RAF's last airfield in France to be abandoned, and then back to Northolt via Croydon.

His report detailing crumbling French resistance in the face of the inexorable German advance, a report for which he was Mentioned in Dispatches, and other intelligence, reinforced Dowding in his assessment that no more fighter squadrons should be deployed in France. Instead they should be held in reserve to bolster the nation's defences, a decision which proved crucial to Fighter Command's success in the Battle of Britain later that summer.

In July 1940 Hamilton was appointed Station Commander of RAF Turnhouse, Edinburgh, as part of 13 Group with its responsibility for the defence of the North of England and Scotland. Under him were over one thousand personnel, alongside small units at outlying stations, and his concern for their welfare seems to have made an immediate impact. 'I was greatly impressed by the fine work you have done at Turnhouse, and the excellent spirit which exists at the station,' the Duke of Kent wrote to him after his visit there in September. 'This reflects great credit on you and your staff.' [4]

Nevertheless there were perennial problems to resolve such as preserving fuel, dealing with breaches of ill-discipline and, most important of all, maintaining security. Although spared the kind of devastation inflicted upon the Glasgow conurbation, especially the attacks on Clydebank in March 1941 which left over one thousand dead and 50,000 homeless, Edinburgh was not immune from the Luftwaffe. It was during a state of alert that an unidentified bomber approached RAF East Fortune in East Lothian one evening. Unable to ascertain whether the bomber was hostile or not, Hamilton felt he could not risk the safety of the entire aerodrome and control tower and ordered all lights to be switched off. The RAF bomber duly came in and crash landed, injuring one or more of the crew, an accident that troubled Hamilton thereafter, although faced with those particular set of circumstances he never doubted that he had made the right decision.

It was during his first few months at Turnhouse that Hamilton inadvertently became embroiled in Rudolf Hess's mission for peace, the result primarily of his friendship with Albrecht Haushofer.

For a man not given to personal feuding and greed, Hess appeared something of a paragon compared to other leading Nazis. Yet for all the sobriety of his lifestyle, his ideological fanaticism made him complicit in some of the most heinous acts of the Nazi regime, not least the reprisals against the SA in 1934, the vicious anti-Semitic legislation and the ruthless subjugation of Poland.

Although his veneration of Hitler had given him a central role in the expansion of the Nazi state and the dissemination of its values, Hess was something of a fading force compared to Himmler, Goering and Bormann as peace gave way to war. His growing political isolation, along with his natural aloofness, exacerbated the quirks in his personality, not least his obsession with medical fads and the occult. While fully committed to Hitler's programme of *Lebensraum*, he deplored war against Britain {and the potential for one against the US} not only because it offended his pro-British sentiments, it also compromised the planned attack of the Soviet Union. With Churchill openly dismissive of Hitler's peace offer of 19 July 1940, and the RAF then engaged in a heroic defence of the homeland against the Luftwaffe, Hess, quite possibly with the Führer's blessing, now took it upon himself to neutralise Britain. At an eight-hour meeting with Karl Haushofer on 31 August he posed the question as to whether peace with her could be achieved through a British intermediary in a neutral country, since a German invasion of Britain could have dire consequences. 'There is a line of reasoning in connection with this which I absolutely must pass on to you,' Karl Haushofer wrote to his son, 'because it was obviously communicated to me with this intention. Do you, too, see no way in which such possibilities could be discussed at a third place with a middle man, possibly the old Ian Hamilton [the veteran of the Gallipoli campaign of 1915 and leading appeaser of Germany during the 1930s] or the other Hamilton?' [5] He mentioned that an opportunity had presented itself to send 'well camouflaged political figures' to Lisbon for its centenary celebrations. By chance their old friend Mrs Violet Roberts, the widow of a Cambridge academic, Ainslie Roberts, had recently sent the family a note of heartfelt greetings and that a reply addressed to her c/o Post Box 506, Lisbon, offered a means of communicating with the British.

Hess developed this theme with Albrecht Haushofer at Bad Godesberg on 8 September.

Ever since the outbreak of war Haushofer had walked a perilous tightrope, trying to balance his work for the Nazi government with his growing links with the German Resistance. Accepting that Hitler's removal during a patriotic war, especially when his country held the upper hand, would be almost impossible, Haushofer's quest for peace continued through the British and German Embassies in Spain, but his efforts had yielded little by the time he met Hess at Bad Godesberg. When Hess asked him to name potential British contacts to open peace negotiations, Haushofer warned that the prospects of peace with Britain were remote while Hitler remained in power given his flouting of previous pacts and contempt of fundamental liberties. He thought that Sam Hoare, the former Foreign Secretary now the British Ambassador to Spain, Sir Owen O'Malley, the British Minister to Hungary, and Lord Lothian, the British Ambassador to the US, were the best options, with Hamilton almost an afterthought.

As the final possibility I then mentioned that of a personal meeting on neutral soil with the closest of my English friends: the young Duke of Hamilton who has access at all times to all important persons in London, even to Churchill and the King. I stressed in this case the inevitable difficulty of making a contact and again repeated my conviction of the improbability of its succeeding- whatever approach we took. [6]

Despite Albrecht Haushofer's presentiments, Hess would not be deterred. He asked him to send a letter to Hamilton delivered via Mrs Roberts. 'Should success be the fate of the enterprise,' he wrote to Karl Haushofer, 'the oracle given to you with regard to the month of August would yet be fulfilled, since the name of the young friend [Hamilton] and the old lady friend of your family [Mrs Roberts] occurred to you during our quiet walk on the last day of that month.' [7]

At Hess's behest, Albrecht Haushofer agreed to write to Hamilton in a form that would incriminate nobody but which would be clear to him. 'I have in the meantime been thinking of the technical route by which a message from me must travel before it can reach the Duke of H [Hamilton],' he informed Hess.

With your help, delivery to Lisbon can of course be assured without difficulty. About the rest of the route we do not know. Foreign control must be taken into account; the letter must therefore in no case be composed in such a way that it will simply be seized and destroyed or that it will directly endanger the woman transmitting it or the ultimate recipient.

In view of my close personal relations and intimate acquaintance with D.H. I can write a few lines to him {which should be enclosed with the letter to Mrs R. without any indication of place and without a full name -an A would suffice for signature} in such a way that he alone will recognise that behind my wish to see him in Lisbon there is something more serious than a personal whim. All the rest, however, seems to be extremely hazardous and detrimental to the success of the letter. [8]

Despite considerable misgivings about contacting Hamilton when the prospects of peace appeared so remote, Albrecht Haushofer wrote to him that same day. He began by commiserating with him over his father's death earlier that year, and that of his brother-in-law near Dunkirk. He continued.

–If you remember some of my last communications in July 1939, you - and your friends in high places - may find some significance in the fact that I am able to ask you whether you could find time to have a talk with me somewhere on the outskirts of Europe, perhaps Portugal. I could reach Lisbon any time {and without any kind of difficulties} within a few days after receiving news from you. Of course I do not know whether you can make your authorities understand so much, that they give you leave.

But at least you may be able to answer my question. Letters will reach me {fairly quickly; they would take some four or five days from Lisbon at the utmost} in the following way: double closed envelope: inside address: 'Dr A.H.' Nothing more! Outside address:

'Minero Silricola Ltd.,

Rua do Cais de Santarem 32/1

Lisbon, Portugal'.

My father and mother add their wishes for your personal welfare to my own....

Yours ever,

'A'. [9]

The letter, dated 23 September, six days after Hitler had called off the invasion of Britain, was addressed to Mrs V.Roberts and dispatched by Hess's brother to the post box in Lisbon to which a reply could be sent. The name was significant because the Roberts had been good friends of the Haushofers and like them had had a son who was a diplomat, Patrick Roberts, whose brilliant career had been curtailed by his death in a car accident in Greece in 1937. Their nephew, Walter Roberts, also happened to be a leading figure in the political and propaganda branch of the Security Intelligence Service {SO1}, prompting future speculation among some historians that Mrs Roberts's letter of 26 July 1940 to the Haushofers might well have been the work of British Intelligence, especially that of S01. 'The fact that the actual letter has not survived is very telling,' commented John Harris and M.J.Trow in *Hess: The British Conspiracy*. 'It is an example of the missing "paper trail" which has so bedevilled research into this work.' They question the rationale behind the recruitment of Walter Roberts, a high-flying stockbroker, to become SOI's Director of Finance and his award of the CBE for his services 'unless those services were actually far more important'. [10] They go on to speculate why Mrs Roberts should write to the Haushofers once their two countries were at war with each other and suggest that her letter of July 1940 offered her services as an intermediary between Hess and a potential British 'peace party'.

According to the historian David Stafford, a leading authority on British Intelligence, there was the possibility by the autumn of 1940 of a British disinformation campaign that quite accidentally caught Hess in its net. The objective of this campaign was probably to help dissuade Hitler from invading the country by suggesting there were moves afoot by the mythical 'peace party' to oust Churchill from power. 'By surreptitiously feeding such beliefs in Berlin, where eager recipients such as the naïve Hess were already disposed to accept them, the British hoped to ward off attack at a particularly desperate stage of the war when, along with the Dominions, they stood alone against Hitler. But even here there is not one iota of evidence to suggest that S01 was deliberately plotting to lure Rudolf Hess to Britain.' [11]

Albrecht Haushofer's letter to Hamilton was intercepted by the British censor on 2 November and sent to MI5, in charge of internal security, which proceeded to lose the original. Photostat copies however were sent to the Foreign Office and Air Intelligence, since Hamilton was an officer in the RAF. The Foreign Office, unaware of Hess's involvement with the letter, showed little interest in it in contrast to MI5 who carried out a series of checks on Hamilton given his pre-war German contacts, especially his friendship with Albrecht Haushofer, whom it suspected of being engaged in espionage.

Those inquiries intensified when it learned that the Lisbon address was a German-controlled corporation actively engaged in the purchase of mineral areas for Germany. As a result the Duke was placed under observation which, according to the historian Hugh Trevor-Roper, himself a member of the Secret Intelligence Service {SIS} during the Second World War, is why he was not shown the letter for five months, the delay explained by it 'being lost in MI5'. [12] The inquiries into the Duke's character and potential subversive activities 'led to nothing', according to Guy Liddell, a senior M15 counter-intelligence officer during the Second World War. His account of Hamilton's correspondence with Albrecht Haushofer [Liddell mistakenly refers to his father Karl] in his war diaries prompted the military historian Nigel West, the editor of these diaries, to dismiss all talk of an elaborate British plot to lure Hess to Scotland. [13]

As for Mrs Roberts, the name meant nothing to the authorities and suspecting that she was in frequent contact with friends in Germany, they placed a check on her correspondence with the Haushofers. Astonishingly, after six months of inquiries the police had unearthed little of substance about her other than she lived at 10 Wilberforce Road, Cambridge, and had written to Martha Haushofer the previous July. It was only when they interviewed her on 14 May 1941 that a fuller picture emerged. A wealthy, educated and sprightly widow in her seventies, Mrs Roberts had, along with her husband, befriended the Haushofers back in 1899 when they had visited Cambridge and thereafter stayed with them intermittently in Munich en route to the Balkans when their son had been based there.

Contrary to conspiracy claims that Mrs Roberts's letter of 26 July 1940 was more than a coincidence, MI5 files released in 2004 show quite clearly that she was in constant communication with Martha Haushofer, although these letters contained little of interest because the latter feared that their correspondence was being scrutinised.

The files also refute the idea that the post box in Lisbon was a mere posting convenience and bore no link to Mrs Roberts. Alerted to a redirecting service provided by Thomas Cook, the travel agents, in Lisbon {Portugal was a neutral state} by a German-born friend of hers in Cambridge, Mrs Roberts had made arrangements with them so that she could continue her correspondence with Martha Haushofer.

Two other facts emerged from the interview. First, Albrecht Haushofer had never written to Mrs Roberts before and second, contrary to the allegations of Picknett, Prince and Prior, she did not know Hamilton.

Having consulted Colonel Vivian of MI6 about Hamilton and arranged with Air Commodore Archie Boyle, Director of Air Intelligence, to send him to Lisbon, Major John Maude decided on 11 January 1941 to hand the case over to Major T.A. Robertson, in charge of deception and counter-espionage at MI5, the much-feared Double Cross system. He emphasised that he had nothing against the Duke - he had been at school with him - but it did appear that the Hamiltons had been 'caught up by the Nazi atmosphere'.

One brother married Prunella STACK and this athletic lady used to be on very good terms with an equally distinguished German athletic lady.

The Duke's mother is a well-known crank. Animals! etc!—

It is impossible to say that the Duke never received the original- since we have lost it. Also we cannot say whether or not he has received any other communications from Haushofer. The delays have been lamentable but so far Fate seems to have prevented that detail spoiling everything. [14]

Robertson decided to proceed with care. He found on reference to Roger Fulford, the journalist-writer and MI5 Officer, that the records of Hamilton before the war had shown him to be an 'advanced appeaser' and even now 'a peace mover'. Thus any information that Albrecht Haushofer had to impart to him would be of interest, but could they be absolutely certain that Hamilton would cooperate with them in view of the fact that their knowledge of Haushofer's letter to him rather cast suspicion on him. Following a meeting between Robertson and his nominal superior, J.C.Masterman, it was agreed that Double-Cross should not get involved; instead Robertson should confer with Archie Boyle and suggest that Hamilton be questioned by Group Captain F.G. Stammers of Air Intelligence about the Haushofer letter. {Robertson was fairly certain that Hamilton had never received it.} Boyle agreed with this plan and asked Robertson to contact Stammers. Robertson did, enclosing a summary of the case.

There is no doubt that ALBRECHT HAUSHOFER is engaged in espionage of some sort or another, actively directed against British interests.

The intercepted letter contains an invitation to the Duke of Hamilton to go to Lisbon so that the writer can put a suggestion to him. As the date of the letter suggests, in all probability HAUSHOFER wished to discuss some sort of peace plan with him.

Our records do not give us any positive proof of any pro-German or anti-British activities, but it is felt that it would not have been surprising if the Duke had allowed himself to be used as an intermediary for these terms during the blackest period of the war last summer. Owing to his prominence in sport and other circles, he had of course many Nazi contacts in this country. [15]

After an inordinate delay caused by the failure of the authorities to establish the true facts about Mrs Roberts, the investigations into Hamilton's past and the dilemma of what line they should take with Albrecht Haushofer, a dilemma they never resolved, Stammers eventually met Hamilton at the Air Ministry on 11 March. When he asked him what he had done with Haushofer's letter, Hamilton, assuming that he was alluding to the one he had sent him from Norway pre-war, told him that he had deposited it in the bank. It soon became clear that they were talking at cross purposes at which point Stammers handed him a photostat copy of Haushofer's intercepted letter. Hamilton read it with surprise never imagining that Haushofer would try and contact him once their two countries were at war with each other.

In *The Rudolf Hess Cover-up*, Picknett, Prince and Prior take issue with the official account of this meeting. They claim that Hamilton received a copy of the letter on 19 February 1941, citing his briefing notes to counsel for one of his libel actions, copies of which can be found in the Hamilton archives. At first sight this appears to be the case, but closer inspection reveals something else. Hamilton's notes, written in rough pencil and difficult to read, do not say Feb19[th], but Feb 1940. He should have written 1941, his confusion perhaps attributable to the letter being originally composed in 1940, but this error hardly suggests a major conspiracy, especially when no other evidence has ever indicated he received the letter prematurely.

Informed by Stammers that the Intelligence authorities considered Albrecht Haushofer an influential person with sources close to the German Foreign Office, Hamilton agreed. As far as he knew he had been sent over to Britain to control Ribbentrop but had given him up as a lost cause. 'In my opinion, while being a patriotic German he did his utmost to exercise a restraining influence, especially before Munich, on the Nazi leaders and I gather after the Munich agreement he was somewhat out of favour.' He confirmed that Haushofer had stayed with him on countless visits to Britain, but had no idea what position he held in wartime. [16]

He also confirmed he knew neither Mrs Roberts nor the firm Minero Silricola in Portugal and when Stammers raised the possibility of sending him on a mission to Lisbon to meet Haushofer he said he would go, but suggested his brother David might be more suitable, given his intimate knowledge of Germany.

Armed with Stammers's report of the meeting and Hamilton's apparent willingness to cooperate, Robertson now pressed for him to go if only to hear what Albrecht Haushofer had to say. He asked Boyle to make the necessary arrangements to give him genuine cover. On 25 April, Hamilton was sent for by the Air Ministry and during the course of a long conversation Robertson asked him whether he could go to Lisbon and once there contact Haushofer with a view to meeting him. Hamilton did not repudiate this plan, but wondered what Britain would get out of it. Robertson replied a good deal of information from Haushofer about how Germany was weathering the war. When Hamilton pointed out that Haushofer was likely to ask similar questions about Britain, Robertson assured him that this was not a problem. They would supply him with a script. Hamilton then said that he would like to think the matter over before informing Group Captain D.L.Blackford of his decision. Robertson told him that if he decided to go he would need to see him again in the company of an expert to discuss political questions with him. He ended an MI5 Report primarily about this meeting with the following observation.

Hamilton at the beginning of the war and still is a member of the community which sincerely believes that Great Britain will be willing to make peace with Germany provided the present regime in Germany were superseded by some reasonable form of government. This view, however, is tempered by the fact that he now considers that the only thing this country can do is to fight the war to the finish no matter what disaster and destruction befalls both countries. He is a slow witted man but at the same time gets there in the end; and I feel that if he is properly schooled before leaving for Lisbon he could do a very useful job of work. [17]

Hamilton never went to Lisbon. Having been advised by his wife's uncle, Lord Eustace Percy, a former diplomat and Cabinet minister, to proceed with care, he did precisely that. He told the Air Ministry he was only prepared to go on the condition that he had the support of the Foreign Office, that the British Ambassador to Portugal was informed about his mission and that Albrecht Haushofer was given a convincing explanation for the seven-month delay in the reply to his letter.

It would be dangerous to allow him to believe that the authorities had withheld his letter from me last autumn and had now released it and had asked me to answer it. That would give the impression that the authorities here had 'got the wind up' now, and want to talk peace. May I therefore have an explanation of the circumstances in which the letter was withheld from me last autumn? [18]

Hamilton's reservations about visiting Lisbon were shared by Boyle, and more importantly Sir Archibald Sinclair, the Secretary of State for Air, who worried that sending a relatively senior serving RAF Officer might be misinterpreted, especially as the British government was not interested in making peace with Germany. Blackford also had his doubts. He asked Hamilton to regard the matter as 'in abeyance' pending further instructions. 'In my own view the delay which has occurred makes it extremely difficult to find a watertight excuse for action at the present time, and although quite a good one has been suggested on the lines of an enquiry from you as to why your previous letters have not been answered, it might not carry conviction and so have undesirable political consequences.' [19] Even Robertson accepted that Hamilton's two objections were 'most reasonable'. According to his biographer Geoffrey Elliott, he was not prepared to open up a link with a near stranger on the off chance of creating a channel through which false information could be fed. [20]

Whatever the machinations regarding MI5 and Lisbon, the idea that British Intelligence was deeply implicated in Hess's visit does not stand up to scrutiny. For aside from the incoherent response not only of the local militia but also of the whole British establishment to his arrival which seemed utterly at variance with an organised plot, the MI5 files show quite clearly that neither they nor Hamilton were involved in any negotiations with Hess, not least because they were unaware that he was behind Haushofer's peace feelers. Even the savvy Robertson was completely in the dark when summoned to the Air Ministry on the afternoon of 12 May 1941 by Air-Vice Marshal Medhurst to be informed of Hess's landing in Scotland.

The files also show that had the Intelligence authorities realised that Hamilton had brought Albrecht Haushofer's letter of July 1939 to the immediate attention of Chamberlain, the then Prime Minister, and Churchill, they would not have had reason to suspect him when Haushofer's letter of 23 September 1940 reached them that November. In the opinion of James Douglas-Hamilton greater transparency could have spared not only his father from every kind of crude insinuation but also that of the country. 'By maintaining excessive secrecy in relation to Second World War matters, those ministers responsible for that secrecy were actually doing Britain a disservice, because Britain had not broken its honourable record and they should have been more transparent in showing that to the British people.' [21]

With the case against the Intelligence Services' role in Hess's flight seemingly flawed, a fact even acknowledged by some of the conspiracy theorists, they now turned to another target: Hamilton and an aristocratic clique seeking peace at all costs. It is to this matter we now turn.

With no reply pending from Albrecht Haushofer's letter of 23 September 1940 and increasingly concerned about the future as Hitler's invasion of the Soviet Union loomed, Hess asked Haushofer to explore other avenues of negotiation. In particular he singled out Carl Burckhardt, the Vice-President of the Red Cross, who had close contacts with the so-called 'peace party' in Britain. It was the failure of these overtures – Albrecht Haushofer met Burckhardt in Geneva on 28 April 1941 - that prompted Hess to fly to Scotland himself to broker peace without Haushofer's knowledge. The question of why he should have risked everything on such a hazardous mission defies rational analysis, but restoring his credentials with Hitler by securing peace with Britain and avoiding a damaging two-front war, appealed to Hess's romantic temperament. According to David Stafford, making dramatic and highly publicised flights for peace had exercised a powerful pull on the popular imagination. 'In the 1930s flying was still novel, daring and perilous, and those who triumphed in the challenge received popular acclaim of almost mystical dimensions.' Recalling Chamberlain's brave if doomed flights to Germany in September 1938 to save Europe from war, Hess, a skilled aviator himself, now looked to follow in his footsteps and succeed where he had failed. [22]

Controversy has raged about Hitler's part in the mission, yet while he may well have known and approved of Albrecht Haushofer's letter to Hamilton of September 1940, there is nothing to suggest any further involvement by him. Not only would Hitler have considered the mission too fraught with danger, Hess, it appears, deliberately excluded him from his plans so that if his mission ended in failure Hitler's reputation would in no way be impaired.

After a brief spell flying the Fokker D-VII in the German Air Force during the final stages of the First World War, Hess gained his private pilot's licence in 1929 and purchased a Messerschmitt M 23 b. In 1934 he won the prestigious air race around the *Zugspitze*, Germany's highest peak, and in October 1940 he was granted permission by his friend Willi Messerschmitt, the renowned aircraft designer, to fly the Messerschmitt BF110 {Me-110}, a brand new twin-engine fighter aircraft developed at his factory at Augsburg. He took lessons from Hans Baur, Hitler's personal pilot, and soon he was flying solo.

Throughout the course of that winter Hess devoted much time to preparing a long-distance flight by installing a 900-litre drop tank under each wing and a new radio. He also pored over weather reports from distant places and familiarised himself with leading landmarks on a large map of Scotland that hung on his bedroom wall. Had the fates been kinder the evidence suggests that Hess would have made his mission back in January, but he was twice forced back because of bad weather, technological deficiencies and, later in April, political commitments.

Conspiracy theorists, both then and later, maintained that Hamilton colluded with Hess over his flight, dating back to an alleged meeting between the two of them at the Berlin Olympics, allegations that Hamilton always denied {see below}. So why did Hess choose him? He would, of course, have heard about him from his adviser Albrecht Haushofer, and as one aviator to another Hamilton's epic flight over Everest would have won his admiration. The fact that Dungavel had an airstrip also appears to have entered his calculations, despite the near impossibility of landing a high-speed fighter on a short grass runway without lights. Above all, his perceived pro-German sentiments as demonstrated by his letter to *The Times* of October 1939, his aristocratic pedigree - German aristocrats were still figures of major consequence in Hess's youth - and access to the King, especially after his appointment as Lord Steward in 1940, convinced Hess that the 'peace party' would be willing to mount a coup against Churchill.

A more eccentric explanation for Hess's motives was advanced by Oliver Brown, Hamilton's former SNP opponent. According to Brown, Hess believed that the aristocracy as the nation's leaders placed the interests of the nation first, which meant in 1940 espousing the nationalist movement in Scotland. Given that there was some opposition to 'England's war' in Scotland, Hess assumed that the Scottish peerage would back nationalist sentiment by suing for peace.

Hess's rationale, while essentially flawed, was not entirely groundless in that there were influential voices in Britain who craved peace- if not at any price. Aside from members of the royal family such as the Dukes of Windsor and Kent, there was David Lloyd George, the former Prime Minister, Lord Halifax, the then Foreign Secretary, his deputy R.A.Butler, Stewart Menzies, the Director-General of MI6, and Max Beaverbrook, the newspaper magnate; there was also the residue of Chamberlain's supporters, many in the City, and various far-right groups spreading defeatist propaganda. Yet as the ferocity of German air raids over Britain united the country behind Churchill's inspirational leadership so it strengthened the Prime Minister's position. Many leading Fascist sympathisers such as Sir Oswald Mosley and Captain Archibald Ramsay were imprisoned, or placed under surveillance, and following the death of Chamberlain in November 1940, Churchill began to remove leading appeasers such as Halifax and Sam Hoare from the Government. It is true that British reverses in Greece and North Africa the following spring, in addition to continued heavy losses in the Atlantic, provided further vindication for a far-right aristocratic clique which remained committed to peace. Yet the Dukes of Buccleuch, Bedford and Montrose hardly spoke for Britain. {Buccleuch, ironically, was compelled to resign as Lord Steward in May 1940 on account of his pro-German sentiments and was succeeded by Hamilton.} Further to this, there is absolutely no evidence to link Hamilton with any of this group, a point emphasised by Albrecht Haushofer in his May 1941 memorandum to Hitler. For as he well knew, any previous sympathy Hamilton might have harboured for Germany would have melted away under the full glare of Nazi depravity, and now, as a serving officer, his loyalties would be fully behind his commander, Churchill.

Saturday 10 May 1941 dawned bright and sunny in Bavaria. After a light lunch with his friend Alfred Rosenberg, a leading Nazi ideologue, during which they conversed in private, Hess, dressed in his Luftwaffe uniform, went upstairs to see his wife who had been confined to bed with a cold. Observing that her bedside reading was Hamilton and McIntyre's *The Pilots' Book of Everest*, an irony if ever there were one, he remarked that Hamilton was very good-looking and courageous. Informing his wife that he had been summoned to Berlin, he promised that he would be back by Monday evening at the latest, a promise she did not find entirely convincing.

Having bid farewell to his family, Hess left in his Mercedes for Augsburg, some forty miles away from his home in Munich, accompanied by his private detective and adjutant, Karl-Heinz Pintsch. En route they stopped off for a brief stroll during which Hess discussed with Pintsch what his mission might achieve, Pintsch being the one person in on his secret since the previous January when Hess had made his first attempt to fly to Scotland. On arrival at Augsburg airport, Hess donned his flying suit and boots, then, having given his adjutant an envelope, and a letter to Hitler, to be opened four hours after his departure, he departed at 5.45pm in perfect conditions for his nine- hundred-mile flight to Scotland.

His route took him over Bonn, Amsterdam and the Dutch coast near Harlingen, heading north across the North Sea until veering north-west on a course to Dungavel, relying first on a radio compass installed in his aircraft and thereafter on visual pilot-navigation, which constituted a remarkable feat of aviation. Some seventy miles off the Northumberland coast he was picked up by coastal radar and designated as a single unidentified aircraft 'Raid 42', perhaps a diversionary one from the main one on London. Then, at 10.23pm, he was detected by the Royal Observer Corps {ROC} post at Embleton, just inland from the Northumberland coast, flying at 300 miles per hour in an Me-110, something they found difficult to fathom since this aircraft lacked the necessary fuel to return home.

In a lightly defended area - the priority was London and the South-East — and helped by a low-lying mist that gave him additional cover, Hess managed to evade two patrolling Spitfires that were ordered to intercept him and a third scrambled soon afterwards from RAF Acklington in Northumberland. None of them were equipped with air-interception radar. Flying very low above English fields to improve his visibility and constantly tracked by the ROC, Hess climbed to 5,000 feet as he crossed the Cheviot Hills into Scotland.

At 10.45pm he passed over Dungavel without recognising it and continued on to the west coast to check his bearings before doubling back, hunted by an RAF Defiant night fighter from Ayr. Unable to locate Dungavel in the darkness and now dangerously short of fuel, Hess elected to bail out at approximately 6,000 feet, his first-ever parachute jump. It proved to be a perilous operation as wind pressure kept him pinned to his seat. Rolling the aircraft over and flying upside down, he managed to eject himself as his aircraft crashed to earth on Bonnyton

Moor, a little to the north of the village of Eaglesham, itself some ten miles south of Glasgow city centre and twelve miles to the north-west of Dungavel. The time was 11.09pm.

As Hess parachuted to safety, he was spotted by the ROC and David McLean, the ploughman at Floors Farm as he prepared for bed at home. He ran to the nearby field and found Hess grappling with his parachute harness. Confirming himself as German and unarmed, he introduced himself in fluent English as Hauptmann Alfred Horn {his brother was called Alfred and his wife's stepfather was Horn}, explaining that he had an important message for the Duke of Hamilton, who unknown to him was not at Dungavel. Having helped extricate Hess from his parachute {he had chipped a bone in his ankle on the aircraft as he fell} and checked there was nobody else on board, McLean escorted him to the cottage he shared with his mother and sister. There he was made welcome and offered a cup of tea {he chose water}. In the rather stilted conversation that followed Hess showed McLean a photo of his son, exuding an air of natural authority, an impression confirmed by the quality of his uniform and his fine leather top boots.

He remained calm when three soldiers and an inebriated special constable brandishing a revolver descended upon the McLean's cottage. They escorted him to an unprepossessing scout hut belonging to the local Home Guard at Busby before transferring him to the Battalion Headquarters at Giffnock close by and placing him in custody. There a German-speaking clerk from the Glasgow Polish Consulate who happened to live close by, interrogated him for two hours in a rather desultory fashion. Hess reiterated his desire to be taken to Dungavel to meet the Duke of Hamilton, claiming he had seen him at the 1936 Olympics in Berlin and that they had a mutual friend. It was a similar message he conveyed to Major Graham Donald, the Area Commander of the ROC. When asked about the nature of the message, Hess replied that it was of prime importance to the British Air Force. Thinking that the face looked familiar, Donald asked if his name was really Alfred Horn and suggested, to some merriment, that he might be Rudolf Hess. He then telephoned the duty commander of his sector, Hamilton's old friend Hector MacLean, requesting that Hamilton be informed that he had interviewed a German prisoner who had an important message for him, and that if the name Alfred Horn meant nothing to him then he should consider Rudolf Hess. {The final part of the message was not conveyed to Hamilton.}

For the previous four nights Hamilton had been on duty at Turnhouse monitoring the German raids across Scotland - Greenock had been badly bombed on the nights of 5/6 May - and consequently was very short of sleep. That afternoon he had flown a Hurricane to Drem Flight Station, North Berwick, and engaged in a mock dogfight over the Firth of Forth with his second-in-command. During the evening he was again on duty at Turnhouse when the ROC reported a lone Me-110 flying across Scotland, a report he assumed to be mistaken given that the Me-110 lacked the necessary endurance to return home. He had watched the Defiant close in on Hess and was disappointed that it had not shot him down. His failure to scramble any fighters to intercept Hess has been seen by some historians as proof of his complicity in his flight, but as Hess never penetrated the sectors under his control the decision was not his to make.

At 11.09pm the operations room was informed that the enemy aircraft had crashed in flames, much to Hamilton's relief. With London under sustained assault that evening which seemed to rule out further attack in his sector, he left the operations room and went home to bed, only to be woken at 2am, according to his official report, {others have put it earlier} by an urgent call from his Senior Controller seeking his return. Who precisely was on the phone is a matter of some dispute, but, according to Hector MacLean, it was he who forced Hamilton from his bed.

'What's all this, Hector?' he inquired tetchily.

'A German Captain has parachuted from a Me 110. He's at Eaglesham Police Station and wants to see you.'

'What does he want to see me about?' continued Hamilton non-plussed. [23]

When MacLean said he did not know, Hamilton sought his advice as to what he should do since there was nothing in the King's Regulations about how a Station Commander should respond to a request from a German pilot to see him. MacLean suggested he should go and see the pilot now held as a prisoner. The fact that Hamilton waited till the following morning attracted some subsequent criticism, as did his failure to send his intelligence officer to interrogate Hess that night, contrary to the normal practice of interrogating aircrew as quickly as possible before they recovered from the initial shock. Had Hamilton known it was Hess, he might well have left for Glasgow immediately, but having sifted through a list of Luftwaffe officers he had met when in Berlin for the Olympics and found no mention of the name Horn he decided the interrogation could wait until the next morning.

A more serious charge seized upon by conspiracy theorists emanated from a story in the *Glasgow Herald* on 16 May 1941. It reported a cryptic encounter between Hess and Hamilton in the presence of the Intelligence Services the night of his arrival during the time Hess was moved from Giffnock to Maryhill Barracks between 2.15 and 2.30am, but there is absolutely no evidence to support this. Indeed the testimony of Graham Donald suggests the very opposite. He recalls speaking to Hamilton at Turnhouse at 2am which, even allowing for some variance in time, discounts any possibility that Hamilton could have been in Glasgow at that hour. [24]

At 10am the next morning Hamilton arrived at Maryhill Barracks with Flight Lieutenant Benson, Turnhouse's Intelligence Officer, and inspected Hess's belongings which had been lodged in the safe. These included a Leica camera, gloves, a map with markings on it to navigate properly - Dungavel was ringed in red- a small torch, an assortment of medicines, family photos and the visiting cards of Karl and Albrecht Haushofer, but no personal letter to Hamilton as has often been alleged. The fact that no letter has ever emerged has led some historians to cite this as another example of government duplicity. They believe it could have provided details of a secret German peace initiative which would have embarrassed Hamilton and the British government, yet even had such a letter existed it is doubtful whether its peace terms would have been any different from those Hess conveyed orally to Hamilton since they were broadly consistent with Hitler's in his Reichstag speech of 19 July 1940: namely that Germany would respect Britain's worldwide interests in return for the British conceding German primacy on the Continent. Later, following the German invasion of the Soviet Union on 22 June 1941, Hess appeared to offer more flexible peace terms when in conversation with Beaverbrook that September, provided Britain joined with the Germans against the Soviet enemy. At no stage, however, did he ever waver in his fanatical loyalty to Hitler, his belief in a Greater Germany or in his hatred of the Jews.

When Hamilton and the Intelligence Officer, along with the Military Officer on guard, were shown in to meet Hess in a small side room, Hess asked Hamilton if they could speak alone. He formally introduced himself and reminded him that he, Hamilton, as a member of the International Olympic Committee, had lunched at his house during the Berlin Olympics, unaware that Hamilton had not been a member of that committee and thus was not present on that occasion. He asked him whether he had seen the photos, thinking that they provided proof of his identity {with his bushy eyebrows and sallow complexion Hess was fairly distinct}, something which Hamilton was not fully prepared to accept. Hess then explained that he was on a mission of humanity. Hitler wanted peace with Britain and Albrecht Haushofer had told him that he, Hamilton, was an Englishman who would understand the German point of view. He had consequently tried to arrange a meeting with him in Lisbon, something which Hamilton had not previously grasped. He went on to say that this was his fourth attempt to come to Britain. The fact that he, Hess, had come in person demonstrated Germany's sincerity in wanting peace. He had come without Hitler's knowledge, but he knew his mind and could vouch for the peace terms he would accept. Could Hamilton assemble the leading members of the 'peace party' and respond to his overtures? Hamilton replied there was now only one party in the country and that was fully supportive of the Churchill government.

Hess continued by indicating the type of peace that Germany was prepared to accept. The two countries should never go to war again, and Britain should abandon its traditional policy of opposing the dominant power in Europe. Hamilton countered by reminding Hess that Germany's constant thwarting of British hopes for peace prior to September 1939 offered no guarantees of future optimism. The interview ended with Hess asking Hamilton to appeal to the King to grant him parole since he had come on his own volition, that his family be informed he was safe and that his true identity be shielded from the press. The last of these requests was soon to be undermined by a German announcement on the evening of 12 May that he was missing.

Fairly convinced from Albrecht Haushofer's description of Hess and from media photos that he had just met Hitler's Deputy, Hamilton told the garrison commander it was possible he was holding a very important prisoner and that he should be moved from Glasgow immediately to a more secure location. With Hess's photos secure in his wallet, he then went to Eaglesham to examine the crashed aircraft before returning to Turnhouse in the afternoon to dictate his report and collect the letter Haushofer had written him in July 1939. According to Mrs Iris Pyne, a WAAF clerk in the operations room, he appeared extremely tense in contrast to his normal relaxed demeanour as he made several telephone calls. [25]

His agitated state was also evident to Sandy Johnstone, a fighter controller at Turnhouse, when Hamilton called him into the controller's rest room. 'Don't think me mad,' he said, 'but I think Rudolf Hess is in Glasgow!'

'Beyond that Douglo said nothing, other than that he must fly to London as soon as possible to report his startling news.' [26]

Hamilton phoned his commanding officer and asked for immediate leave to communicate with Sir Alexander Cadogan, the Permanent Under-Secretary of the Foreign Office. In his official report Hamilton claimed that his fractious conversation with one of its officials regarding his request was his first contact with the Foreign Office, or any other government department, over the mystery German officer. His account is corroborated by Churchill in his *History of the Second World War,* and Cadogan, whose diary for that day records a phone call to his country cottage at 5pm informing him about a matter of great importance. The unaccountably long delay in contacting senior ministers about the extraordinary capture of Hitler's Deputy has mystified many historians. According to John Costello, 'There appears to be only one convincing explanation: that higher authorities knew, either from the Duke himself or from other channels, that Hess was in Britain. It is simply not credible that a commanding officer of a fighter sector with the political experience and contacts that Hamilton had would not have reported the affair to his superiors before he claims he did, late that Sunday afternoon.' [27]

Certainly from John Colville, Churchill's private secretary, we get a different account. In his memoirs he recalls walking over to the Foreign Office at 11 o'clock on the Sunday morning and finding the Foreign Secretary Anthony Eden's deputy private secretary on the telephone to Hamilton. It was a heated conversation because the deputy secretary John Addis – not Nicholas Lawford as Colville has it - appeared unreceptive to Hamilton's request that he should meet Cadogan that evening.

On seeing Colville, Addis beckoned him over and asked him to speak to Hamilton. He did, but Hamilton, according to Colville, would not be specific, remarking only that something extraordinary had occurred, which Colville bizarrely relates to a dream he had had the previous night about a leading Nazi parachuting into Britain. In Hamilton's account he recalls Colville telling him that the Prime Minister had sent him over to the Foreign Office because he had been informed that he, Hamilton, had some interesting information to impart. Both accounts agree that Colville then asked Hamilton whether somebody had arrived, to which Hamilton replied, 'Yes'. [28]

Colville then contacted Churchill and he agreed to see Hamilton that evening, but rather than have Colville meet him at Northolt he arranged for Hamilton to be diverted directly to Kidlington airfield near Oxford.

Although he confuses the deputy secretaries and appears to resort to fabrication over his dream, Colville's account is given some credibility by the memoirs of Sir Ronald Tree MP, a friend of Churchill's and his host on numerous occasions at his Oxfordshire home, Ditchley Park. He was away that weekend, but when he returned a few days later his wife Nancy told him of the strange request by the Prime Minister on Sunday morning, that the Duke of Hamilton spend Sunday night at their home. 'Nancy was totally mystified as to why this peer from remote Scotland was being so suddenly and importantly injected into Mr Churchill's counsels. Hamilton duly arrived, but still the reason for his visit was not stated.' [29]

Nancy Tree's confusion about why Hamilton should suddenly be given such privileged treatment has been echoed by others. But this is to miss the point, for whatever his status in the RAF or otherwise, he was Scotland's premier peer, the Lord Steward, a former Unionist MP and, most important of all, a good friend of Churchill's. At the House of Commons' dinner to honour the Everest flight it was Churchill who had sat next to Hamilton, and it was to him that Hamilton had turned on receipt of Albrecht Haushofer's letter in July 1939.

After a quick return home to collect that letter and a brief conversation with his wife about the day's events, Hamilton left Turnhouse just before 5pm in a Hurricane to fly down to Northolt in North London. On arrival there he was handed an important message in a sealed envelope instructing him to fly to Kidlington. A technical hitch to his aircraft caused by a mechanic priming his carburettor with a hand pump necessitated an hour's delay while a replacement was found. Arriving at Kidlington in a Miles Magister, Hamilton was met by an official black car and chauffeur, who informed him that their destination was Ditchley Park, a well-secluded Georgian mansion close to Blenheim Palace. It was at Ditchley that Churchill stayed on moonlit nights when Chequers, the Prime Minister's official weekend residence, was deemed unduly exposed to German air attacks, and on this occasion he and Sir Archibald Sinclair were among the thirty guests of Sir Ronald Tree's son. The previous night's assault on London, the worst of the war, had resulted in the deaths of over 1,400 people and the House of Commons being burnt to the ground, but far from being demoralised by these reverses, Churchill seemed positively bullish. Greeting Hamilton at the end of a black-tie dinner, he said, 'Now come and tell us this funny story of yours.'

'Sir, I cannot possibly tell you in public. It's necessary I talk with you in private.'

Churchill agreed as the other guests dispersed, leaving Hamilton, still dressed in his crumpled flying suit, to brief him and Sinclair on the day's events. When he had finished a long silence ensued before Churchill asked him with studied emphasis, 'Do you mean to tell me that the Deputy Führer of Germany is in our hands?'

Hamilton showed him the photos of Hess and assured him that they fitted the prisoner he had interviewed that morning.

'Well, Hess or no Hess, I am going to see the Marx Brothers,' Churchill replied. [30]

Exhausted by his exertions, Hamilton slept soundly through the film and awoke only when it was all over, at which point Churchill subjected him to a thorough grilling. During the course of the next two hours Hamilton gave a full explanation as to why he believed the prisoner to be Hess. The key, he believed, was his exact resemblance to the description offered by Albrecht Haushofer and that his peace offer was consistent with the general tenor of Haushofer's two letters to him of July 1939 and September 1940.

Unsure how he should respond to Hess, Churchill asked Hamilton to accompany him to London the next morning. They left Ditchley at 9.15 driving at breakneck speed through the capital's bombed-out streets. On arrival, Churchill gave Eden the gist of the weekend's events and then Hamilton visited the Foreign Office to have the photos checked. Having heard a full account of what had happened from Hamilton, Eden suggested that they should send for Sir Ivone Kirkpatrick, a former First Secretary at the British Embassy in Berlin, who spoke fluent German and knew Hess. Kirkpatrick identified him from the photos before Eden asked him to accompany Hamilton up to Scotland so he could do it formally.

Following another meeting at the Foreign Office that afternoon, Hamilton and Kirkpatrick left London at 5pm in a Flamingo aircraft. Delayed by headwinds they were forced to refuel at Catterick. On arrival

at Turnhouse at 9.40pm, their first priority was to get some food having not eaten since lunchtime, but an emergency call from Sinclair to
Hamilton put paid to that. A German broadcast that evening to the
effect that Hess was missing made it a matter of the utmost priority to
identify the prisoner and let London know as soon as possible.

After a lengthy drive during which the driver lost his way on the
blacked-out roads, they eventually arrived at Buchanan Castle, the military
hospital at Drymen, near Loch Lomond, to which Hess had been transferred that afternoon. The time was midnight. There the commandant
led them up a winding stair to the dimly-lit attic bedroom where they
found Hess asleep on an iron bedstead. Woken up by the guard, he did
not recognise Kirkpatrick, but when Kirkpatrick reminded him of their
previous encounters, he greeted him warmly. Then speaking from copious notes he had prepared that day, Hess launched into a fierce diatribe
about past German grievances against Britain. Refusing to rise to his bait,
Hamilton and Kirkpatrick, seated on hard wooden chairs, absorbed all
the barbs in silence, but at 1am the latter was called to the phone to speak
to Eden, still in emergency session with Churchill and Cadogan in the
Cabinet Office. Kirkpatrick confirmed that the prisoner was definitely
Hess. He returned to find Hamilton comatose as Hess continued his rant
on why Germany would definitely win the war. It was in this context
that he had come to Scotland, without Hitler's knowledge, to convince
the British to make peace by giving Germany a free hand in Europe in
return for Germany leaving the British Empire intact. These proposals,
he emphasised, would not apply to any government led by Churchill.

After a welcome snack in the hospital before they left, the exhausted
pair drove back to Turnhouse, arriving at 6am and Kirkpatrick telephoned the Foreign Office at 8.30am to report on their interrogation.
It was undoubtedly Hess, he declared, but he had yet to fathom why he
had come. The next day Kirkpatrick accompanied Hamilton on a visit
to HMS *Victorious* in the Firth of Forth only to be stopped short by
instructions from Eden to continue their talks with Hess. They found
him in a tetchy state, unhappy about the slow pace of the negotiations
and treatment that he deemed shoddy for someone of his status. Having

heard Hess utter more demands - Britain should leave Iraq - and more threats if she continued the war, Hamilton departed for London leaving Kirkpatrick to conduct one final unsatisfactory interview the next day. Aside from a failure to supply any useful information, Hess in his own fanatical loyalty to Hitler, seemed oblivious to Britain's refusal to countenance peace with a Germany under his control, a rationale which convinced Hamilton that he was both stupid and ignorant.

If Hess was creating a poor impression in Scotland it was nothing compared to the one he had left behind in Germany. When Karl-Heinz Pintsch arrived at the Berghof, Hitler's Alpine retreat at Berchtesgaden, on the morning of 11 May to inform him about the flight, he reacted with uncontrolled fury, fearful that it would undermine national morale and reveal the secrets of his planned attack of the Soviet Union. While Hess's staff were rounded up, including the Haushofers whom Hitler held primarily responsible for the botched expedition, a communiqué was released at 10pm the following evening depicting Hess as mentally unstable. And yet for all the embarrassment his captivity caused the Nazi leadership the British government was caught cold by his arrival and did not know how to respond. On one hand Churchill was minded to let the facts speak for themselves, thereby highlighting German division and irresolution in the face of unremitting British defiance, while on the other Eden favoured something more devious. He saw it as an unexpected opportunity to undermine the German-Soviet rapprochement by hinting at a peace accord between London and Berlin. These divisions were laid bare following a German radio announcement on 14 May.

Hess embarked on his flight with the intention of proceeding to the estate of the Duke of Hamilton and Brandon in Lanarkshire, and as a matter of fact landed in the vicinity of the estate.

——. Hess had made the acquaintance of the Duke at the Olympic Games, Berlin, in 1936, and believed that the Duke belonged to the British group in opposition to Churchill as representative of the clique of warmongers. Hess further believed that the Duke possessed sufficient influence to be able to wage an effective fight against the Churchill clique— The object of his journey to Great Britain was to explain to these circles {around the Duke}, which he believed possible [sic] by reasonable arguments, the real position of England and also the position of Germany. [31]

The broadcast sparked a furious row between Churchill and Eden as how best to respond. With Eden, supported by Beaverbrook, a fellow member of the War Cabinet, successfully blocking Churchill's statement to the House of Commons, the Government's policy of silence provided fertile soil for speculation and insinuation to germinate, much to the detriment of Hamilton and his reputation.

So riled were the British-American press corps about this failure to respond to Goebbels that Walter Monckton, the Director General of the Ministry of Information, felt compelled to release details about Hess's previous attempts to contact Hamilton.

The next day the *Glasgow Herald* took up the baton and ran with that story. 'The Duke had met Hess on one or two occasions before the war in connection with matters of sport in which they were both interested. During the Olympic Games at Berlin in 1936 the Duke {then the Marquis of Clydesdale} met Hess when dining with Hitler. For the Games the German authorities placed cars and various houses at the disposal of the Marquis and members of the Douglas-Hamilton family.' [32]

The *Scotsman* carried an interview with David McLean, the ploughman, who revealed that Hess had told him he knew the Duke well and had flown to Dungavel to give him valuable information. The *Daily Mail* also reported Hess's claims of a previous acquaintance with Hamilton, as did the *Daily Express*, a Beaverbrook newspaper. Under the headline 'Boxing Marquis dined with Hess', it stated that it was Hamilton's 'interest in the British Youth movement that brought him in touch with Hess and other German leaders. He attended several of the great Nazi youth displays and Hess and he dined together and had long talks over political problems'. [33]

Although Hamilton had met Baldur von Schirach, the leader of the Hitler Youth, at the World Congress on Leisure Time and Recreation in

Rome in June 1938, there was nothing else in the story that was remotely accurate. Had the *Express* simply not checked its facts or was there something more sinister? According to Anne Chisholm and Michael Davie, Beaverbrook's most recent biographers, Hamilton's failure to support his Empire Crusade back in 1930 had never been forgiven. [34]

Their opinion was later echoed by the historian Richard Davenport-Hines in *An English Affair: Sex, Class and Power in the Age of Profumo.* Calling Beaverbrook's *Express* newspapers 'seedbeds of ancient rancour', Davenport-Hines wrote that 'For a quarter of a century his newspapers inserted disobliging paragraphs about the Duke of Hamilton, partly because he was a duke, but chiefly because Hamilton as a young parliamentary candidate had rejected an offer of Beaverbrook's support during a by-election'.[35]

As a leading appeaser who had met Hess himself and who had been in contact with pacifist elements of the ILP during the East Renfrewshire by-election of 1940, Beaverbrook's position remained a matter of some discussion during the spring of 1941. An opportunity therefore to shift attention away from his own association with Hess by focusing on Hamilton was one the ever devious Beaverbrook was quick to exploit. At a press lunch at Claridge's that same day he repeated the claims of his newspaper, while Alfred Duff Cooper, the Minister of Information, added fuel to the fire by saying something similar to the BBC. Even Churchill's proposed statement of 14 May, for all its reference to Hamilton's conduct as 'honourable and proper' in every respect, acknowledged that he had met Hess before.

Others laboured under the same impression. Harold Nicolson told his wife that Hess had years ago made friends with Hamilton and his brother Geordie. 'They had discussed the possibility of an alliance between Germany and Britain. The memories of these conversations came back to him.' [36] Two of Hamilton's parliamentary colleagues at the Olympics, Kenneth Lindsay, who did interview Hess, and 'Chips' Channon, both affirmed that the two had met, and Brendan Bracken, the then Minister of Information, said something very similar at a New York press conference in August 1943. Later the author Ian Colvin in his biography of Sir Robert Vansittart claimed that Vansittart's wife had introduced Hamilton to Hess at the Chancellery dinner. [**37**]

The allegations taxed Hamilton and possibly sowed a seed of doubt in his mind. For despite his genuine denials about meeting Hess before 11 May 1941, the possibility remained that he might have inadvertently overlooked a fleeting encounter five years earlier at a time when he was meeting all and sundry. He told Sinclair that the two of them might have been at the same function, but had no recollection of them being introduced. Later when he drew up his statement in the libel action he initiated against the London District Committee of the Communist Party, he changed it from an initial categorical denial of any encounter with Hess to something slightly more flexible; 'It is possible that he was at one of the large parties which I attended but I did not recall his name or consider him a person in particular I wanted to see.'

Hamilton's claims were corroborated by Hess himself, contrary to his earlier comments to him after his arrival. 'It is untrue to say that I knew the Duke of Hamilton,' he later told Colonel Eugene Bird, the American Commander of Spandau Prison. 'I had never met the man, never dined with him. If he was in the same room as I was during the Berlin Olympic Games, we never conversed. I of course knew about him and his flying.' [**38**]

When Bird cross-examined him on a further occasion Hess stated that 'It was the Haushofers who knew the Duke of Hamilton. Contrary to what books say since I flew, I had never met the man. —When I flew I took Haushofer's visiting card with me to present to him.' [**39**]

Further confirmation of Hess's reminiscences came from his son, Wolf Rüdiger Hess, in a letter to James Douglas-Hamilton of 23 August 1980, a few weeks after they had met in London. He told him that he had asked his mother whether his father had come across Hamilton during the Berlin Olympic Games and she confirmed that they had never met before May 1941 in Scotland. {He was to prove much more equivocal in his memoir of his father several years later, claiming that Hamilton had played a prominent role in the conspiracy to lure him to Britain.}

As speculation mounted about the real motive behind Hess's mission, Hamilton was placed in an almost impossible position. 'The poor Duke of Hamilton feels acutely the slur of being taken as a potential Quisling - which he certainly is not,' Colville confided to his diary as early as 13 May, and on the same day George VI wrote in his diary: '— I went to London. Alec H. [Sir Alexander Hardinge, his private secretary] told me Hess had landed 2 miles from Clydesdale's home, I should say the Duke of Hamilton's, as they knew each other before the war.— My Lord Steward, Hamilton, has only been appointed for a year—,' he continued rather ominously. [40/41]

By the time Hamilton met Duff Cooper two days later to set the record straight his stock had depreciated ever further with the additional allegation circulating that Hess had been permitted to fly across Scotland unopposed. A contrite Cooper offered to help draft an official statement that Churchill would give to the House of Commons or prepare a reply to a planted question. The next day Hamilton mulled over the two options with the King when lunching with him at Windsor, the King favouring the second one. 'The Duke of Hamilton came to see me, & explained the reason why his name has been mixed up with the arrival of Hess,' he wrote in his diary. 'As my Lord Steward, he felt it was right to come and see me. He told me he had never met Hess in Germany before the war, but that he had had talks with a Professor Haushofer who was a great friend of Hess. On the latter's arrival he {Hess} had asked at once to see Hamilton, who did see him. Hess gave a fictitious name to the farmer who captured him of "Alfred Horn" but revealed his true identity to Hamilton. Hamilton showed me a copy of his interview with Hess, & two interviews Kirkpatrick had had with him.— Hamilton also told me that Hess had asked him to ask me to give him his 'Parole' while he was here!!—' [42]

Three days later Hamilton returned to the Foreign Office and the day after that he was granted the briefest of interviews with Churchill as they travelled together in the Prime Minister's car from Downing Street to Buckingham Palace. Alluding to the pummelling he had taken in the press, Hamilton pointedly asked Churchill: 'What do you tell your wife if a prostitute throws her arms around you?' Churchill was much amused by his analogy and while imploring him to keep his own counsel, he promised him a public show of solidarity. [43]

On 22 May, in the Commons, Sir Archibald Sinclair robustly refuted press claims that Hamilton and his three brothers had previously met Hess or had been in correspondence with him. 'It will be seen that the conduct of the Duke of Hamilton has been in every respect honourable and proper,' he said to loud cheers. When a Labour MP sought an assurance that Hess had not written to Hamilton before his arrival in Scotland, Sinclair retorted that he could not say that; only that no letter had reached Hamilton or any responsible party. [44]

That same day Sinclair, on behalf of the Air Ministry, wrote a formal letter of complaint to Duff Cooper at the Ministry of Information. He informed him how shocked he was to hear that the story published in some newspapers, that Hamilton had been in correspondence with Hess, had been inspired by his department.

There was no truth whatever in the story. The Duke had assured him personally that he had never received a letter from Hess. He expressed surprise that his Department should have given currency to a story that affected the reputation of a serving officer in the Royal Air Force without consulting him. He hoped he could rely on him to ensure that no such a thing ever happened again.

In its reply the Ministry fully acknowledged the nub of Sinclair's complaint: that Hamilton had never received any correspondence from Hess. Its statement had been drafted with a view to protecting him by avoiding any suggestion that the letter addressed to him - Albrecht Haushofer's one of 23 September 1940 - was actually written or signed by Hess. {Hess had of course, unknown to Hamilton, been the instigator behind it.} Hence its statement that he had received the letter and passed it on to the security authorities rather than it had been intercepted.

Five days after Sinclair's statement, Harold Nicolson, Duff Cooper's deputy, under fierce questioning from a Conservative MP, sought to clarify matters in the Commons. The information supplied to the BBC was erroneous. The true facts were those stated by the Secretary of State for Air on 22 May. 'There is no question of any imputation on the Duke of Hamilton's personal conduct. He has acted with the utmost circumspection and carefulness. For any statement for which my Ministry is responsible which may have led to any doubts about his integrity we must apologise, and we do so now.' [45]

As far as Hamilton was concerned, these two parliamentary exchanges should have settled the whole matter once and for all, but Sinclair's and Nicolson's assurances, far from quelling speculation, only added to it. In an Adjournment Debate on 17 July, the left-wing MP Sidney Silverman raised the whole question of Hess and complained about the unsatisfactory nature of the replies given to questions in the House. The people were entitled to know from the Government Hess's motives for coming. Did he or did he not bring a peace plan? Another Labour MP and prominent appeaser, Richard Stokes, challenged the official line that Hamilton did not know Hess. From all that he had heard from people who had flown and visited Continental flying clubs there was no possible doubt that the two knew each other.

Prior to this, Hamilton had been preoccupied by various allegations outside Parliament. Anne Chisholm and Michael Davie relate how post-22 May Hamilton's solicitor, Godfrey Norris, called on John Gordon, the editorial chief of the *Sunday Express*, to urge him to withdraw damaging statements that Hamilton had met Hess both before the war and once it had started. He agreed to do so, but at their next meeting his attitude had changed. Having conferred with the management he declared that Sinclair's Commons statement was false and that the *Sunday Express* would be prepared to defend itself in the courts. [46]

The fact that Hamilton did not respond to this rebuff is significant to conspiracy theorists, especially as Beaverbrook was one of the four recipients of his secret report about Hess's arrival. Certainly Hamilton did contemplate legal action until mollified by Nicolson's apology of 27 May. 'There appears to be no doubt that the Minister of Information got hold of the wrong end of the stick and gave the press a false impression,' he wrote to Norris on 30 May. 'I think, however, that Harold Nicolson's recent statement should have cleared the matter up sufficiently.' [47]

Four days later he was less philosophical when alerted by Norris to a leaflet entitled *Why is Hess Here?* It alleged that Hamilton had colluded with the enemies of his country and was sympathetic to the Nazi government because he wanted to suppress the working class. Did the authors seriously believe this? Perhaps, but at a time when the British Communists were under bitter attack for 'sitting out' the war in conformity with the Nazi-Soviet Pact until Hitler's attack of the Soviet Union, they sought scapegoats everywhere they could to deflect attention from their quiescence. Advised by counsel to ask for damages and an injunction, Hamilton, believing the article to be a slur on his character, did precisely that. Having secured the support of the Air Ministry, he issued the writ against Harry Pollitt, Ted Bramley and Marston Printing Company. Later he issued another one against Howard Goodman, publisher of the Communist journal *World News and Views,* and the author Ivor Montagu for similar allegations.

The decision unnerved Herbert Morrison, the Home Secretary, who fretted that the defendant might call Hess as a witness with all the potential embarrassment he could cause the British government. Hamilton had every right as a citizen to go to court, he informed Sinclair, but he wondered what he would gain by a libel action, especially since his reputation had been entirely cleared by Sinclair's statement in Parliament.

He asked Sinclair to use his influence to persuade Hamilton to withdraw. Sinclair duly wrote to Hamilton expressing sorrow that he had been unable to keep his name out of the 'squalid' controversy about Hess. Nobody, however, could control the Communists and he was not surprised at his indignation at their 'mendacious' pamphlet. He felt obliged to send him a copy of Morrison's letter, but sought to reassure him that he was in no way coercing him to abandon his action. If he decided to go ahead with it, he would fully support him.

After considering the matter Hamilton replied that as the libel had been issued after the statement in Parliament, and as it was such a gross one, he conceived it his duty to bring proceedings against the authors 'and I am sure that you will not disagree with my reasons'. He would withdraw if Morrison declared it to be in the national interest, 'but to withdraw the actions after having commenced them would place me in a very difficult position and would undoubtedly give rise to further statements which might be more objectionable than those which are the subject of the present proceedings'. [48]

On 26 June, Hamilton served the writ with Churchill's blessing as well as Sinclair's, the latter telling colleagues that if he withdrew now, the Communist Party would be encouraged to repeat its allegations much to the detriment of Hamilton, the RAF and, quite possibly, the Government itself. After an interminable delay, the case was eventually settled out of court when the defendants, in the absence of any evidence, were forced to apologise publicly. {Pollitt was exonerated on the grounds that he had no part in the slurs.} In a statement in *The Times* on 19 February 1942, they accepted 'That they had no intention whatever of impugning the character or loyalty of the plaintiff [Hamilton], and unreservedly accept the plaintiff's assurance that he had no sympathy with the Nazis or the Government in Germany; that he had never met Hess; and that he has never received any letter from Hess at any time. The defendants therefore regret and unreservedly apologise for any of the statements made by them which could be interpreted as reflecting personally on the plaintiff'. [49]

Hamilton had won an important battle, but the war to clear his name had only just begun. The trial did nothing to eradicate Soviet suspicions of British complicity in the Hess affair. The failure of the Chamberlain government to unite with the Soviet Union against Germany at the time of Munich, and its subsequent efforts to destabilise the Molotov-Ribbentrop Pact of August 1939, gave some substance to Soviet fears when they heard about Hess's arrival in Britain bearing peace proposals for Hamilton, especially since the two were allegedly in contact prior to that. The Intelligence sources for such information were notoriously unreliable, with much of it emanating from the double-agent Kim Philby, who later defected to the Soviet Union, but the British government's deliberate campaign of disinformation about Hess in order to try and win over Stalin served only to convince him of perfidious Albion. According to John Erickson, a leading authority on the Soviet Union, the Hess affair with all its conspiracy theories never died. 'For Moscow the German attack on 22 June 1941 confirmed an inextricable link between war and the circumstances of Hess's flight to Britain.' [50] A Soviet Intelligence report submitted to Stalin in October 1942 based on information supplied by Colonel František Moravec, the head of Czech Military Intelligence, placed responsibility for Hess's flight squarely at the door of British Intelligence. The Soviet version refuted the idea that Hess had arrived unexpectedly in London. Long before his flight he had corresponded with Hamilton about it as well as the absolute priority of an Anglo-German truce given Germany's plans to attack the Soviet Union. However Hamilton himself took no part in the correspondence. It was the Secret Service who answered in his name as part of its device to lure Hess to Britain.

These allegations of a British Intelligence plot gave Stalin a stick with which to beat Churchill, something he proceeded to do whenever they met, especially given his government's failure to place Hess on trial for war crimes. According to Oliver Harvey, Eden's secretary, it brought Anglo-Soviet relations to a new low. 'The presence of Hess here is now being made a source of offence,' he wrote on 26 October 1942, '— Do the Russians seriously think we are keeping him for some anti-Soviet move? Hess is quite mad and useless for any purpose.' [51]

The Hess affair rumbled on throughout the war. It was to quell the feverish allegations that had mushroomed in the US that Brendan Bracken gave his notorious press conference there in August 1943, in which he disclosed the reasons behind Hess's flight to Britain, information that had been withheld from Parliament. When MPs bristled at this breach of parliamentary etiquette, Eden reassured them that Bracken had not intended any slight. The Government had withheld information in the earlier stages and made no apologies for so doing 'because we thought a certain amount of perplexity was not unhealthy for Germany'. He went on to reveal the bare facts of the affair and the desire of Hess to make peace with Britain. [52]

Eden's statement, and a brief interview by Hamilton with the *Daily Mail*, which disclosed little, generated a stack of dramatic headlines, but it did not kill off the speculation as Hamilton discovered in April 1945 when he was forced to cancel a trip to the US on behalf of Scottish Aviation. Concerned as to how he would cope with the grilling he was likely to receive from local journalists, he had asked Bracken for a covering letter. Bracken obliged proposing letters to leading American media magnates testifying to Hamilton's sterling character and asking the head of the British Information Services, New York, to help him during press conferences. Bracken's idea, however, that Churchill provide Hamilton with a special testimonial was brusquely rejected by the Prime Minister. Having recently been subjected to a stream of vitriol from Stalin about the duplicity of the British Secret Service in enticing Hess to Britain, Churchill had no wish to reopen the controversy in a country where Hamilton's character had been impugned.

In the climate of confusion that greeted Hess's arrival in Britain in May 1941, it was not long before rumours started circulating back to the US. A memorandum from J.Edgar Hoover, the Director of the FBI, told of a conversation with an unnamed source close to the German Ambassador that mentioned the existence of a peace group which numbered Hamilton among its members. It was this group that Hess was trying to contact with a view to terminating hostilities between Britain and Germany.

Other rumours of this type abounded in the US, exacerbated by the British government's silence on Hess's whereabouts, and in October 1941 the Dutch-American journalist Pierre Van Paassen, in a book entitled *That Day Alone,* accused Hamilton of conspiracy. 'With the Duke of Hamilton, a British Fascist, Rudolf Hess had carried on an assiduous correspondence ever since the beginning of war. Before September, 1939, they visited each other, hunted together, planned together, and held discussions and conferences with mutual British friends.' [53]

Only alerted to the offending publication many months later, Hamilton was furious that his good name both as a serving officer and private citizen had once again been called into disrepute. When Godfrey Norris reminded him that American libel laws were very weak, he replied that he would go over there if necessary and consult Eddie Eagan, by then a leading attorney. Instead he took advice from the New York solicitors, Baldwin, Todd and Young. They pointed out that under New York state law any proceedings against libel had to be brought within twelve months of the libel, which effectively ruled out any action against the Dial Press, the original publishers, since the book was published the previous year. This left the option of action against the much less wealthy *Omnibook Magazine*, which had published an abridged version of *That Day Alone* in its January 1942 edition, but here again they urged caution. Although Hamilton could expect exemplary damages this would no doubt involve drawn-out litigation and publicity. What is more, the amount he was likely to win would be small given that Hamilton was relatively unknown to the average New York juror and that the case dealt with events far from New York.

This advice, and the fact that the money meant much less to him than his reputation, explains why Hamilton, having filed for £25,000, settled for something much less. On 17 March 1943, Van Paassen made a public retraction and apology in the Federal Court, agreed to reimburse Hamilton for the cost of two libel suits and remove the offending passages from the book. {The English version of Van Paassen's book, published in 1943, did not contain any reference to Hamilton or Hess's visit in May 1941.}

This was not the end of the matter. An article in the extreme right-wing *American Mercury* in May 1943 alleged that Hess had been in touch with friends in Britain prior to his flight, and representatives of British Intelligence were waiting for him at Dungavel, a summary of which was published by the prestigious *Reader's Digest* in its July edition. Owing to the fairly general nature of the allegations, Hamilton was advised not to press for libel but rather to turn his fire on a damning article in the June edition of the little-known *Democratic Action News Letter*. A writ was issued against the editor and publisher, J. Redfern Collins, on 4 November 1943, and advised by his solicitor that he had no defence, Collins accepted responsibility in an out-of-court settlement.

With this history of controversy about Hess in the US, and continuing Russian sensitivities about the matter, it is perhaps understandable why Churchill acted as he did in April 1945, but cancelling Hamilton's visit at the eleventh hour left him distinctly unimpressed. 'This step, I fear, will prove more harmful than any reaction there may or may not be on my visit,' he protested to the Prime Minister. 'Already I have reason to be seriously concerned regarding the effect of this matter on my personal reputation and this assumes wider proportions in view of my position in Scottish Aviation matters.'[54]

He could conceive of no satisfactory explanation he could give to the representative bodies that were expecting him and with his departure due for the next day, he hoped he would receive Churchill's permission to leave before then.

He did not. At the request of Sinclair, Hamilton contacted the Air Military Police only to hear that they had barred him from travelling to the US. 'As I clearly cannot say publicly that the Prime Minister had my journey cancelled on the grounds of political implications and it would be undesirable to question the Air Ministry's decision in giving me this leave of absence,' he wrote to Sinclair in high dudgeon, 'I find myself in a most awkward position.'

Regarding the Hess incident, I have been most reluctant, while the war is in progress, to intrude my personal position. I hope, however, that you will forgive me for bringing it up now. I am indeed most grateful to you for the steps you took on my behalf at the time, and especially for the way you dealt with this matter in Parliament. It is, however, becoming increasingly clear that I am regarded with suspicion fairly widely in America, and I feel that some further action should be taken to counteract this. [55]

In reply Sinclair told him that he thought that, after full consideration of all the circumstances, the Air Ministry's reasons for not releasing him at that stage of the war were strong and conclusive. He admitted that he had known nothing about his plan until it had been brought to his attention by the protests of some of his colleagues on other grounds. It would have been embarrassing to have had the Hess controversy stirred up yet again.

He took issue with Hamilton's claim that he was regarded with suspicion in the US, but warned that the Hess episode was still a subject of curiosity and had the potential to excite suspicion in other countries, and arouse feeling in Germany which might be detrimental to the interests of British prisoners still languishing in German hands.

He concluded by assuring Hamilton that every effort would be made to safeguard his position when the full story of the Hess affair could be told, and he, Sinclair, would always be ready to give his testimony, but while Britain remained at war with Germany the less said about Hess the better.

Hess, meanwhile, was struggling in captivity, dismayed that he could not see Hamilton again or gain access to the King. After a brief stay at the Tower of London in May 1941, he was transferred to Mytchett Place, a country house near Aldershot, where he was interviewed by Lord Simon, the Lord Chancellor, in great secrecy. His message remained a defiant one: Britain should submit or be destroyed by Germany. Later, when interviewed by Beaverbrook that September, he shifted his focus to a proposal of joint German-British cooperation in the war against the Soviet Union.

He remained closely guarded as his behaviour became ever more mercurial - he apparently tried twice to commit suicide - as he struggled to come to terms with his captivity and the failure of his mission. After moving to Maindiff Court Military Hospital, Abergavenny, South Wales, in June 1942, he was flown to Nuremberg in October 1945 to stand trial as a war criminal along with nineteen others. Despite claims of amnesia, he was found guilty of making preparations for war and was sentenced to life imprisonment in Berlin's Spandau Prison, many years of which were spent in solitary confinement.

Hess's flight had caught Albrecht Haushofer completely unawares and not surprisingly he reacted with despair to the news. Not only did he discern the futility of the mission, he had lost his leading protector in the brutal aftermath. A furious Hitler held him and his father responsible for Hess's apostasy and both were drummed out of public life.

While hopes of an understanding with Britain remained even a remote possibility, Albrecht Haushofer had his uses but his growing links with the German Resistance and General Beck, one of its leaders, for whom he wrote a peace plan, placed him in ever greater peril. Following the failure of the von Stauffenberg Bomb Plot, an attempt by senior German officers to kill Hitler in July 1944, the Gestapo went after Albrecht Haushofer and captured him that December while hiding in Bavaria. From there he was taken to Berlin and subjected to rigorous interrogation which established his guilt beyond doubt.

As he awaited his fate in the desolate confines of Berlin's Moabit Prison, his written confessionals revealed an essentially decent man out of his depth when dealing with the machinations of the Nazi era. On 21 April 1945, as the Russians pounded the outskirts of Berlin, Albrecht Haushofer met his tragic end, shot by the SS, leaving his father a broken man. The following March he and his wife committed suicide near their home, two more victims of a creed that had consigned 60 million to death and many others to untold misery. 'The death of your brother Albrecht deeply distressed me,' Hamilton later wrote to Heinz Haushofer, Albrecht's brother and a fellow captive before being freed by the Russians, 'for had he lived, I believe he would have made a great contribution in these difficult days.' [56] He asked for a copy of Albrecht's poems and his photo and derived pleasure from the fact that Heinz sent his son to Gordonstoun.

Although in one sense Hamilton viewed his involvement with Hess as a four-day affair it continued to tax him thereafter. An allegation in the February 1950 edition of the American magazine *Truth* that he had been engaged in treasonable correspondence with Hess was quickly disowned in the next edition, along with a very public apology, following a letter from Hamilton's lawyers. Later that year he wrote to Churchill asking him to make alterations to his war memoirs after extracts had appeared in the *Daily Telegraph* stating that he had met Hess before the war.

Part of Hamilton's problem lay in his inhibitions about telling his side of the story. Back in 1946 he confided to Eddie Eagan that he would like to give an interview about Hess, but would need to wait until such time as he had the blessing of the Foreign Office. Nothing further was heard from him until April 1961 following the release of German Foreign Office documents that pinpointed the role of Albrecht Haushofer in giving Hamilton's name to Hess. In a front-page interview with the *Scottish Daily Mail*, Hamilton revealed the existence of Haushofer's two letters and was quoted as saying that had the second letter been promptly delivered the war might have ended five years earlier, a statement that roused him to immediate action. 'I have never suggested anything so absurd as that any meeting that might have taken place between myself and Hess could have altered the course of the war,' he wrote in indignation to the *Scotsman* and *Glasgow Herald*. [57]

It was now in light of all the inaccurate reporting about the Hess affair that Hamilton felt inclined to tell his side of the story and began to jot down a few incidents, but the book never materialised. The following year he turned down the offer of an interview on Canadian television about his role and later declined to participate in a full-length BBC documentary about Hess. He also asked his friend Sandy Johnstone to confine himself to operational matters when he touched on Hess in his autobiography. He did, however, cooperate with the German writers Roger Manvell and Heinrich Fraenkel in their biography of Hess and with his son James when he came to write his *Motive for a Mission*. David Douglas-Hamilton recalls that his father was initially reluctant to talk about the episode, but in response to James's persistent questioning he relaxed his guard, and in the end was more than happy to give his side of the story. *Motive for a Mission* was published in 1971 to favourable reviews, including one from the radical journalist and historian Owen Dudley Edwards. He recounts how some time afterwards he and his wife were invited to dine at Lennoxlove, the family seat near Haddington, during which Hamilton spoke with great insight about the events in James's book. Although fully admiring of his stoicism and humility, Dudley Edwards could not help thinking that he had been badly scarred by his treatment, let down by people who should have known better.

With the British government reluctant to release all the files on Hess and the Soviet Union continuing to entertain suspicions about the affair, talk of a cover-up gained credence. The 1990s saw a number of publications peddling various accounts of this theme, few of which did justice to Hamilton. Now that all the files have been released and show Hamilton to be guilty of nothing more untoward than naivety, his place in history is due for considerable reappraisal.

Hamilton also kept his distance from the Hess family. When Ilse Hess contacted him after the war, requesting the return of the photos of her husband's flight, he did not reply but passed the letter to the Foreign Office. Similarly, when Wolf Rüdiger Hess, on a visit to Britain in 1967 organised by the *Daily Express*, sought Hamilton's help in getting his father released from Spandau, Hamilton did not believe there was any useful purpose in the two of them meeting. He did, however, write to George Brown, the then Foreign Secretary, to register his unease about Hess's continued incarceration after so many years and when clearly he was no longer a threat. While he did not think he was the person to take up the matter, not least with the Russians who remained suspicious about the whole affair, he hoped others would.

From the time that Hess became the sole occupant in Spandau in September 1966, support for his release gathered pace with only the Russians objecting, partly because it gave them a continued presence in West Berlin and partly for fear of what secrets Hess might divulge, especially in relation to the Molotov-Ribbentrop Pact of August 1939. Faced with Russian obduracy, Hess was condemned to another twenty years of misery until committing suicide in 1987, the final act in a life of perpetual incarceration ever since that fateful May evening nearly fifty years earlier.

8. $\mathcal{D}$ISTANT HORIZONS

On 30 May 1941, Hamilton returned to Turnhouse newly promoted. According to Mrs Pyne, there was great delight at HQ when he came in with the insignia of a Group Captain on his sleeves and cap. 'Obviously whatever may have been said in the corridors of power did not adversely affect him. In fact the 'Waafery' [the WAAF personnel] decided we should throw a party for him- we did and he had a jolly good time I remember. He was able to relax by then. The station returned to normal after that, and the whole Hess affair was no longer spoken of.' [1]

Within three months Hamilton was on the move again to take command of the Air Training Corps {ATC} in Scotland. The ATC, founded in February 1941, grew out of the Air Defence Cadet Corps, the first official organisation established by the Government to train fifteen to eighteen-year-olds in aviation skills, either in the air or on the ground. The ATC in Scotland was run by Sir Edward Tennant, and following his death in an aircraft accident in the Cairngorms that August, Hamilton, who sat on its Advisory Council, was considered his obvious successor. Before the Council's next meeting on 20 August, its chairman, Lord Glentanar, conferred with him to ascertain his reaction to such an appointment. Hamilton replied that he was an officer and did what he was ordered to do. He would give up his operational control with very great regret, but appreciated the importance of the new position.

When the question of Tennant's successor as Commandant was raised, the Council was unanimous in proposing Hamilton. 'It will be a very popular appointment both with Officers and Cadets,' Glentanar informed Sir Archibald Sinclair. [2] 'The Air Training Corps is, I am convinced, an organisation of fundamental importance not only for the present but for the future,' Sinclair wrote to Hamilton. 'It's foundations in Scotland were laid by Edward Tennant and I can think of no one more fitted to carry on the work than yourself.' [3]

Hamilton's main responsibility was to travel around Scotland to encourage the young to sign up and provide them with the best possible training facilities, but first he was immersed in administrative matters. At his first meeting on 17 September, he declared that a great amount of work fell on the area commanders and he felt it necessary to appoint regional officers to certain areas such as Glasgow and the South-West where recruitment was poor. The next month he submitted a short report to the Air Ministry requesting permission to set up training centres for Scottish officers at certain aerodromes, an ATC headquarters in Glasgow and the post of District Inspecting Officer for Scotland. By December these were all approved and he could now turn to recruitment.

In November 1941 he wrote to the main Scottish newspapers to advertise the scheme and the following February he spearheaded a recruitment week. Nearly 15,000 had signed up so far, he reported, and the quality had been high, but the number from the Glasgow area remained disappointing. Overall, many more were needed. Stressing the importance of air power and its revolutionary potential post-war regarding trade and travel, he called the ATC a great youth movement whose specialist training in leadership, self-discipline and good citizenship would equip them for a career in the services. Seventy-five per cent of ATC cadets went airborne and the fact that 40 per cent of those joining the RAF had only had an elementary education amply demonstrated that it was a career open to all types. Within a month recruitment was up by nearly one thousand, but while numbers continued to grow the shortage of gliders and instructors meant it would be possible to run only one glider school in Scotland and that was at Dungavel.

In June 1942 Hamilton hosted a successful five-day visit to Scotland by his old friend Wavell Wakefield, the Director of the ATC, who pronounced himself most impressed by the physique and standard of Scottish cadets. Weeks later the two of them were locked in emergency talks following Hamilton's opposition to attempts to centralise the direction of the whole Corps at the Air Ministry. He sent a memorandum to the Ministry reminding it that local government in Scotland was administered separately from the Secretary of State and that each region had its own distinct style of organisation. So seriously did he feel about it that he contemplated resignation until Glentanar asked him to hold fire while he broached the matter with Sinclair.

Hamilton's reservations, which were shared by Glentanar himself, were enough to make Wakefield see sense. After talks between him and Hamilton it was agreed that the latter would continue to issue orders to Scottish units as hitherto. The only change would be the exercise of a right previously not used - and one that Hamilton accepted - the issuing of major orders to the whole Corps under the signature of the Permanent Under-Secretary.

With his officer training schools proving a great success, Hamilton continued to innovate, establishing the Scottish Educational Board and Chaplain's Committee to give guidance on educational and religious matters affecting the ATC in Scotland. He also formed the Scottish ATC Boxing Association and presided over rising standards of fitness in recruits.

A frequent speaker at schools and colleges, Hamilton attended ATC camps all over the country and tried to increase the opportunities for flying, which inevitably were restricted by the lack of aircraft available. By September 1943 the number of cadets had risen to about 18,500, but with interest beginning to lag in Scotland, as elsewhere, Hamilton launched a fresh appeal in Edinburgh for several thousand more. He raised hopes of better glider facilities with two stations about to come into operation and four others under consideration, hopes which were partially realised.

Well aware that some of the outlying areas of Scotland struggled under more difficult conditions than other parts of the country, Hamilton won commendation from district officers for his help tending to their needs. His resignation in August 1945 in order to devote more time to his many other commitments was the cause of much regret, not least in Scotland. According to Air Marshal Sir Leslie Gossage, Wakefield's successor, there was no doubt that his Command had thrived during the period that he had been in charge; his presentation of particular difficulties to Scotland and his suggestion for meeting them had been particularly welcome and acceptable to everyone at the Air Ministry.

During the war Hamilton and his brothers made history by becoming the only four brothers in the RAF to be professional instructors and Squadron Leaders. After serving as Dowding's Chief Intelligence Officer and Director of Training at the Air Ministry, Geordie was appointed a group captain in East Africa countering the German U Boat task force operations near Ceylon. He had a close shave on the way out when five Ju88 long-range fighters attacked his Wellington bomber over the Bay of Biscay and shot his windscreen away, but a combination of rapid retaliation and cloud cover enabled him to survive.

Malcolm spent two years as a flight instructor in Rhodesia before returning to lead No 540 Photographic Reconnaissance Squadron on dangerous aerial missions, exploits that won him the Military Order of the British Empire and the Distinguished Flying Cross.

David also began the war as a flying instructor, the prelude to his command of 603 {City of Edinburgh} Spitfire Squadron in Malta at a time when the island was under sustained attack from the Axis powers. Despite being greatly outnumbered and suffering heavy casualties, the squadron absorbed everything the enemy threw at it, and retaliated in kind to ensure that the island, vital for strategic operations in the Mediterranean, remained in Allied hands. After having given his all to 603, David joined Malcolm at RAF Benson, leading some thirty photographic reconnaissance sorties over German-occupied Europe. On 2 August 1944, he and his navigator were returning to base from a hazardous mission in Southern France on one engine after their Mosquito had been badly damaged by anti-aircraft fire. As they prepared to land at Benson the second engine gave out, causing the aircraft to crash. Both pilot and navigator were killed instantly.

David's death was a devastating blow to his family and many friends. 'It is indeed an irreparable loss to us all and especially to his wife and little boys,' Hamilton wrote to a friend. 'Having come through some of the heaviest fighting in Malta, we had hoped that he might have been spared to enjoy the fair future which seemed to lie before him and to play his part in building up this shattered world after the war. He now joins that gallant company who have given their lives for what indeed is the one Crusade worth dying for.' [4]

Ever since its inception Hamilton and McIntyre had dreamed dreams about Scottish Aviation Limited {SAL} becoming both a major international airline operator and leading manufacturer which would accomplish for aviation what the Clyde had done for shipping. The war went some way towards realising their vision as the company's manufacturing business increased dramatically and Prestwick became the main base for American military aircraft. With crossings taking place at over one thousand per month by 1944 it was incumbent upon the airport to develop its facilities to the standard required for this massive increase in traffic. The runways were enlarged, the Transatlantic Area Air Traffic Control Centre took up residence there and passenger facilities in the terminal building were greatly improved.

With Prestwick now among the best-equipped airports in the country, Hamilton and McIntyre, its Station Commander during the war, saw its potential in the new lucrative transatlantic market in which their company could play a leading role. As early as 1942 they were trumpeting it as a transatlantic airport to the Air Ministry and in their Development Plan the following year they made clear their intention to form a Scottish International Airlines. The Air Ministry, however, was deaf to their overtures, claiming that only one international airport was affordable and that was Heathrow.

At a board meeting in March 1943, Hamilton intimated that the Secretary of State for Scotland, Tom Johnston, was actively interested in the prospect of Prestwick becoming a designated international airport, provided SAL's motives were not simply profit-driven. In order to convince the Air Ministry that their overriding priority was a flourish-ing aviation industry in Scotland, he sought board approval to write to Johnston offering company cooperation in the form of a public utility corporation to run the airport.

His proposals were supported by his brother Geordie and McIntyre, but other shareholders including W.E.Nixon, the chairman, baulked at a policy that did not equate the development of aviation with private enterprise. {They also considered the plan for Scottish International Airlines to be financially flawed.}

Hamilton duly met Johnston and secured an undertaking from him to lobby the Air Ministry on behalf of Prestwick and its international status. He then discussed with Nixon his proposals that SAL become a public company to develop an airline, well aware that it would clash with the interests of de Havilland, which had airline operators among its customers. An amicable parting of the ways ensued with Hamilton becoming SAL's chairman and the Hamilton trustees, now with more capital available, buying out the existing shareholders.

At a dinner at Prestwick on 29 November 1943 to mark the third anniversary of the first American arrival there, Hamilton, with Tom Johnston, the principal guest, expressed his belief that making Prestwick an international airport would promote trade, employment and prosperity in Scotland. A radio documentary in February 1944 featuring Prestwick's wartime development was the prelude to the company hosting British and American journalists at the airport. The journalists liked what they saw. 'Group Captain McIntyre and the Duke have every reason to be proud of Prestwick Airport,' opined the *Glasgow Evening News*. 'It is their dream come true.' [5]

Yet for all the accolades heaped upon Prestwick, the Air Ministry remained unconvinced about its future place in the sun, something that naturally perturbed SAL. Speaking at Milngavie in February 1945, Hamilton stressed the importance of giving immediate encouragement to the conversion, assembly and production of aircraft in Scotland and having an international airport there. He received support from Scottish MPs of all persuasions when the future of civil aviation was debated in Parliament that April. At first the Government appeared to pour cold water on the project by claiming that Britain could only afford one top-class airport and that would be Heathrow. The next month there was a partial reprieve when the Under-Secretary of Civil Aviation announced that Prestwick would be designated as one of the terminals for international traffic.

In practice the future of both the airport and SAL remained in jeopardy, a situation exacerbated by the election of a Labour government in July 1945 committed to the nationalisation of both airports and airlines. At a lunch hosted by the company to bid farewell to Transcontinental and Western Airlines, two of the US's largest airlines, Hamilton expressed deep regret that they were moving from Prestwick to the Irish Republic, the result of the British government's refusal to subscribe to an international agreement on civil airline deregulation. The fact that Britain was likely to be bypassed by all American airlines was to him extremely serious. It was time that aviation was developed as an implementation of peace rather than war. McIntyre added that British aviation was at a crossroads. It must choose between being a monopoly or American-regulated competition. SAL was in the vanguard of those who wanted the latter.

The company continued to receive the backing of the Scottish press with the *Daily Record* declaring that in the growing development of civil aviation there must be a prominent role for the world's greatest all-weather airport.

On 19 October, Hamilton was part of a delegation from the Scottish Council for Development and Industry and SAL that met Lord Winster, the Minister of Civil Aviation {MCA}, in London to make the case for Prestwick as a peacetime airport. Winster assured them that he bore the airport no hostility, but the Ministry announced that December that it intended to assume the position of landlord of Prestwick and compulsorily purchase the company's airport holding from 1 April 1946.

The chill winds blowing out of Whitehall galvanised Hamilton and McIntyre into a fresh round of lobbying. At a civic lunch hosted by the Glasgow City Chambers before Christmas, Hamilton not only made the case for a transatlantic airport and SAL's own airline company, Scottish Airlines, but that both should be based in Scotland. Unless the country grasped the opportunities presented by civil aviation it would become a decadent, disgruntled poverty-stricken corner of Britain.

He returned to this theme of decentralisation when addressing the Aberdeen Chamber of Commerce in the New Year. 'London, to my mind, is becoming a great gangrenous growth, spread like a disease, and sapping the vitality of other parts of the country.' [6] It was only through great pressure from Scotland that Prestwick had been designated a transatlantic airport. That had been admitted, and now the country wanted control of both its airports and airlines.

It was not a political matter as it could be brought in just as easily by a Labour government as a Conservative one, but there were too many politicians in both parties who could hardly see beyond the mist of London. When Scottish MPs and peers met local authorities and members of the Scottish Council for Development and Industry at Edinburgh City Chambers, they unanimously supported an adequate devolution of power for the administration of airports and operation of air services in Scotland.

On 14 February, in a debate on Scottish Airlines in the House of Lords, the Earl of Glasgow introduced a motion requesting that the Government set up a Scottish corporation to administer Prestwick and a second one for Scottish Airlines. A failure to do so, he warned, could encourage the formation of a strong separatist movement in Scotland. Explaining that he was unable to do so because it ran counter to the Government's policy of nationalisation, Winster declared that a Scottish corporation would be a retrograde step and very expensive to run. More controversially, he questioned SAL's contention that if Prestwick were made sufficiently attractive many more American operators would use it, particularly on the route to the countries of Northern Europe. Had they wanted to come, he declared, they would have been able to do so.

Two days later, at a dinner to mark the tenth anniversary of SAL, Hamilton was scathing in his response. The fact was that two foreign operators had applied in December for permission to use it and they were refused permission by the MCA. He challenged the minister to deny the accuracy of this statement.

Had the British government given American operators equal commercial freedom to use Prestwick as the Irish government had offered them for Rineanna {Shannon}, they would have continued to use Prestwick as their Atlantic terminal instead of the Irish Republic. 'This is the issue which is constantly evaded by Government spokesmen, and instead of telling us the facts about the British Government closing Prestwick's door, while Rineanna's door was wide open, they conceal this fact with half truths about American operators expressing a preference for Rineanna.' [7]

The pressure seems to have paid off for weeks later Prestwick was designated as Britain's second airport, the gateway, as far as Hamilton and McIntyre were concerned, for operating airline services. The main problem they now faced was the nationalisation of Britain's airlines which prevented them from operating their own scheduled services. Resorting to charter work, they operated various routes from Prestwick to venues such as Belfast, Paris and Amsterdam, which brought them some success at first until such time as these routes were taken over by national airlines.

It was a similar story with the factory. Although Liberator and Dakota conversion work was some compensation for the rapid cancellation of government contracts at the end of the war, it could not disguise the overall shortage of orders. With the bank overdraft nearly at its limit and liquidation deteriorating fast, Hamilton warned his board in March 1948 that SAL's position was serious. Already the previous May the Hamilton trustees had registered their unease about the company's plight by seeking a recall of their £50,000 loan. Hamilton had managed to persuade them to back off and even to extend their loan until the litigation over the rent and compensation for the compulsory purchase of Prestwick, SAL's main asset, had been settled.

Although the Government had requisitioned the airfield in 1941, no settlement had ever been reached. In 1947 the company attempted to break the deadlock by settling out of court for a minimum compensation of £300,000, but the MCA would only offer £87,000. A revised offer the next year of £175,000 was still far short of company expectations, and it took the matter to litigation with all that which entailed in further delays.

With the financial situation declining ever further throughout the summer of 1948 the Hamilton trustees, as a matter of urgency, called for a comprehensive report of the company's assets from an independent party. That report, describing the overheads at the factory as terrifying, painted a sombre picture of future prospects. In their desperation to salvage their company Hamilton and McIntyre managed to persuade the trustees to defer execution once again. With SAL continuing to bleed money, not least its disastrous association with Hellenic Airlines, much depended on the negotiations over Prestwick and getting an acceptable settlement as soon as possible.

In August 1950 Hamilton informed the board that it had been decided to separate the airlines section of the company's activity, but on legal advice he had agreed not to proceed in case it might prejudice the arbitration. {Part of SAL's claim for compensation was based on the airport's value as a utility and total going concern.}

Against this background and pressure from the trustees, relations between Hamilton and McIntyre became somewhat frayed. With his vision, charisma and drive, McIntyre was the galvanising force behind SAL and its principal asset during its rise to prominence. At the same time his willingness to fly close to the sun, especially over the loss-making airlines, appeared unduly reckless in the eyes of his critics who did not share his enthusiasm for the airlines and wanted it discontinued.

Hamilton had always sympathised with McIntyre's vision more than most, but with heavy losses continuing to accrue to its London service, begun in 1951, he informed him the following March that this service should be terminated as soon as possible. McIntyre resisted, and with the company solicitors, Allen and Overy, advising against closure he was given another lifeline.

That September the Hamilton trustees raised grave reservations about McIntyre's purchase of three York aircraft at £8,000 each, reservations shared by Hamilton, especially since the purchase was not made conditional on a contract from the Air Ministry. At the next board meeting he read out a statement about the purchase. He recognised that McIntyre had indicated his intention to make the offer in the Managing Director's Weekly Report on 25 August, which might have given the impression that he was directly authorised to proceed. As it happened he, Hamilton, did not see the report until much later. The purchase of aircraft was much too important to be dealt with by indirect authority and on general grounds he was opposed to it. He regarded it as essential that there be no purchase of aircraft and other capital expenditure without the direct authority of the board.

Hamilton's note was approved and adopted as a resolution by the board, but the admonition seems to have left some lingering resentment with McIntyre. In a letter dated 10 October 1952, he complained to Hamilton that he appeared to lack confidence in him. That breach was soon to widen as McIntyre began negotiations with the new Conservative government to find a way of granting certain internal services to SAL. If the Government agreed to his proposals he assumed it would be happy to settle the acquisition favourably and place an order for the Twin Pioneer, SAL's small reconnaissance aircraft with its short take-off and landing capacity. Keen to go down this route in order to release money to prop up his floundering airline, McIntyre worked closely with Reginald Maudling, a junior minister at the MCA. A talk with the latter on 12 November appeared to have secured a breakthrough and following a telephone call to Hamilton the next day to brief him on developments, the gist of which Hamilton failed to grasp, McIntyre wrote to the Minister not only to offer a compromise but also to state a figure. When two directors found out about McIntyre's letter, written without board approval, they were not amused, especially since they were opposed to a settlement that merely provided further capital for Scottish Airlines. Under pressure from the Hamilton trustees, the board submitted two draft letters prepared for McIntyre at their next meeting instructing him to withdraw. He refused and received support from Tom Overy, the company's solicitor, who advised that his letter did not affect the compensation claim from a business point of view.

The New Year did not bring an upturn in fortunes. On 22 January, Hamilton was warned by the company secretary J.R.Hogarth that the financial situation was dire, and unless they were able to get a rapid settlement to the acquisition it would be absolutely essential to obtain some more liquid capital.

That settlement appeared as elusive as ever and by March 1953 the company was on the brink as the bank demanded repayment of £60,000 of its additional overdraft. Hamilton felt they had no option but to comply, but McIntyre was not willing to lie down. Following a meeting with the bank the next week the former felt obliged to reconsider.

At the board meeting on 14 October 1953, Sir Ian Bolton, representing the Hamilton trustees, insisted that the company should compel its subsidiary to close down its airline activities without further delay. When McIntyre claimed that the air services had contributed to the Twin Pioneer, Hamilton not only disputed this but amended the draft minutes highlighting that disagreement, a decision that vexed McIntyre. He assumed that Hamilton had amended the draft in a hurry and did not appreciate that his disagreement with his factual statement on the Twin Pioneer amounted to disbelief. He wrote to him to question the rationale behind his disagreement. Could he suggest how else the Twin Pioneer design was created?

He sought a candid discussion between the two of them regarding their relationship. It had taken a great deal of initiative and constant effort to bring their company through to its present position. Yet it would be extremely difficult to make the most of these opportunities if factual statements made by the Managing Director on points of some importance to the company were disbelieved by its Chairman.

The next day the board secretary told Hamilton he thought it most unfortunate that the disagreement over the Twin Pioneer should appear in the minutes and advised him to delete it, advice which Hamilton accepted.

Amidst the gloom there was a ray of hope. Not only did the recommencement of the Berlin airlift throw Scottish Airlines a lifeline, the dispute over Prestwick was nearing its end. Advised by Baillie Gifford fund managers that the terms were fairly satisfactory, the board, while considering the land sale most disappointing, agreed to accept the Arbiter's findings. Those findings, finally completed in November 1953, awarded SAL £343,835 for the airport land and buildings along with £100,000 for other claims arising out of compulsory acquisition together with a ninety-nine-year lease of the factory site.

At the next board meeting Hamilton warmly congratulated McIntyre on his skilful negotiation. The Hamilton Estates loan was paid off, unprofitable contracts ceased and the company returned to profit. Successful trooping contracts to Malta, Cyprus and Egypt enabled Scottish Airlines to become a separate company, but after a promising start the wheel turned again in 1956 with the end of these contracts together with the failure of the Twin Pioneer to attract the volume of orders anticipated. This had serious ramifications given the level of investment in it which far exceeded company resources. A £100,000 loan from the Finance Corporation for Industry {FCI}, a government-established body, had increased to nearly £2.5 million by 1957.

In this unforgiving climate McIntyre made every effort to boost sales abroad. It was while flying the flag in North Africa in December 1957 that his Twin Pioneer crashed in Libya, the result of metal fatigue in the port wing. He and the other five on board were killed instantly. 'Mac was a grand chap and quite irreplaceable,' was Hamilton's succinct but accurate assessment of the loss of his great friend. [8] Not only had the company lost its leading talisman, but also the circumstances of his death badly dented market confidence in the Twin Pioneer. As orders plummeted and SAL's losses for 1958 reached nearly £800,000, the FCI announced its unwillingness to grant it any further loans.

With the company once again standing perilously close to the brink the directors were faced with painful choices at the January 1959 board meeting. Hamilton thought SAL had no legal alternative other than cease operations and go into voluntary liquidation as FCI was by far its largest creditor. The directors, however, on the advice of Bernard Boxall, a professional consultant from Production Engineering Ltd and the new deputy chairman, decided to ask the FCI for a stay of execution pending a substantial order for the Twin Pioneer. The FCI was amenable and even increased its loan, but for all Hamilton's deep gratitude to Boxall for saving the company from imminent peril, the respite proved brief as the Portuguese order failed to materialise. With his colleagues accepting closure it required all the resilience of the general manager, T.D.M.Robertson, to persuade them to soldier on.

At a meeting of the company's major creditors, Robertson convinced them that with their help SAL could survive and prosper. A Downing Street summit at the end of the year led to the Ministry of Aviation purchasing four additional Twin Pioneers, but aside from enhanced orders for the Pioneer, the road to recovery lay in greater diversification and expanding Scottish Express air transport. Gratified by the improved financial position, Hamilton decided to relinquish the chairmanship to Boxall in April 1961 and become President. A measure of the esteem in which he was held came the following year when the company gave the Hamiltons a Georgian silver salver to mark their twenty-fifth wedding anniversary. Looking back on SAL's first twenty-five years, its historian Alan Robertson concluded that for all the turbulent times it had encountered it had successfully realised its founders' objectives by establishing at one time or another in Scotland all the major branches of the aviation industry.

In July 1962 Hamilton was appointed by the Minister of Aviation, Julian Amery, to chair an independent committee on the training of pilots for civil aviation. Given his experiences at SAL, his lifelong presidency of the British Airline Pilots' Association {BALPA}, the professional organisation representing the majority of pilots, and his presidency of the Air League, an aviation society promoting the cause of British aviation, he was more than qualified for this important role. With safety as ever at a premium, the standards of training at civilian flying schools and the methods of selecting recruits had assumed an ever greater importance, given the substantial decline in the number of recruits from the services.

Beginning work that October, the committee consulted various government departments, took evidence from twenty-four bodies and written evidence from sixty-eight witnesses. On top of that it supplemented its written and oral evidence by inspecting training facilities for professional pilots, not least in the US.

The report, published in June 1963, recommended a 'Junior Wings' scheme designed to introduce boys and girls to flying while still at school if necessary. Up to one thousand scholarships would be provided each year for sixth formers to obtain up to ten hours' flying instruction and to make a first solo flight. Without a suitable scheme, the committee stressed, future recruitment for professional pilots and other civil aviation posts would inevitably suffer, especially in competition with other industries and professions. Recruitment of sixth formers needed to be encouraged if they were to attract those of calibre. Those eligible for the scheme would need to have five O levels with passes in English, maths and one of the sciences.

Another proposal concerned the need to improve the salaries paid to both ground and flying instructors. The cost of the scheme it estimated to be £50,000, much of which would be borne by the Treasury, but recommended that employers of pilots should make a significant contribution to the cost. The recommendations were fully implemented.

Hamilton's work did not end there. As President of BALPA for the rest of his life, he attended its annual technical symposium. In 1964 he represented it at the International Federation of Airline Pilots' Associations Conference in Manila and in 1970 helped organise its conference in London. In January 1973, weeks before he died, he unveiled a plaque at Prestwick to commemorate its proud past. SAL was not to survive much longer as an independent concern, becoming the Scottish Division of British Aerospace in 1977, and eventually BAE, but it should forever be remembered for its pioneering role in creating an aviation industry in Scotland.

9. In THE SERVICE OF ALL

During the war Ferne remained a great centre for the Douglas-Hamilton family, as well as acting as a home for bombed-out children and an animal sanctuary for evacuated cats and dogs.

It was in these circumstances that Miss Lind's influence increased. Elizabeth Hamilton recalled the occasion they arrived at Ferne only to find the drawing room door locked. It had been handed over to Miss Lind as her private apartment. On another occasion when visiting Ferne, Hamilton was worried at the deterioration of the building. Some nasty-looking black mushrooms had appeared on the ceiling of the top floor and with Nina's permission he called in an architect to make a report. The black mushrooms were due to damp being pumped through the outer wall by an enormous Virginia Creeper growing up the outside. It must be removed. With his mother's consent, Hamilton proceeded to cut through the stem. As soon as he had done so water bubbled up through it. At this point Miss Lind, who was staying in the house, walked onto the terrace with a face like thunder. 'Douglo,' she said. 'This was a thing of beauty and you have destroyed it.' He explained that it was damaging the building and the architect was insisting it must be removed. She replied: 'Architects are there to make you spend money, doctors to make you ill, lawyers to make you quarrel, and clergymen to make you sin.' After pronouncing her credo, she went indoors having done her best to demolish not only the authority of the architect, but the medical and legal professions as well as the Church. To Elizabeth, Miss Lind, whatever her past achievements, was now a self-obsessed megalomaniac. 'It seems incredible that Nina could have so abdicated common-sense as to have allowed herself to come under such a doom-laden influence – The worst thing Miss Lind did was to destroy Nina's faith, not in God or the Christian Faith, but in the Church.' To support Miss Lind she stopped going to church and lost her respect for the clergy. [1]

In 1949 Hamilton was best man at Geordie's wedding to Audrey {Wendy} Sale-Barker, an alpine skiing champion and prominent aviator who flew for the Air Transport Auxiliary during the war. It proved to be a happily-enduring marriage during which Geordie, now Earl of Selkirk, held Cabinet office and enjoyed success as UK High Commissioner for Singapore and Commissioner General for South-East Asia before becoming an active member of the House of Lords.

The wedding, held at St Giles' Cathedral, Edinburgh, was the last major family event that Nina attended. She remained fully committed to her work and in November 1950 received a papal blessing when she presented an appeal for the proper treatment of domestic animals.

Weeks later she developed a non-malign throat condition and could not swallow. She was put on an aureomycin drip and began to recover, but when she realised aureomycin had been discovered as a result of experiments on animals, she dispensed with the drip in her ankle and refused further medical treatment. She died slowly of starvation with Miss Lind and her followers around her yet unwilling to help her or get her the treatment she needed, a shocking state of affairs. Hamilton went to London to be with his mother during her final days and Elizabeth joined him there after her death. Seeing her mother-in-law lying there on her bed she could not believe that this skeletal form was anyone she had ever known. It was a most distressing sight and one that continued to haunt her for the rest of her life. [2] At Nina's funeral in Salisbury Cathedral the grief on display from family, friends and retainers for this much-loved woman was palpable, but while Hamilton fully shared in that grief he did not allow sentiment to get in the way of her legacy. Dismayed that his mother had left Ferne and its grounds to animal charities to maintain the animal sanctuary there, he was determined that valuable family possessions did not fall into the wrong hands. In no time he had the removal vans down to Ferne and the possessions transferred to his new home at Lennoxlove.

These possessions included a vast collection of the Fisher papers which the Admiral had bequeathed to Nina. Shortly before she died she expressed her wish that these papers be housed at Lennoxlove; then in 1955 George, Viscount Lambert, Fisher's literary executor who served as Civil Lord of the Admiralty between 1905 and 1915, asked Hamilton to assume responsibility for all of Fisher's papers. He duly consented and there they remained at Lennoxlove until after Hamilton's death when they were received by the Government instead of estate duty on his estate. In 1980, following a recommendation by the Royal Commission on Historical Manuscripts, the papers were allocated to Churchill College, Cambridge.

Throughout the duration of the war Hamilton and his family had spent little time at Dungavel, which had been used as a convalescent home for the WAAF. Now with the war over and austerity in vogue the task of maintaining such an establishment became ever harder. Certainly Elizabeth never cared for its forbidding features and intemperate climate which she blamed for the children's colds. She wanted something smaller that could be considered a family home and yet large enough to house the Hamilton heirlooms, not least their fine art collection. In the summer of 1947 they purchased Lennoxlove, a historic house a mile south of Haddington in East Lothian, for £4,000, but getting rid of Dungavel proved no easy business. Generous offers first to the Church of Scotland for a boys' school there, and then to the Hamilton Presbytery for an eventide home, were reluctantly declined because neither could afford the cost of the alterations required. Eventually, in 1950, it was bought by the National Coal Board as a training college for miners, much to the consternation of one of Hamilton's tenants, the left-wing Hugh MacDiarmid, who found paying rent to a nationalised industry a more taxing proposition than living rent-free off a Duke! Later Dungavel was acquired by the Government who used it first as an open prison and then as an immigration removal centre, the only one in Scotland to date.

Standing in attractive parkland and originally called Lethington Tower, Lennoxlove had been the property of the Maitland family since

1345, and they transformed it from a medieval keep to a substantial house. One of its owners, Sir Richard Maitland, the blind poet who served both King James V and his wife, Mary of Guise, was responsible for restoring it after the damage wrought by the invading English during the 1540s, and his son William was Secretary of State to Mary, Queen of Scots. Another son, John Maitland, became Lord Chancellor under James VI and his grandson, the 1st Duke of Lauderdale, was virtual ruler of Scotland under Charles II. It was during the latter's ownership that a new wing was built and substantial improvements made to the interior including prison-chambers for Covenanters.

Following the expiry of the Maitland line, Lethington was purchased by the trustees of Frances Teresa Stuart, Duchess of Richmond and Lennox, a society beauty known as La Belle Stuart and much admired by Charles II. Dying childless, she bequeathed it to her nephew Alexander, 5th Lord Blantyre, an impecunious soldier, with the stipulation that it be called Lennox's love to Blantyre, in time shortened to Lennoxlove.

The Blantyres lived there for two centuries and prospered as benevolent landlords. On the death of the 12th and last Lord Blantyre without a male heir in 1900, the house passed to his daughter, Ellen Stuart, and her husband, Sir David Baird. Their son, Major William Baird, commissioned the eminent Scottish architect Sir Robert Lorimer to undertake a major restoration, especially its Great Hall, in 1912.

Having bought a house steeped in history it said much for Elizabeth's artistic taste that she managed to both preserve its ancient splendours and give it an intimate feel conducive to raising a family there. Not only did she convert the dungeon into a delightful chapel, she also commissioned the illustrious Scottish interior designer John Fowler to refurbish its state apartments. {He later renovated their private apartments at Holyrood.} Hamilton for his part arranged the fine collection of family portraits, persuading Robert Baird, the previous owner, to part with the portrait of La Belle Stuart, and established a museum containing photos of his flight over Everest and mementoes from Hess's flight to Scotland.

In 1953, to help pay for the upkeep of Lennoxlove and its market gardens, Hamilton decided to open it to the public for 2 shillings

{10 pence} per person. It proved to be a popular innovation, especially when he himself acted as a guide. On one occasion when an old lady was having difficulty negotiating the stairs he put his arm around her and carried her down much to the appreciation of her husband waiting at the bottom. 'Thank you, my man,' he said as he pressed half a crown into the Duke's pocket. Not everyone was so sensitive, and when somebody entered the Duchess's bedroom while she was changing Hamilton closed the house down there and then. It was not to open again to the public during his lifetime.

While life at Lennoxlove lacked the grandeur of Ferne or Dungavel, the Hamiltons lived there in a certain style with a butler, cook and chauffeur, and entertained the Queen Mother {several times}, King Gustaf VI of Sweden and Sir Learie Constantine, the renowned West Indian cricketer who later became Rector of St Andrews University. Family, too, featured highly with Elizabeth's sister Diana, Duchess of Sutherland, and David Douglas-Hamilton's two sons, Diarmaid, later an astrophysicist of rare brilliance at Harvard University, and Iain, the renowned elephant conservationist, regular guests. Others who appreciated the generous hospitality at Lennoxlove were Malcolm Douglas-Hamilton's children, Diana, Fiona, Niall and Alasdair, all of whom were very fond of their Uncle Douglo.

For all their prominence the Duke and Duchess were private people, happy to live life away from the public glare. When in residence there was nothing that Hamilton enjoyed more than donning old garb and heading into the woods to plant trees. He took a great interest in the estate, not least his herd of Cadzow white cattle, and spent much time in the estate office.

Fortunate to have men of real calibre in Alan McDonald, Factor of the Hamilton estates, and Stuart Chalmers, Factor at Lennoxlove, Hamilton in turn was an excellent employer. He knew all his staff and looked after their welfare, providing them with a generous pension scheme and decent accommodation. Mindful that George Sked, the gamekeeper, had an artificial leg, he asked Jimmy Miller, his head forester, to take over his driving commitments to Edinburgh and to walk in the line at shoots. {When hosting shoots at Lennoxlove or Archerfield, Hamilton always made his guests very welcome and gave them the best positions in the butts.} According to Chalmers, it was impossible to find anyone who had a bad word to say about him, a view fully endorsed by Miller, who recalls him as a wonderful man with no side to him. One of the accolades that meant most to the Duke was being an elder at his local church, Bolton, and when it needed timber to repair the roof he supplied it free of charge.

Always receptive to sound advice, Hamilton, on Chalmers's suggestion, built a timber treatment plant to supply timber to the building trade and for motorway fencing, a business that became very successful. Another profitable enterprise which he fully supported was his factor's policy of buying up farms in East Lothian and the acquisition of the 2,500-acre Archerfield estate in 1963, the bulk of which was later sold off for the development of an exclusive residential-golf complex there. According to Miller, there was no better-run estate than Lennoxlove when the Duke was alive.

During the 1930s, Hamilton, along with his other brothers, had pooled their assets into a family fund in which he had become the largest shareholder. In time further adjustments were necessary, not least the 1947 Settlement which split a large chunk of his personal shareholding into four separate funds and helped preserve Lennoxlove.

Not all Hamilton's investments were quite so successful. In 1945 he bought the Hebridean island of North Uist from Sir Simon Campbell-Orde, supposedly to stop a whisky baron from obtaining it, only to sell it again sixteen years later to Earl Granville, a cousin of the Queen. It was during this time that he invested £80,000 in a basking shark fishery on Soay, an island off the south-west coast of Skye, owned by the writer and conservationist Gavin Maxwell, a cousin of Elizabeth's. The business proved to be a flop and Hamilton called time on the venture, much to Maxwell's frustration. His decision to voice his criticism publicly in his celebrated book *Harpoon at a Venture* so outraged Hamilton that he never spoke to him again.

Another misguided venture involved investing in underdeveloped property in the Bahamas, following advice to Hamilton from a fellow peer to remove his assets from the country to safeguard them from a left-wing government. Alan McDonald invested far more than intended, but the Hamilton Estates in time were able to extract themselves, thereby limiting the damage.

With the Hamilton tradition of service and his leading position in society it is not surprising that the 14th Duke should be associated with so many worthy causes. He formed a close bond with George VI and in 1946 was awarded the Grand Cross of the Royal Victorian Order. Later, in 1951, he was admitted to the Order of the Thistle, Scotland's great order of chivalry with its complement of sixteen knights. The death of the King the following year greatly upset him, but he soon came to revere his successor, the young Queen Elizabeth. At her coronation, he held the canopy for the Queen's anointment and then played a leading role in the ceremony north of the Border.

To mark the Queen's post-coronation visit to Edinburgh at the end of June, the Honours of Scotland, the ancient relics of Scottish royalty, were to be presented to her at a National Service of Thanksgiving and Dedication at St Giles' Cathedral. Intended to be a great national celebration, the event became mired in controversy following Buckingham Palace's announcement that the Queen would wear day clothes, a *faux pas* that offended Scottish sensitivities. Another grievance concerned the insignia E11R on the pillar boxes since the new Queen was in fact only the first Elizabeth to rule over Scotland. Amidst acts of vandalism to pillar boxes which carried the new insignia, Hamilton wrote letters to Sir Alan Lascelles, the Queen's private secretary, and Churchill, the Prime Minister, advising that the controversy be handled tactfully. The numeral as it now stood acknowledged the ancient English Royal Line, but the only explanation that had hitherto been given ignored the Scottish Royal Line from which the Queen was descended and Scotland's history as an ancient kingdom. Failing some assurance to use whatever numeral in England or Scotland were the higher, he warned that the present agitation would continue with potentially embarrassing consequences.

His words initially fell on deaf ears, Churchill believing that Hamilton's proposals would bind the Sovereign and government of the day in a way which would be contrary to precedent. A month later, however, the Prime Minister appears to have had second thoughts, for on 15 April he told the Commons that in future it would be reasonable for the Sovereign to use either the English or Scottish number whichever was the higher.

With James Stuart and Alec, Earl of Home at the Scottish Office ensuring that new pillar boxes thereafter carried only the Crown of Scotland image, all these spats were forgotten by the time the Queen visited Scotland at the end of June. It fell to Hamilton as hereditary bearer of the Crown of Scotland, to be one of the bearers of the Honours, and, accompanied by his two eldest sons as pages, he rode in pomp through Edinburgh's crowded streets to St Giles'. Inside, he led the Royal Procession down the aisle along with his fellow bearers, Lord Home {Sword of State} and Lord Crawford {Sceptre}, before presenting the Crown to Dr Charles Warr, the Minister of St Giles' and Dean of the Chapel Royal in Scotland, who placed it on the communion table. There it remained till the end of the service when the Dean presented the Honours to the Queen, who in turn returned them to the bearers while they knelt in homage before her.

As Lord Steward, the leading officer in the Royal Household, Hamilton had responsibility for the organisation of all state banquets, issuing invitations, supervising all arrangements and presenting all the foreign dignitaries to the Monarch, a role he carried out with his customary aplomb. His one minor hitch came in 1960 when asked by Iain Macleod, the Colonial Secretary, to chair a commission into constitutional reform in Uganda since he was a friend of the Kabaka, widely known as King Freddie. Keen to accept, he was ultimately forced to decline following royal concerns that substantial differences between the two countries would intrude into the political sphere. When Hamilton retired in February 1964 in an attempt to reduce his commitments the Queen was sorry to see him go. She invested him with the Royal Victorian Chain, a personal token of high distinction and esteem from the Monarch, and invited him and Elizabeth to a private lunch with herself and Prince Philip.

This was not the end of his royal duties. As Hereditary Keeper of the Palace of Holyroodhouse, he had responsibility for welcoming the Queen there at the beginning of her annual stay and often hosted the final leg of state visits, his guests proving an interesting mix. King Olav of Norway was welcomed cordially owing to the wartime connection; President Khrushchev of the Soviet Union amused Hamilton with his compliments on Scottish women and his strong opinions about tea; King Hussein of Jordan's entourage was entertained by the Corries, a well-known Scottish folk group, and proved adept Scottish dancers; Idi Amin, President of Uganda, exerted an oppressive control over his terrified advisers before leaving with the idea that he might take up residence there and become King of Scotland!

Within Holyrood, Hamilton was always friendly and helpful to the Palace staff. He won the loyal support of its High Constables, a small corps of ceremonial guards for royal visits, by attending their dinners and greatly encouraging them in all their duties. According to Sir Charles Fraser, sometime Purse Bearer {head of the household} to the Lord High Commissioner to the General Assembly of the Church of Scotland, it was his grace and courtesy that really stood out. He recalled how during General Assembly week he would make it his business to visit Holyrood on the final day to meet the Lord High Commissioner and check that everything had functioned properly. In 1970 the Lord High Commissioner happened to be Margaret Herbison, the daughter of a miner, a Labour minister and the first woman to hold the position, and Hamilton addressed her as Your Grace, the correct form of address, with great humility.

On one particular occasion Fraser himself happened to be the beneficiary of this humility. Parked outside St Mary's Church, Haddington, in driving rain, he was having trouble manoeuvring his car out of a confined space, whereupon Hamilton got out of his car and received a soaking while he directed Fraser. 'Everyone mattered to Douglo,' he recalled.

In 1953 Hamilton was appointed Lord High Commissioner to the General Assembly of the Church of Scotland. Although this largely ceremonial appointment was usually entrusted to one of Scotland's established families, Hamilton was uniquely qualified, not only because of his close links to the Crown, but also because of his strong attachment to the Kirk as an elder.

For a week every May {then it was ten days} the Lord High Commissioner takes up residence at Holyrood where he entertains in style, carries out a number of functions and is greeted with a bow or curtsey. Although unable to influence debates, he presides over the General Assembly and addresses it at the beginning and end of its deliberations.

As Scotland's only national forum at that time, the General Assembly's views on a range of moral and political issues attracted great coverage in an era when religious observance was much more paramount. Yet even then the seeds of spiritual indifference were beginning to sprout, something which Hamilton alluded to in his opening speech to the Assembly.

Recalling that his own forbear, the 1st Duke of Hamilton, had represented the Crown at the historic Glasgow Assembly in 1638 when episcopacy had been overthrown, he drew satisfaction from the contrast with those turbulent times. Not only had the Church's spiritual independence been secured, its relations with the monarchy were much improved and now, on the eve of the coronation, they looked forward to the new reign with hope.

Reflecting on his twenty-year association with the Assembly, Hamilton opined that the Church had endured many vicissitudes during that period. Now confronted with a more materialistic age, he suggested that its position would be immeasurably strengthened by a greater participation of the laity in its worship, work and fellowship.

In a week full of symbolism he hosted numerous events at Holyrood, the most spectacular of which was a garden party for eight thousand, an event blighted by torrential rain. With his natural charm and interest in all things Scottish, he proved the most popular of hosts to clergy and laity alike. He also took a keen interest in the Assembly debates, and in his closing speech, he spoke up for an increase in ministerial stipends, as well drawing great encouragement from the welcome accorded to two bishops from the Episcopal Church. The road towards organic unity, he remarked, was a long and winding one, but they were travelling towards the dawn.

It was a theme he returned to in his opening speech the following year when he contrasted the sense of unity within the Commonwealth fostered by the coronation, with those countries that languished under atheist regimes and menaced the free world. Underlying all these problems that confronted them was a tragic truth that man's intellectual activities had outstripped his moral capacity. The advance in science and technology had been meteoric but who could claim a corresponding advance in wisdom and goodness. Their failure in spiritual advancement had meant that their power to destroy in bitterness and strife had increased more rapidly than their power to create love and happiness. The development of nuclear power was in itself a challenge to every Christian to give to the Church wholesale service and devotion for never in the course of history had man been so called to put on the whole armour of God.

Amid the usual round of debates, services and entertainment, including another wet garden party, Hamilton invited the tenants of Lennoxlove to tea at Holyrood and the opportunity to watch the RAF band 'Beating the Retreat'.

In an Assembly dominated by nuclear politics and the Very Rev George MacLeod's abortive amendment to renounce war, Hamilton's closing speech referred to the dreadful burden that it had placed upon their souls. He appealed to more young people to enter the ministry for if the call went unheeded a serious crisis would soon emerge. 'In his second term of office, the Duke of Hamilton has again shown the keenest interest in the affairs of the Assembly,' commented the *Scotsman,* 'and with the unstinting help of the Duchess carried out with distinction the numerous engagements of Assembly week.' [3]

That August Hamilton was the only lay member of the Church of Scotland delegation to the Second Assembly of the World Council of Churches at Evanston, Illinois. He found it to be an occasion of great American warmth and hospitality, and concern for Christian unity at a time when the denominational barriers to inter-Communion still proved highly divisive. As a strong believer in ecumenicalism, he thought the most poignant and hopeful event there was the open Communion celebration according to the rites of the Church of South India.

His experiences there formed the basis of his opening speech to the General Assembly the following year when he acted as Lord High Commissioner for the third year in succession, the last such person to do so. A clue as to why this honour was bestowed upon him was given by Dr Ronald Selby Wright in a pre-Assembly service at Canongate Kirk. The General Assembly was the most Christian parliament in the world, and the Duke and Duchess of Hamilton set a standard of Christian living that was an example to all in Scotland.

The 1955 General Assembly was notable for following in the footsteps of the renowned American evangelist Billy Graham and his historic All-Scotland Crusade at the Kelvin Hall in Glasgow. For six weeks he had addressed capacity nightly audiences and now, as Hamilton's special guest, he was present, along with thirteen past Moderators, in a crowded Assembly Hall to hear him appeal for Church unity. Evanston was an event of incalculable importance to the whole Christian world, but until the challenge of inter-Communion was fairly faced, the seeds of the ecumenical movement would quickly wither. Expressing his pleasure at the hope that the 'Tell Scotland' campaign had given the nation, Hamilton tempered that pleasure with a warning. To find true hope they had to look beyond churches and into individual homes to find the heart from which flowed the lifeblood of their spiritual life. Having referred to the centenary of the birth of Sir William Smith, the founder of the Boys' Brigade, he once again appealed to those in the vigour of youth to give full service to the Church.

By the end of an Assembly marked by fine weather, Hamilton felt compelled to warn Christians of succumbing to the twin dangers of escapist pietism on the one hand and political activism on the other, the latter primarily a reply to George MacLeod, one of the Kirk's most controversial figures. The rush to storm the citadels of poverty and injustice was fraught with danger, especially when the will of God was subordinated to the will of Caesar. Surely the great tragedies of history had sprung from a failure to recognise this truth. Heretics had been burned and blood cruelly shed, not because men had sought to do God's will, but because in their pride and self-sufficiency men decided what He ought to want.

By the time Hamilton returned to office in 1958, a late replacement for his successor, Sir Walter Elliot, the former Unionist Cabinet minister, who had died earlier that year, his pessimism about the state of the world had grown more pronounced.

Never had their politicians and statesmen borne so heavy a burden, nor had there been a greater need of the spiritual resources that only the Church could provide. Yet such resources were scarce to be found in a Church when it succumbed to the hungry call for trite political formulae. ' The Church stands weakened in its witness before all the world, because it is in itself torn with disunity, so that when the Church preaches reconciliation, the world turns to it and says- "Physician heal Thyself".'

How could the Christian seeking truth expect to find it when even his fellow Christians were so divided that they could not go together in the central act of the Christian faith to Him who was truth?

In striving to find unity they must first find God and he commended the words of the Cambridge historian Sir Herbert Butterfield, 'Hold to Christ, and for the rest be totally uncommitted'. [4]

According to the Moderator, John A. Fraser, the Duke had never spoken in the General Assembly with greater power or relevance. On the great issues of peace and unity which so confronted them all, the sense of urgency had been given a notable and moving expression.

Hamilton remained preoccupied with ecclesiastical matters over the next several years owing to his chairmanship of the Iona Appeal Trust, which brought him into an uneasy partnership with its leading light, George MacLeod, Socialist, pacifist and great spiritual visionary.

In 1938 MacLeod had founded the Iona Community as an ecumenical Christian community to find new ways of living out the Gospel and rebuilding the medieval abbey on the Hebridean island of Iona, the symbolic centre of Scottish Christianity originating from its association with St Columba in the sixth century. In June 1959 the Abbey was close to completion and a new appeal was launched to endow for all time the upkeep of all the buildings. The Appeal would be the responsibility of a new body, the Iona Appeal Trust, which comprised representatives of the Cathedral trustees and Iona Community.

When approached about becoming Chairman of the Appeal trustees in July 1958, Hamilton was reluctant to oblige on grounds of lack of time, but MacLeod would not be deterred. At a meeting between the two of them that September he asked him to think again. Hamilton told him he would do so but only if his colleagues insisted he was the best available candidate. They did, not only for his position as a former Lord High Commissioner and elder of the Kirk but also for the respect he commanded, MacLeod assured him.

Given the Iona Community's well-known radical colours Hamilton appeared to be acting out of character, but he had always been impressed by the ecumenical nature of the venture, and this to him outweighed his misgivings about its politics on the understanding that any appeal with which he was associated was free of a party label. MacLeod assured him that although Labour himself other trustees held Tory sympathies.

After discussing the matter with Dr Charles Warr, Hamilton allowed his name to go forward provided he was not expected to attend more than two meetings a year, a condition to which MacLeod readily agreed, knowing that his value lay elsewhere.

Yet Hamilton, for all his detachment from day-to-day events, would prove no cipher and it was not long before he and MacLeod were embroiled in a gentle altercation over the Appeal brochure, which many of the trustees thought too political.

Worried that it would neither inspire confidence nor attract the right sort of response from a wider public, Hamilton told MacLeod that if the Iona Community were to have the backing of the trustees he felt it must be scrupulously careful to keep them clear of political controversy. 'If it is desired to develop a philosophical thesis, I feel that this should be dealt with separately by the Community as such, and due care taken not to involve the trustees in any expression of views that they might feel they could not sincerely support.' [5] His words appear to have had an effect. When Mike Stuart, the Chairman of the Appeal Committee, asked MacLeod to redraft the brochure he complied and Hamilton added some amendments before its publication.

A serious leg operation prevented Hamilton from attending the launch of the Appeal on 28 June 1959, but his facsimile signature appeared on a covering letter together with the brochure that was sent out to 30,000 individuals. Inevitably the driving force behind the Appeal would be George MacLeod, but for all his eloquence and charisma he was a divisive figure seeming to endanger the pillars of the temple.

Since touring Africa in 1953, MacLeod had trenchantly opposed the white-dominated Central African Federation, a semi-independent state comprising Northern Rhodesia, Southern Rhodesia and Nyasaland, established that same year. In 1958 he persuaded the General Assembly to set up a Special Committee to consider Central African interests and the following year, as the situation deteriorated in Nyasaland where African nationalism was on the march, he won Assembly backing for his motion calling for a radical revision of its constitution. His victory generated much publicity and caused unease within the Church of Scotland as the Macmillan government convened the Monckton Commission to recommend changes to the constitutional workings of the Federation. Into the fray stepped Dr R.H.W. Shepherd, a respected missionary from South Africa, the Moderator of the General Assembly in 1959-60 and member of the Monckton Commission, who resented his original exclusion from the Special Committee. In a dramatic debate at the 1960 Assembly he pleaded for delayed judgement on the main proposals of its Special Committee until the Monckton Commission had reported later that year.

Shepherd's amendment was seconded by Hamilton. He accepted as a church they stood for the advancement of the rights of all Africans, but that advancement, as with all groups, depended on the maintenance of the rule of law and inviolability of witnesses. Thus it followed that intimidation of witnesses should be condemned. Why, he wondered, had such instances not been brought to the attention of the Assembly by reports that in the past had no more theological content and no greater claim to unbiased objectivity than the average political pamphlet?

The Church, now as always, had this duty to challenge the state when its enactments violated the moral law; equally the Church had a duty to resist pressure from those who would use it for political ends.

To agree to this deliverance as it stood would be to endorse a political manifesto in the name of the Church on information demonstrably inadequate for such a purpose.

Having asked that the very specific political demands be removed, he concluded: 'This is not a Forum for mere political debate. That Church is not Scotland's, it is not ours - it is His who founded it, and it is in His Name that we speak.' [6]

Shepherd and Hamilton spoke for the majority of the General Assembly because in a significant shift of opinion from the previous year it narrowly rejected MacLeod's motion, much to his dismay and Hamilton's delight. 'The Assembly acted much more in character with its traditions and common sense prevailed over oratory and extremism,' he informed Iain Macleod, the Colonial Secretary. 'The real difficulty which we now face in the Church is that of finding a way of expressing some kind of common mind without giving the impression that we are forsaking the Church in Central Africa with whom the Church of Scotland has of course such historic and intimate ties.' [7]

Away from the politics the task of financing Iona continued. Hamilton wrote to Lady Wakehurst, wife of the Governor of Northern Ireland, to see whether she could help MacLeod on his fundraising tour of the province that October. MacLeod in turn approached Hamilton to ascertain whether he could accompany him on his North American tour early in 1961, promising not to mention Central Africa once, not even on the plane. Various commitments prevented Hamilton from doing so, and in any case the two men were soon at loggerheads again as the Kirk celebrated the four hundredth anniversary of the Reformation in Scotland with a visit by the Queen to a special meeting of the General Assembly. What marred the occasion was a pungent article entitled 'How to Celebrate the Reformation' in the *Glasgow Herald* by MacLeod, which concluded with a diatribe against the bomb. 'As we watch, appalled, its ever-gathering strength and its unimaginable lethal potential, we may come nearest, in terms of our day, to the biggest problem that was theirs – namely, when is it God's purpose that his people should rebel against lawful authority? That for years was John Knox's great agony.' [8]

Drawing inspiration from Knox's ultimate willingness to rebel against legal authority, he called for a unilateral uprising against the bomb.

MacLeod's words, aside from their general furore, caused deep unease among leading figures on the Appeal Committee at a time when his political partisanship had deterred many potential donors from giving. Concerned at his impending visit to Northern Ireland and the courtesy to be shown to him by the Governor, partly at his request, Hamilton wrote MacLeod a stiff note clarifying his position. 'May I have your assurance that you will not at any time use the Iona Appeal as a platform for such a line of argument? Were this Appeal to become in any way interpreted as presenting treason as a Christian alternative in the world of today I am afraid I should no longer be able to associate myself with it.' [9]

While MacLeod assured Hamilton he would not embarrass the Iona Appeal in Ireland, he expressed frustration at a church that had nothing to say about non-violence and racial inequality, values that stemmed directly from the Cross. He wanted to see a movement within the Church which grappled with the challenges of the modern world and that movement, he asserted, happened to be the Iona Community.

He understood the frustration his pronouncements had caused him and accepted he would never make him happy, but he wanted him to stay part of the Appeal not because of his position but because of his personality.

Hamilton stayed but continued to trade blows with MacLeod in a protracted correspondence about his article.

In detail your views may ultimately be proved right, but in present circumstances I do not think this allows you to present treason as a Christian alternative, or civil disobedience as a responsible course.

The Christian must acknowledge that the principle of earthly authority and government is under a divine sanction and is rightly to be exercised in obedience to the Divine Law. Treason may be justifiable in the face of the violence by the State of the individual's right to be true to his religious convictions and conscientious beliefs, but in a country where there is religious and political toleration and scope for an effective opposition these prerequisites are lacking. [**10**]

Whether Hamilton's admonition had any effect is unknown, but MacLeod's relationship with his committee seems to have improved thereafter. His world tour raised £7,000 and by 1963, the fourteenth hundred anniversary of St Columba's arrival on Iona, the Appeal had raised £80,000. The Abbey was completed in 1965 and in more recent times the responsibility for its maintenance has passed from the Iona Cathedral Trust to Historic Scotland.

For all his English connections Hamilton was very proud of his Scottish ancestry and the institutions which defined it. He had always fought hard for a thriving aviation industry north of the Border and now he played his part in ensuring that two important events in Scottish history should be properly commemorated.

In 1954 he joined forces with other leading Scots to contribute to a granite memorial tablet to Sir William Wallace, the great Scots patriot whose resistance to King Edward I ended in gruesome circumstances at Smithfield in 1305. An appeal committee was formed, and all its efforts came to fruition two years later when a memorial tablet was unveiled on the outer wall of St Bartholomew's Hospital, West Smithfield, to the sounds of 'Flowers of the Forest'.

Hamilton also inaugurated a little garden in Edinburgh's Grassmarket dedicated to the Covenanter martyrs of 1689, and those who in Convention under his ancestor, William, 3rd Duke of Hamilton, helped overthrow King James VII. Those martyrs included the Cameronians, the regiment founded in 1689 by another of his ancestors, the Earl of Angus. When the regiment was disbanded in May 1968, victim of defence cuts,

Hamilton, as its commander-in-chief, presided over its disbandment parade at Douglas.

Aside from his public duties and SAL, Hamilton held a number of other important business positions: Governor of the British Linen Bank, a Scottish bank bought by Barclays in 1919 but still maintaining its independence, Chairman of the Norwich Union {Scotland}, a director of Securicor {Scotland} and President of the Building Societies Federation. It was when representing the latter in Washington that he had a chance encounter with President Kennedy at the White House.

For a man not given to great commercial acumen it might seem rather anomalous that he rose as far as he did in the business world. The reason, according to Sir Charles Fraser, was the tradition of insurance companies having a landowner on the board, and whatever he lacked in acumen he more than compensated with his common sense and total integrity. Under his leadership, the British Linen Bank merged with the Bank of Scotland in exchange for Barclays acquiring a 35 per cent shareholding in the enlarged bank. When he retired in 1970, the bank wanted a portrait of him for the boardroom and somebody proposed Oskar Kokoschka, the great Austrian expressionist whose work Hitler had denounced as degenerate. In the end the bank commissioned the Scottish artist Alan Sutherland and a studio copy remains at Lennoxlove, but Hamilton, on the advice of his son Hugh, decided himself to commission Kokoschka, a friend of Yehudi Menuhin, to paint a double-portrait with Elizabeth. Although rather touching to the naked eye, the result was not entirely to their liking, especially Hamilton, who was made to look rather haggard. The painting now hangs in the Scottish National Portrait Gallery in Edinburgh.

In January 1948 Hamilton was appointed the thirty-third chancellor of St Andrews University, following the death of Stanley Baldwin, his predecessor. 'No honour could bring greater honour than this one conferred on me by Scotland's most ancient University with which I have already family ties,' he wrote to Sir James Irvine, the Principal. 'The significance and greatness of my new appointment have much awed me and I am very conscious of my inadequacy when I contemplate all that the office stands for and the outstanding personality whom I follow.' [11]

Even allowing for his indifferent academic record when young, Hamilton was being unduly modest about his qualifications to be Chancellor. No slouch intellectually - he read widely, appreciated art and heraldry and had a good grasp of the philosophy of religion - his high personal standing, his sterling work for youth welfare and his close family ties with the university did much to compensate. Aside from his ancestor John Hamilton, a well-known Archbishop of St Andrews in the sixteenth century and fervent supporter of Mary, Queen of Scots, his brother David was a leading figure there in the early 1930s. Accustomed to flying to RAF Leuchars when visiting, Hamilton would signal his arrival by flying over St Salvator's Tower before joining the boxing team for a training session and consorting with students of all ages thereafter. Later he trained the University Air Squadron and received a Doctor of Laws in 1946.

On the day of his installation, appropriately enough St Andrew's Day 1948, Hamilton was given the warmest of welcomes from the students who crowded into the Younger Hall. Having paid a gracious tribute to Baldwin, Hamilton declared that the university was passing through an age of expansion. It behoved it to remember the immense power for good or ill which was inherent in its work and that it exercise that power discreetly.

It was obvious to all that education to an unprecedented extent was being directed towards the production of experts whose services would be of immediate benefit to the state. 'It will be an evil day for learning and equally an evil day for Scotland and the Commonwealth if any university education becomes fettered to the needs of national industry and of export trade. Admittedly, the universities can play a part in restoring industrial prosperity, but a university's first function surely is to attain the aims and ends of true learning.'

A university's function was to train minds in an atmosphere of intellectual freedom, and the state's first duty was to provide trained minds with opportunity.

To make the most of such opportunity, however, the mind should be trained not merely in one direction but in a broad and comprehensive spirit. In universities, in particular, specialisation should be accompanied by a large measure of general culture.

Turning to the wider field of knowledge, Hamilton remarked that the universities shared a common identity with the Church in their joint search for truth. That quest had evolved down the ages against many changing backdrops. Recent generations of scientists and political reformers had ushered in much that was good. Yet for all their achievements, man trod the edge of a precipice, his faith forgotten in the speed and clamour of modern life. Only with the survival of his religious beliefs could he face with equanimity the insignificance of his tiny planet and the vast loneliness of a universe whose immensity was equally beyond the scope of his comprehension. 'Those are truths that encompass the essential dignity of man and the sanctity of life. In our generation we have seen them disastrously denied, and witnessed the brutalities that spring where they are not heard. The universities are Shrines of truth. May they thrive, prosper and shed the light.' [12]

Despite Hamilton's later admission that he looked forward to the installation ceremony as one of the biggest ordeals of his life, the speech went down well with Irvine, who thought it struck the right balance between dignity and friendliness.

In September 1950 Hamilton welcomed Queen Elizabeth to St Andrews to celebrate the five hundredth anniversary of St Salvator's College, Scotland's oldest college; then in June 1955 he welcomed the new Queen and the Duke of Edinburgh to University College, Dundee, but in between these pleasantries there were some nasty squalls to negotiate.

Following the death of Sir James Irvine in 1952, Malcolm Knox, the Professor of Moral Philosophy, was appointed Acting Principal. It was a pivotal time to be in charge, given the continuing frisson between St Andrews and University College, Dundee, a constituent college of the former since 1889, chiefly over the desire of the latter for independence. Responding to the 1951 Royal Commission which recommended unity through diversity and parity, the St Andrews Act of 1953 dissolved the governing body of University College and placed its property and endowments in the hands of a reconstituted Court {the governing body in a Scottish university}. It also established two College Councils, one for St Andrews and one for Queen's College, Dundee, the replacement for University College, as well as instituting the office of Principal of the University in its own right.

Formally appointed Principal and Vice Chancellor of this reconstituted Court and inducted by Hamilton in November 1953, Knox made it his priority to weld together both sides of the university. As part of his bid to win the confidence of Dundee, a graduation ceremony was held there in February 1954. Having opened the Ewing Building School of Electrical Engineering and Botany, Hamilton expressed the hope at a civic lunch that Dundee's interest in the university would grow each year and that civic pride would be enhanced by academic achievement. 'The city of Dundee and the University of St Andrews stand side by side with a great task before them- a shared responsibility in the furtherance of university education in Scotland, and it is only in friendship and understanding that we can hope our highest endeavours will be crowned with success.' [13]

Acknowledging the different traditions of St Andrews and Dundee, he stressed the need for tolerance and goodwill if those differences were to be successfully resolved. One of those differences was Dundee's objection to the Court's ruling that the College headships should be academics, since this ruled out Major-General Douglas Wimberley, University College's abrasive Principal. When invited to get embroiled in the dispute, Hamilton refrained other than to express the hope that the authority of the new Court should be supported. In time the Statutory Commissioners, called in by Dundee to settle the dispute, endorsed the authority of the Court much to Hamilton's relief. One initiative with which he was associated was the attempt to entice Ronald Selby Wright, the Minister of Canongate Kirk, to become the university's first chaplain such was his admiration for his rapport with the young. Selby Wright was flattered by the offer and gave it serious thought, but ultimately his loyalty to the Canongate, and especially to its Boys' Club {of which Hamilton was president}, precluded him from accepting.

Between 1957 and 1960 Hamilton's chancellorship rather receded from public view during a three-year absence which did not go unnoticed. In October 1960 he was subjected to a critical letter from one student in *Venture*, the university journal. Not only had he failed to attend the Installation of Bob Boothby as Rector in April 1959 - illness had forced him to withdraw at the last minute - but he did not attend graduation ceremonies and expressed no message in any university publication. Could anyone enlighten him as to why this was so? As he was the titular head of the university, he felt that Hamilton should at least take some interest in its life.

Had Hamilton deigned to reply he could have justifiably claimed a greater commitment to his university than some other chancellors, yet even allowing for the constraints on his time it was surely incumbent upon him to give such a prestigious position his all. Year after year he rejected invitations to the Student Representative Council dinner and that of the University Air Squadron, much to the genuine disappointment of the students who always appreciated his company on those rare occasions they encountered him. According to Wilfred Taylor, an alumnus of St Andrews and *Scotsman* columnist: 'The reason why he seldom exercised his right to preside over graduations was probably that he genuinely dreaded the obligation to reel off all those slightly ridiculous slabs of presumptuous, synthetic Latinity which are supposed to make graduands feel holier-than-thou.' [14]

In fairness to Hamilton, he used his influence behind the scenes, such as his recommendation to the Scottish Secretary that Knox receive a knighthood or to get the Queen Mother, an honorary Graduate of the university, to open the new Queen's College in October 1961. He also played a leading part in two university appeals. In March 1962 he presided over a dinner at St Andrews to launch the university's £1 million appeal, the first of its kind by a Scottish university, to help finance a major expansion in numbers over the coming decade. Wilfred Taylor, a fellow passenger on the train from Edinburgh, noted his careworn expression as he spent all the time working on his notes and 'preparing himself for what to some other, less sensitive, men would not have been much of an ordeal'. [15]

Describing the university's aura of eternal youth as proof of the vigour of its survival, Hamilton hoped that the Appeal would ensure St Andrews a future worthy not only of its illustrious past but also 'of this present generation, who must now face the immense responsibilities and challenges that the world's widening horizons must inevitably bring to them'. [16]

That May he spoke at a fund-raising dinner at the Café Royal, and prior to that attended a press conference in which he tried to discount the idea among graduates that expanding St Andrews meant destroying its family atmosphere. By virtue of some discreet lobbying he not only succeeded in extracting a £100 donation from the Queen Mother for the Appeal, but also persuaded her to attend a cocktail party for 350 at the Merchant Taylors' Hall in March 1963. Although the Appeal raised only £622,000- some way short of its target- Hamilton thought the amount was very gratifying in the circumstances.

The publication of the 1963 Robbins Report advocating an immediate expansion in higher education, and a new university in Scotland, had profound implications for St Andrews. Having spent the previous decade successfully bringing Dundee in from the cold, Knox now felt compelled to change course. At a meeting of the Court in October 1964 he not only recommended separation as quickly as possible, but also announced his resignation to make way for someone younger and more sympathetic to the spirit of Robbins.

Knox's resignation as Principal saddened Hamilton, especially since he was privately opposed to separation. Prior to his departure in September 1966, Knox asked him whether he could persuade the Queen Mother to become the first chancellor of Dundee University, a city she knew well because of its close proximity to Glamis, her childhood home. Although aware that she had recently declined the chancellorship of Stirling because of her extensive commitments as Chancellor of London University, Hamilton depicted Dundee as a special case in his submission to her, not only for the boost it would give the city, but also for higher education in Scotland.

After obtaining assurances from Hamilton that her duties would be light compared to those she undertook at London, the Queen Mother consented to become Chancellor for a limited time. In the event she remained for ten years and won admiration for the unflustered way she dealt with a group of unruly students at her Installation.

Knox's successor as Principal was the distinguished Oxford historian J. Steven Watson and in addition to working constructively with his opposite number at Dundee, he struck up an instant rapport with Hamilton, helping to make his final years as Chancellor his most satisfying.

10. SECURING THE FUTURE

Away from the public eye Hamilton's main priority was his family, spending time with them at Lennoxlove or at Ryvra, their holiday retreat at North Berwick, where they engaged in much outdoor activity. James Douglas-Hamilton recalls a boat trip to the island of Craig Leith in the Firth of Forth which went badly wrong when the weather turned distinctly nasty. Rowing back home in mountainous waves, Hamilton faced a Herculean task but gradually got the measure of the elements and only reluctantly acceded to the assistance of the North Berwick pilot boat. Having been safely towed ashore, James walked home along the beach reflecting this had been a great adventure. 'My father on the other hand did not see it in quite the same light. All he said on the way back to our house was 'No need to say anything about this to your mother!' [1]

Although he and Elizabeth provided a loving and stable environment in which their children could flourish, raising a family of five boys in changing times proved quite taxing. This was especially the case with Angus, his son and heir, whose ambivalence towards his ducal inheritance never deserted him.

In many ways Angus appeared blessed by the gods to lead a charmed life. Handsome, wealthy and intelligent, he read Mechanical Engineering at Oxford, stroked the Balliol VIII and was a qualified pilot by his twenty-first birthday, an occasion of sumptuous celebration at Lennoxlove. In scenes reminiscent of his father's twenty-first at Hamilton, a champagne lunch was held for four hundred friends, employees and tenants who plied Angus with gifts. In one of several toasts Alan McDonald, the Factor at Hamilton, told him that in his family's long history there was not one of his ancestors who could stand comparison with the present Duke. It was meant as a great compliment, but may well have had the opposite effect, given Angus's inhibitions about following in his father's footsteps and living up to expectations. 'The trouble with father is that he's done everything,' he had confided to the *Scottish Daily Mail* days before. 'Naturally I want to emulate him, but I will have to find something new in the way of adventure.' [2]

Something of a rebel at Eton, an institution he later confessed to loathing, Angus was, according to his housemaster, James Parr, difficult and self-willed. Although Parr recognised his courage and honesty, Angus failed to form a great rapport with his peer group and in his final year was passed over for election to the House Debating Society {a junior level of house prefect}. His rejection prompted Hamilton to write to Parr to warn him that such a humiliation would merely discourage Angus from participating in house activity and leave him feeling embittered about Eton.

Although only working spasmodically, Angus passed into Balliol, his father's old college, and aside from his success on the river distinguished himself in the University Air Squadron. He began to toy with the idea of a career in the RAF, an idea that found favour with Hamilton, and to persuade him to enlist he promised to indulge his passion for motor racing by buying him a racing car. After some hesitation Angus did enlist, but always his own man his relationship with his father remained a troubled one, his many accomplishments as a pilot, first in the Far East with the RAF then as a test pilot for SAL, somewhat overshadowed by a chequered personal life.

While Angus fretted about his inheritance, James, the next in line, was more at home with pageantry, although he, like Angus, disliked being treated differently on account of his background. In his memoirs he tells of the thrill of being a page to his grandmother, Helen, Dowager Duchess of Northumberland, Mistress of the Robes, at the coronation of Elizabeth 11 in 1953 as he walked behind her in the Queen Mother's Procession. Afterwards he saw Winston Churchill in the Royal Gallery of the House of Lords and became an avid devotee from then on.

Weeks later James was again in the spotlight when he and Angus acted as pages to their father during the Procession of Honours at St Giles'. More conventional and compliant than his elder brother, James enjoyed a close relationship with his father and followed increasingly in his footsteps. Having been taught the basics of boxing by him on the beach at North Berwick it became his leading sport - rather to his mother's disapproval – at both Eton and Oxford. Possessed of a steely resolve that enabled him to absorb many of the blows that came his way, an apt metaphor for his later political career, James became a redoubtable opponent in the ring, and in 1962 enjoyed his crowning moment when he boxed Oxford to victory against Cambridge. Giving away the prizes afterwards, a proud father could not help but comment on 'a jolly good show'. [3]

It was not the end of James's Oxford triumphs. Well versed in the Hamilton tradition of leadership and tutored in the art of debating at Eton by that fine schoolmaster Willie Gladstone, he was a rigorous attender at the Oxford Union and became President in 1963. This era may have been the iconoclastic 1960s, but there was no deviation from the Toryism of his father and Uncle Geordie, a much-respected First Lord of the Admiralty in the Macmillan government. Parliament was only a matter of time.

A keen historian, James leaned on his father for much information for his book on Hess and thereafter became the guardian of Hamilton's legacy through the interminable controversies surrounding his relationship with Hitler's Deputy.

With the three younger children Hamilton's influence was less marked as Hugh, Patrick and David gravitated more towards the cultural and artistic interests of their mother. None of them experienced particularly easy childhoods with such an eminent father. Hugh was a charming, intelligent young man with a great passion for Scottish history and architecture, but was never quite the same after university in South Carolina, suffering badly from depression, an illness which greatly disturbed his father as he struggled to come to terms with it. The experience made him more sympathetic towards the plight of his younger children. Neither

Patrick nor David liked boarding school, and when David was asked to leave Eton he recalls Hamilton being very supportive, especially in his refusal to accept an Old Etonian tie.

In July 1964 tragedy was to strike the family when the aircraft carrying Malcolm Douglas-Hamilton and one of his sons crashed in Cameroon. It brought to an end the life of a talented man whose later years were dogged by fluctuating fortunes.

Shattered by the death of his brother David in the war, Malcolm retreated to the Highlands, his depressed state placing a strain on his marriage. In 1945 he succeeded Hamilton as Commandant of the ATC for Scotland and found fulfilment training cadets in the Cairngorms. It was during this period that he played a leading role in the development of the area for winter sports.

Having fought the safe Labour seat of Greenock at the 1945 election, he now turned his sights to winning Inverness for the Unionists, a seat that had been held by Liberals of various persuasions since 1918. He moved the family to Findhorn on the Moray Firth to nurse the constituency and his efforts paid off at the 1950 election. Within eighteen months he had increased his majority to over 10,000 and won acclaim for his work on behalf of the Highlands, but the long hours, the inadequate pay and a liaison with a twice-divorced American socialite, Natalie Paine, put paid to his marriage. Although Hamilton and Geordie tried to talk him out of divorce, both for the sake of his family and his own political future, Malcolm felt honour-bound to marry Natalie. The news of his divorce from Pam, the mother of his four children, caused consternation within his constituency party and losing the confidence of a significant clique, including the chairman, proved his undoing. He resigned in 1954 and repaired to the US where he and Natalie, now his wife, founded the American-Scottish Foundation dedicated to promoting cultural ties between the two countries.

Desperate to clear his debts, made no easier by an exacting divorce settlement, Malcolm started a charter flying company in New York supplying aircraft to people and companies all over the world, delivering many of them himself. It was an industry he knew much about, but the work was both arduous and dangerous, especially to someone no longer in the flush of youth. Natalie disliked his frequent absences, and a business trip from New York to the Congo in July 1964 was not one she viewed with equanimity. She pleaded with him not to go, but tired and worried though he was, Malcolm would not be deterred, insisting it was his duty.

On 22 July 1964, he was flying the first of two Twin Beech aircraft his company had sourced to Air Congo from Monrovia, Liberia, to Kinshasa, accompanied by his son Niall, a newly qualified pilot, and a passenger. As they reached Douala in Cameroon, their destination for that evening, they ran into a vast thunderstorm, veered off course and crashed into the side of Mount Cameroon. When air traffic control became aware that the aircraft was missing a massive search went into operation and Hamilton flew out with other relatives to help, but in such inhospitable terrain their efforts yielded nothing. Soon everyone feared the worst and exactly two years later Malcolm's remains were found amid aircraft debris by a native hunter high up Mount Cameroon, his body identified by his signature ring bearing his name. It seemed the cruellest of ironies that Hamilton's three youngest siblings were now dead, Malcolm and David victims of the very activity they all loved. He felt that Malcolm's remains should be buried where they were found, but Natalie was desperate to have them back in New York, and consequently he was laid to rest in the beautiful churchyard of Hewlett, Long Island.

During the mid-1960s a subtle change took place in the Hamiltons' marriage. For years Elizabeth had proved an ideal foil to her husband in his public duties, helping him write his speeches and entertaining one and all either at Holyrood or Lennoxlove. An intelligent, forceful person in her own right, she now found an outlet for her energy and took centre stage while he supported her, a role he played with characteristic generosity, founding the Haddington Garden Trust in 1972.

Aware from her own church that communal life in a largely rural area was threatened with decline, Elizabeth looked to renew it in a meaningful way. According to her son David, it was probably a family visit to

Iona in 1966 which determined the course of her life. Inspired by the way that George MacLeod had restored the derelict Abbey there, she aspired to something similar with St Mary's Church in Haddington, a magnificent fourteenth century church, the largest in Scotland. Known in medieval times as the Lamp of Lothian, it was badly damaged by the siege of Haddington in 1548-49 and although it continued as the parish church, complete with a new roof, its choir and transepts remained open to the elements.

After gathering around a group of influential people such as the cellist Joan Dickson, the broadcaster Tom Fleming and the actress Lennox Milne, Elizabeth founded the Lamp of Lothian Trust in 1967 to restore for communal use some of Haddington's finest old buildings. These buildings included Jane Welsh Carlyle House, Haddington House and Poldrate Mill, functional until 1968 before its conversion into a community arts centre, but overriding all this was the restoration of St Mary's. Through her good friends Sir John and Lady Kennedy, Elizabeth met Yehudi Menuhin, the world- famous violinist, and persuaded him to perform at the inaugural concert at St Mary's. He came at three weeks' notice and returned many times thereafter bringing many artists with him. Thanks to his enthusiasm, Elizabeth's flair as an indefatigable fundraiser- she would not take no for an answer- and the efforts of St Mary's Kirk Session, the church was restored to its ancient splendour and thereafter staged many a memorable concert.

For all Elizabeth's attempts to get Hamilton to slow down he remained wedded to the concept of public service with links to over eighty institutions. No sooner would he sever his attachment to one and another would come knocking at his door. In 1959 he had turned down the presidency of the Boys' Brigade, but the trustees kept pressing him and finally, in 1963, he succumbed to their blandishments. It was the same with the chancellorship of St Andrews. In November 1968 he told the Principal of his intention to retire. 'Twenty years is a long time to remain in office and from the personal point of view I am finding my time overcommitted and feel I should endeavour to reduce the number of claims upon me.' [4]

His letter filled Steven Watson with gloom. Could they at least talk it over, he wondered? No record of their conversation at Lennoxlove survives, but it must be presumed that Steven Watson was successful in his entreaties as the subject was never mentioned again. Moreover, it was during Hamilton's final years in office that he performed his greatest service to the university.

The separation with Dundee had serious implications since it deprived St Andrews of half its strength in departments, students and endowments, thereby undermining its potential to provide value for money. Consequently, the Court agreed to run another appeal to fund a further expansion in residential accommodation and a new graduate centre. It was launched at the North British Hotel in Edinburgh on 30 January 1970 followed by a reception in Hamilton's apartments at Holyrood. Capitalising on the university's close links with the US and Canada, it was decided to tap into the resources of 1,500 alumni who lived there and after a preliminary visit by the Principal in 1970 he asked Hamilton whether he would consider a visit there. 'The point is that your appearing in the United States, either with me or with the Appeal officer would give a very desirable extra impetus to our campaign there.' [5]

Hamilton was immediately taken with the proposal and agreed to accompany Steven Watson and his wife, and the Appeal officer the following April. Beginning in San Francisco and Los Angeles, they headed on to Canada making direct appeals to alumni, industrialists and St Andrew's societies. Whenever possible a film of the university was shown at meetings, after which letters enclosing brochures would be sent. With the local economy in recession and American-Canadian private educational funds struggling, it was not the ideal time to be fundraising, a task that did not come easily to Hamilton in any case. On one occasion at a lunch in Toronto hosted by the Bank of Nova Scotia, he was almost apologetic for raising the matter of finance, even within the walls of a bank, and did not press the matter.

Despite the gruelling pace of the tour and the time spent preparing official speeches, Hamilton seemed to enjoy meeting fresh faces every night and answering questions about Hess and aviation, as well as loan-financed residences or scholarships. On the day of his departure - he missed the British Columbia leg because of his commitments at the General Assembly of the Church of Scotland- the party was entertained to lunch by a group of businessmen and without warning he was invited to speak. Without a note he spoke of his great love for St Andrews, of the unique contribution the university had to make to international education and his dream of a scholarship linking Canada and the US with Scotland, similar to a Rhodes scholarship at Oxford. The sincerity and eloquence of his words made a great impression on his audience, who spontaneously rose to him.

The tour, aside from raising £1 million, also deepened his friend-ship with Steven Watson as the latter's note of gratitude makes clear: 'It was not simply that you worked so hard with us but you made it all such a pleasure. When you had gone back we were much less cheerful, the work seemed harder- in short we missed you very much and realised how much we owed you.' [6]

In July 1972 Hamilton paid his final visit to St Andrews and he and Elizabeth were royally entertained by the Steven Watsons. 'It was indeed a great honour for me to perform the Graduation ceremony of Medical Degrees,' he wrote afterwards, 'although I felt it was somewhat sad that St Andrews should lose the Medical Faculty. We are, however, living in an ever-changing world.' [7]

That same year saw him perform the last of his royal duties when he played host at Holyrood to Queen Juliana and Prince Bernhard of the Netherlands and to the Grand Duke of Luxembourg. On a personal note, the year brought happiness with Angus's marriage to Sally Scott, with whom he had four children, and James's election to Edinburgh Corporation for the Murrayfield/Cramond Ward, Hamilton being given special dispensation to attend the count at the Edinburgh City Chambers.

The New Year began with a nostalgic trip to Prestwick to unveil a plaque in the International Departure Lounge commemorating the Orangefield House, the former terminal building. His last major pub-lic appearance was handing over the first of 132 Bulldogs to Air-Vice

Marshal Cook, the Director of General Training, most of which were destined for the Central Flying School.

Hamilton had always said he wanted to go quickly and like a light. On 3 February 1973, he had celebrated his seventieth birthday and appeared in buoyant health, so much so that he had rather procrastinated over taking out an Annuity to live on and making over the rest of his personal estate, then valued at approximately £1 million. {His failure to do so meant that the estate became liable for very heavy death duties.} That March Hamilton booked himself into St Raphael's Nursing Home in Edinburgh for a routine prostate operation. When James arrived unexpectedly to visit his father on the eve of the operation he was nowhere to be seen. 'Oh he could be anywhere except Blackford Hill,' he was told. James smiled. He knew exactly where his father was and, sure enough, he found him striding down the windswept hill looking fitter than ever.

The next day the prostate operation went badly wrong because Hamilton was allergic to the drugs he was given, causing him to haemorrhage severely. After a second operation some twelve hours later he asked to see James. James, in London en route to a skiing holiday, flew back immediately. As he went in to see his father he found him completely grey as though life was ebbing away, and Hamilton did not find it easy to talk. Nevertheless he treated his condition as being of little or no importance. 'I am alright, James,' he said, 'Take your mother home.' He then turned over to sleep and James went into the adjacent room where his mother was waiting. Some twenty minutes later a nun came in, clasped her hands in prayer and told them that Hamilton was dead.

The sudden nature of Hamilton's death left Elizabeth and the family shattered. After an unplanned service in the chapel at Lennoxlove, staged at the request of the estate workers, and a private funeral at Warriston Crematorium, Edinburgh, Hamilton's ashes were scattered from the air by Angus and James besides 'The Politicians Walk', Lennoxlove, ironically enough on the fortieth anniversary of his great triumph over Everest. As letters of condolence poured in from family and friends the obituaries praised his courage and commitment to public service. 'The

Duke was kind and gentle in nature, with immense stamina,' declared *The Times*. ' He overcame his inborn modesty only to help other people and to carry out the many duties – both ceremonial and in business, but more particularly in social welfare and in setting a public example – that his historic role and personal aptitude properly fulfilled in contemporary Scotland.' [8]

Similar sentiments were expressed by the *Scotsman:* 'The Duke carried on a distinguished family tradition of leadership which dates back over centuries of Scottish history, and by his own record added personal distinction in diverse fields of activity. He was not a man who sought the limelight, yet his name frequently broke into the headlines of the newspapers, aside from any reference to his notable public services.' [9]

'The Duke of Hamilton was a familiar figure in East Lothian,' commented the *East Lothian Courier,* 'and commanded the respect of all who knew him. No one could hold him in more esteem than his own estate workers and tenants at Lennoxlove.' [10]

A month later over one thousand mourners crammed into St Giles' Cathedral for Hamilton's memorial service, which featured a reading from the broadcaster Tom Fleming, a lone piper playing 'My Home', the Cameronian slow march, and music specially composed by his son Patrick. In his address, the Moderator of the General Assembly of the Church of Scotland, Ronald Selby Wright, doubted whether so many people from so many walks of life had ever gathered together in one place to pay tribute to one man. 'He will surely be remembered by those who knew him best for his quiet kindliness and his real goodness. Nothing was ever too much trouble for him provided it was for the benefit of a person or a cause. Here was a man who did surely what the Lord required of him- a man who did justly and loved kindness and walked humbly with his God.' [11]

For Elizabeth who built a house on the Lennoxlove estate, there was at least the consolation of the Lamp of Lothian to preoccupy her, a communal service that gained her an OBE. She also continued to chair the Yehudi Menuhin School of Governors until 1989 and later compiled an anthology of verse and prose entitled *Lamplight* with her friend the Rev Charles Robertson, Minister of Canongate Kirk. In July 2007 she was present when the Queen and Duke of Edinburgh visited the Lamp of Lothian Centre to mark its fortieth anniversary. It was to be her last public appearance because the following year she died aged ninety-two. In recognition of all her work on behalf of the Lamp of Lothian, the Poldrate Arts and Crafts Community Centre was renamed The Elizabeth Hamilton Buildings.

For Angus the opportunity to be Laird of Lennoxlove was not something that greatly appealed, especially without the necessary help to run such a place. Within a few years he and his family had moved to a farmhouse on the Archerfield estate, keeping his distance from Lennoxlove, but alive to its spiralling costs, he turned it into a charity in 1987. Later, in 2006, he oversaw a major renovation of the property that has restored it to its former glory, giving it more scope to host weddings, conferences and luxury weekend-breaks.

A warm, generous man in private, Angus shunned the limelight as much as possible. He did, however, rise to the occasion when duty required, not least when bearing the crown at the opening of the new Scottish Parliament by the Queen in 1999, and quietly supporting a number of charities. After two failed marriages and a battle with alcohol, a battle he eventually won, he found happiness with Kay Carmichael, a former nurse and fellow animal lover, who nursed him devotedly during his final years when afflicted by dementia. On his death in 2010, his elder son, Alexander, inherited the dukedom.

For James, the lure of politics has remained as intense as ever. Elected to Parliament in October 1974 for Edinburgh West, he put in a lengthy stint at the Scottish Office during the Thatcher and Major governments, rising to become Minister of State in 1995. Losing his seat in the Labour landslide of 1997, he served in the Scottish Parliament for eight years, before devoting himself to the House of Lords where he sits as Lord Selkirk of Douglas. In 2011 he was appointed Lord High Commissioner to the General Assembly of the Church of Scotland for 2012-13, the office which his father served with such distinction.

If the years 2008 and 2010 were unhappy ones for the descendants of the 14th Duke of Hamilton with the death of his wife and elder son {Hugh had died in 1995}, 2011 was an occasion for joy with the marriage of Alexander to Sophie Rutherford at Canongate Kirk. Weeks later the new Duke was back there to read the lesson in the presence of the Queen and the Duke of Edinburgh, a telling reminder that after centuries of fluctuating fortunes the Hamiltons are still a force to be reckoned with, something that would have given Alexander's grandfather immense satisfaction.

ℭONCLUSION. A TRUE SCOTTISH PATRIOT

'I hope the Hess affair has now died a natural death,' Hamilton wrote to one of his superiors on 26 May 1941.[1] It proved to be a forlorn hope as Hess continued to trouble him intermittently for the rest of his life and beyond. In retrospect, it is easy to see how his reputation was compromised, given his German connections pre-war and the leaden response of the British government to Hess's arrival, a silence that enabled speculation to thrive.

Hamilton's wholehearted support of the Baldwin-Chamberlain governments' appeasement policy towards Germany was well-known. He had met intermittently with Nazi leaders and was a much-feted guest at the Berlin Olympics. Less overt but more significant was his friendship with Albrecht Haushofer, Hess's foreign policy adviser, and their respective attempts to forge closer relations between their two countries. It was in this context that Hamilton wrote his letter to *The Times* in October 1939 proposing peace with a Germany devoid of Hitler and becoming in turn the innocent recipient of a German peace initiative, an initiative that ended up in the clutches of MI5.

That letter, written by Albrecht Haushofer and instigated by Hess, subjected Hamilton to rigorous scrutiny by the British Secret Service, a scrutiny that completely exonerated him, and when Hess flew into Scotland asking to see Hamilton, he once again became an object of suspicion. Rumours soon abounded that the two had met during the Berlin Olympics and that Hamilton had helped arrange Hess's flight.

The question of that supposed encounter in Berlin has dogged Hamilton ever since as many contemporaries and historians, unwittingly or not, accepted it as fact. The Duke, while acknowledging that both of them had been present at two official functions and that he might have been pointed out to Hess, always maintained that they had never met before 11 May 1941. Hess later supported him in his contention, yet even if they had met its effect would surely have been merely symbolic as their conversation would have amounted to little more than a few pleasantries in the company of others.

As to the charge that Hamilton colluded with Hess in his flight to Britain there is absolutely nothing to support this. To have done so would have given credence to those who accused him of having Nazi sympathies. While there is no doubt that some of his circle possessed far-right views, a mere glance at Hamilton's record, both in public and private, shows a consistent opposition to Fascist totalitarianism as the suppressor of individual freedom and racial equality. In perhaps the most uncompromising speech he ever made, he told the Boys' Brigade annual rally in May 1939 that they were the antidote to authoritarian paramilitary organisations that reeked of godless doctrines and cruel deeds. The fact that Albrecht Haushofer, well aware of Hamilton's deep-seated antipathy to Hitler, warned Hess about the futility of his peace overtures to him is further testimony for the defence. That Hess chose to ignore these reservations, convinced that Hamilton would rally the 'peace party' in a coup against Churchill's government, reveals all too clearly his ignorance of British politics. For while there were clearly those who advocated peace with Germany they were few in number and presented little threat, especially by May 1941.

As far as the events of Hess's flight are concerned and its immediate aftermath, certain discrepancies in the account have helped foment the conspiracy theories. Whether Hamilton should have waited till the following morning before interviewing Hess, or whether Churchill knew about his arrival earlier than he claimed, is ultimately immaterial. What mattered was the response of the British government. Its failure to offer clarity both at the time and later did Hamilton and itself no favours. Not only was his patriotism called into question, it fuelled Russian suspicions of an Anglo-German conspiracy against the Soviet Union, suspicions compounded by Hitler's invasion of their country weeks later.

It is now only in more recent times with the release of Foreign Office and MI5 files refuting many of the allegations that Hess was enticed to Britain by its security services, that a more sober assessment of Hamilton's career can be made. An aristocrat with a social conscience, a prize boxer who won the Scottish Championships {middleweight} and a distinguished aviator who found enduring fame with his flight over Everest, he was a respected MP, not least for his work on behalf of Scottish affairs and his constituents. Focusing increasingly on foreign policy, his undue faith in diplomacy as a means of curbing the Nazi lust for conquest was flawed, especially given his strong reservations about the nature of the regime.

That said, if Hamilton is to be condemned for his appeasement of Germany, a charge that could be levelled against most of the British establishment of that era, he could equally claim credit for exposing the deficiencies of the nation's air defences. His passionate advocacy of rearmament, his leadership of 602 Squadron, his mission to France in May 1940 at some personal risk, and his leadership of the Scottish ATC all helped defeat the Nazi threat from the air.

Once the war was over he continued to be closely involved with aviation through SAL and the campaign to get Prestwick designated as an international airport, a campaign that eventually bore fruit in 1946. As Chairman of SAL through the late 1940s and 1950s, Hamilton played second fiddle to David McIntyre as they struggled to operate their own airline, but despite only limited success they compensated in the field of aircraft manufacturing, producing the Prestwick Pioneer, the Twin Pioneer and the Bulldog training aircraft.

A loyal family man who successfully relocated the family seat from Dungavel to Lennnoxlove in East Lothian, Hamilton's essential decency commanded respect wherever he went. A devotee of worthy causes, he served the Crown with great dignity both as Lord Steward and Hereditary Keeper of Holyroodhouse. He also featured prominently in business, youth welfare and higher education, crowning his lengthy tenure as Chancellor of St Andrews with a highly successful fundraising tour of the US and Canada.

His aristocratic bearing and social poise made him an ideal candidate to be Lord High Commissioner to the General Assembly of the Church of Scotland on four separate occasions, but more pertinent was his genuine commitment to the Kirk by virtue of his twenty-year stint as an elder.

It was this same pride in his country's heritage that encouraged him to support its art, its traditions and its regiments, and speak with such eloquence to Scottish societies on the other side of the Atlantic. Although his reluctant part in the Hess affair has continued to preoccupy historians this was not Douglas Hamilton's true legacy; rather it was pride in serving his country and its people fully in the tradition of a true Scottish patriot.

INTRODUCTION

1   David Stafford [ed], Flight from Reality: Rudolf Hess and his Mission to Scotland 1941, Pimlico, 2002, p.11

CHAPTER 1

1   Ruddock Mackay, Fisher of Kilverstone, Clarendon Press, Oxford, 1973, p.142
2   Lanarkshire, 8 August 1903
3   Strother's Glasgow, Lanarkshire and Renfrewshire Xmas and New Year Annual 1910-11
4   Los Angelone, 17 May 1941
5   Quoted in Laddie Lucas, Thanks for the Memory, Stanley Paul and Co, 1989, p.232
6   J.H.M.Hare House Book, Eton College, December 1918
7   Lanarkshire, 15 January 1919
8   Frances Stevenson, Lloyd George: A Diary [ed A.J.P.Taylor], London: Hutchinson, 1971, p185
9   Admiral Lord Fisher to Sir William Watson, 19 December 1919, Hamilton Papers
10 A.J.Marder [ed], Admiral Lord Fisher to Sir Ernest Hodder-Williams in Fear God and Dread Nought. The Correspondence of Admiral of the Fleet Lord Fisher of Kilverstone, Vol 3, London: Jonathan Cape, 1959, p620
11 Eton Chronicle 1920-21, p 990
12 Ibid, p.995

13 NA KV2/1684, 11 January 1941
14 Record of Service Book, Eton College, Ref No SCH/CCF/9/1

CHAPTER 2

1   The Times, 10 March 1922
2   Isis, 15 March 1922
3   Ibid, 6 December 1922
4   Edward Eagan, Fighting for Fun, London: Lovat Dickson, 1932, p.168
5   Isis, 14 March 1923
6   Glasgow Herald, 2 April 1923
7   Scotsman, 2 April 1923
8   Lanarkshire, 27 March 1924
9   Evening Times, 22 March 1924
10 Ibid
11 Scotsman, 22 March 1924
12 Daily Record, 16 April 1924
13 Scotsman, 16 April 1924
14 Lanarkshire, 17 April 1924
15 Weekly Record, 19 April 1924
16 Lanarkshire, 10 May 1919
17 Ibid, 24 December 1925

CHAPTER 3

1   Geordie Douglas-Hamilton's diary, 31 May 1927, Hamilton Papers
2   The Marquis of Clydesdale to Malcolm Douglas-Hamilton, 15 February 1927, Hamilton Papers
3   Glasgow Evening News, 7 July 1927
4   The 14th Duke of Hamilton to Noel Capper, 19 March 1963, Hamilton Papers
5   Douglas McRoberts, Lions Rampant: The Story of 602 Spitfire Squadron, London: William Kimber, 1985, p.31
6   Strictly the Conservative and Unionist Party following its opposition to Irish Home Rule in the 1880s, it was known as the Unionist Party in Scotland during this era.

7   The ILP was affiliated to the Labour Party between 1906 and 1932. Particularly strong in Scotland with the advent of the Red Clydesiders during the 1920s, it became increasingly disenchanted with the moderation of Labour under Ramsay MacDonald and voted to leave in 1932.

8   The Marquis of Clydesdale to J. Rossie Brown, 7 July 1927, Hamilton Papers

9   Robin MacDonald to the Marquis of Clydesdale, 15 November 1927, Hamilton Papers

10 The Marquis of Clydesdale to T.H.Hoste, 31 December 1927, Hamilton Papers

11 Evening Times, 11 May 1929

12 Ibid, 25 May 1929

13 Govan Press, 31 May 1929

14 Sir John Gilmour to the Marquis of Clydesdale, 6 June 1929

15 Daily Record, 5 November 1930

16 Glasgow Herald, 28 November 1930

17 Renfrew Press, 28 November 1930

18 Glasgow Herald, 24 November 1930

19 Scotsman, 15 October 1931

CHAPTER 4

1   Dougal McIntyre, Prestwick's Pioneer: A Portrait of David F.McIntyre, Woodfield Publishing, 2004, p.23

2   Scotsman, 6 October 1932

3   The Marquis of Clydesdale and David McIntyre, The Pilots' Book of Everest, William Hodge and Company Ltd, 1936, p.14

4   Ibid, p.16

5   The Times, 15 March 1933

6   The Marquis of Clydesdale and David McIntyre, The Pilots' Book of Everest, p.135

7   The Times, 4 April 1933

8   Ibid

9   Daily Telegraph, 4 April 1933

10 Times of India, 4 April 1933

11 Central European Times Zurich, 10 April 1933

12 Quoted in James Douglas-Hamilton, Roof of the World: Man's First Flight over Everest, Mainstream Publishing, 1983, p.123

13 Ibid, p.161

14 Ibid, p.170

15 Air Commodore P.G.M. Fellowes to Nina, Duchess of Hamilton, 18 April 1933, Hamilton Papers

16 The Times, 24 April 1933

17 Scots Observer, 27 May 1933

18 The Marquis of Clydesdale to Lady Houston, 24 May 1933, Hamilton Papers

19 The Marquis of Clydesdale to Colonel S.V.L.Blacker, 27 May 1933, Hamilton Papers

20 Patrick G. Zander, Wings over Everest: High Adventure, High Technology and High Nationalism on the Roof of the World 1932-1934, 20th Century British History, 2010, 21 [3], p.300-329

CHAPTER 5

1 Glasgow Herald, 17 March 1934

2 Douglas McRoberts, Lions Rampant: The Story of 602 Spitfire Squadron, p.29

3 Hector MacLean, Fighters in Defence: Memories of the Glasgow Squadron, Squadron Prints Ltd, 1999, p.29

4 Sandy Johnstone, Adventure in the Sky, William Kimber, 1976, p.21

5 The Student, 22 October 1935

6 The National Party of Scotland merged with the Scottish Party in 1934 to become the Scottish National Party

7 Glasgow Evening News, 7 November 1935

8 Scotsman, 12 November 1935

9 Paisley and Renfrewshire Gazette, 16 November 1935

10 The Marquis of Clydesdale to David Patterson, 22 June 1936, Hamilton Papers

11 Daily Record, 27 April 1938

12 Paisley and Renfrewshire Gazette, 21 May 1938

13 Home Journal, 27 July 1935

14 Pearson's Weekly, 24 August 1935

15 Elizabeth, Duchess of Hamilton, Nina: Some Recollections, p.7, Hamilton Papers

CHAPTER 6

1 I.G.C.Hutchison, Scottish Politics in the Twentieth Century, Palgrave, 2001, p.49

2 Richard Griffiths, Patriotism Perverted: Captain Ramsay, the Right Club and British Anti-Semitism 1939-1940, London: Constable, 1998

3 Martin Pugh, Hurrah for the Blackshirts, Fascists and Fascism in Britain during the Wars, Jonathan Cape, 2005, London: Pimlico, 2006, p284

4 Gavin Bowd, Fascism in Scotland, Birlinn, 2013

5 In his libel action of 1942 Hamilton instructed his lawyer to state that he had never been a member of the Anglo-German Fellowship. Picknett, Prince and Prior claim there is a receipt for membership for that year in his private papers, although according to James Douglas-Hamilton, this may well have been a receipt for the dinner of 14 July 1936 which he attended. Official records in the National Archives of the Anglo-German Fellowship show no evidence of his membership for 1935-36 or any other year.

6 The evidence given for Nina, Duchess of Hamilton's membership of the Nordic League is rather sketchy. In her book *Feminine Fascism: Women in Britain's Fascist Movement 1923-1945*, London: I.B.Tauris and Co, 2000, Julie Gottlieb refers to a Lady Douglas-Hamilton as a member of the Nordic League on page 307.
In his book *Blackshirt: Sir Oswald Mosley and British Fascism,* London: Viking, 2006, Stephen Dorril mentions Nina, Lady Douglas-Hamilton accusing Neville Chamberlain of selling out to the Jews on page 450. Aside from the wrong title, no date and place is given for this speech although the assumption is that it is sometime in the spring of 1939.

7   News Chronicle, London, 4 May 1939

8   Lynn Picknett, and Clive Prince and Stephen Prior, Double Standards: The Rudolf Hess Cover-up, Little Brown and Co, 2001, p312

9   Ibid, p313

10 Sandy Johnstone, Spitfire into War, William Kimber, 1986, p.272

11 Glasgow Herald, 22 August 1936

12 Quoted in James Douglas-Hamilton, The Truth about Rudolf Hess, p.66

13 Notes taken by the researcher Dr John Campsie while working for the 14th Duke of Hamilton, p.9, Hamilton Papers, National Library of Scotland

14 The Marquis of Clydesdale to Albrecht Haushofer, 8 March 1937, Hamilton Papers

15 The Marquis of Clydesdale to Albrecht Haushofer, 30 May 1938, Hamilton Papers

16 Prunella Stack, Movement is Life: An Autobiography, Collins and Harvill Press, 1973, p.110

17 Renfrew Press, 28 October 1938

18 Salisbury Journal, 31 March 1939

19 Liverpool Post, 30 March, 1939

20 The Marquis of Clydesdale to Douglas Simpson, 1 June 1939, Hamilton Papers

21 Albrecht Haushofer to the Marquis of Clydesdale, 16 July 1939, Hamilton Papers

22 Quoted in James Douglas-Hamilton, The Truth about Rudolf Hess, p.99

23 Malcolm Douglas-Hamilton to the Marquis of Clydesdale, 20 September 1939, Hamilton Papers

24 Quoted in Prunella Stack, Movement is Life, p120

25 The Marquis of Clydesdale to Lord Halifax, 30 September 1939

26 The Times, 6 October 1939

27 James Douglas-Hamilton, The Truth about Rudolf Hess, p.101

CHAPTER 7

1   Dundee Courier, 22 March 1940

2   J.S.M.Jack to the Duke of Hamilton, 26 March 1940, Hamilton Papers

3   James Maxton to the Duke of Hamilton, 20 March 1940, Hamilton Papers

4   The Duke of Kent to the Duke of Hamilton, 19 September 1940, Hamilton Papers

5   Karl Haushofer to Albrecht Haushofer, 3 September 1940, Quoted in James Douglas-Hamilton, The Truth about Rudolf Hess, p.117

6   Albrecht Haushofer: Top Secret Memorandum. Are There Still Possibilities of a German-English Peace? 15 September 1940, Ibid, p121

7   Rudolf Hess to Karl Haushofer, 10 September 1940, Ibid, p.123

8   Albrecht Haushofer to Rudolf Hess, 19 September 1940, Ibid, p.123

9   Albrecht Haushofer to the 14th Duke of Hamilton, 23 September 1940, Hamilton Papers

10 John Harris and M.J.Trow, Hess: The British Conspiracy, Andre Deutsch, 1999, p.154

11 David Stafford [ed], Flight From Reality, p.11

12 Ibid, p.162

13 Nigel West [ed],The Guy Liddell Diaries, Volume 1: 1939-1942, Routledge, 2005, p.147

14 NA KV2/1684, 11January 1941

15 Ibid, T.A. Robertson to Wing Commander F.G.Stammers, 22 January 1941

16 Ibid, Statement of the Duke of Hamilton, 11 March 1941

17 NA KV2/1685, Statement of T.A. Robertson, 29 April 1941

18 Ibid, The Duke of Hamilton to Group Captain D.L.Blackford, 28 April 1941

19 Ibid, Group Captain Blackford to the Duke of Hamilton, 3 May 1941

20 Geoffrey Elliott, Gentleman Spymaster: How Lt Col Tommy 'Tar' Robertson Double-Crossed the Nazis, Methuen, 2011, p.164

21 Scotsman, 9 November 2004

22 David Stafford [ed], Flight from Reality, p.15

23 Hector MacLean, Fighters in Defence, p.138

24 Cited in Lynn Picknett, Clive Prince and Stephen Prior, Double Standards: The Rudolf Hess Cover-up, Little Brown and Co, 2001, p.216

25 Quoted in James Douglas-Hamilton, The Truth about Rudolf Hess, p.146

26 Sandy Johnstone, Spitfire into War, William Kimber, 1968, p.270

27 John Costello, Ten Days That Saved The West, London: Bantam, 1991, p 415

28 John Colville, Footprints in Time, Collins, 1976, p.111, The Duke of Hamilton, Report written for Submission to the International Military Tribunal, 1945

29 Ronald Tree, When the Moon was High: Memoirs of Peace and War, Macmillan, 1975, p.149

30 Quoted in James Douglas-Hamilton, The Truth about Rudolf Hess, p.150

31 German broadcast, 14 April 1941, Hamilton Papers

32 Glasgow Herald, 15 May 1941

33 Daily Express, 15 May 1941

34 Anne Chisholm and Michael Davie, Beaverbrook: A Life, Pimlico, 1993, p.408

35 Richard Davenport-Hines, An English Affair: Sex, Class and Power in the Age of Profumo, Harper Press, 2013, p.199

36 Stanley Olson [ed], Harold Nicolson. Diaries and Letters 1930-1964, New York, 1980, p.209

37 Ian Colvin, Vansittart in Office, London, 1965, p.109

38 Quoted in James Douglas-Hamilton, The Truth about Rudolf Hess, p.66

39 Ibid, p.67

40 John Colville, On the Fringes of Power: Downing Street Diaries 1939-1955, London, 1985, p.460

41 RA GVI/PRIV/ DIARY/1941: 13 May 1941

42 RA GVI/PRIV/DIARY/1941:16 May 1941

43 Quoted in James Douglas-Hamilton, The Truth about Rudolf Hess, p.163

44 Hansard, 22 May 1941

45 Ibid, 27 May 1941

46 Anne Chisholm and Michael Davie, Beaverbrook: A Life, p.410

47 The Duke of Hamilton to Godfrey Norris, 30 May 1941, Hamilton Papers

48 The Duke of Hamilton to Sir Archibald Sinclair, 24 June 1941

49 The Times, 19 February 1942

50 David Stafford [ed], Flight from Reality, p.55

51 John Harvey [ed], War Diaries of Oliver Harvey, London: Collins, 1978, p.172

52 Hansard, 23 September 1943

53 Omnibook, January 1942, p.3

54 The Duke of Hamilton to Winston Churchill, 4 April 1945

55 The Duke of Hamilton to Sir Archibald Sinclair, 10 April 1945

56 The Duke of Hamilton to Heinz Haushofer, 3 September 1948, Hamilton Papers

57 Scotsman and Glasgow Herald, 25 April 1961

CHAPTER 8

1 James Douglas-Hamilton, The Truth about Rudolf Hess, p.164

2 NA AIR 2/633, Lord Glentanar to Sir Archibald Sinclair, 20 August 1942

3 Ibid, Sir Archibald Sinclair to the Duke of Hamilton, 28 August 1942

4 The Duke of Hamilton to a friend, 9 August 1944, Hamilton Papers

5 Glasgow Evening News, 20 March 1944

6 Glasgow Herald, 12 January 1946

7 Scotsman, 18 February 1946

8 The Duke of Hamilton to Brian Thynne, 23 January 1958, Hamilton Papers

CHAPTER 9

1 Elizabeth, Duchess of Hamilton, Nina: Some Recollections, p.8, Hamilton Papers
2 Ibid, p.9
3 Scotsman, 27 May 1954
4 Ibid, 21May 1958
5 The Duke of Hamilton to George MacLeod, 16 March 1959, Hamilton Papers
6 Speech to the General Assembly of the Church of Scotland, 26 May 1960, Hamilton Papers
7 The Duke of Hamilton to Iain Macleod, 28 May 1960
8 Glasgow Herald, 11 October 1960
9 The Duke of Hamilton to George MacLeod, 11 October 1960, Hamilton Papers
10 Ibid, 28 October 1960, Hamilton Papers
11 The Duke of Hamilton to Sir James Irvine, 16 February 1948, University of St Andrews Library, Special Collections, UY875/ Irvine/ Box File acc 508
12 Inauguration speech as Chancellor of St Andrews University, 30 November 1948
13 Scotsman, 13 February 1954
14 Scotsman, 4 April 1973
15 Ibid
16 Glasgow Herald, 17 March 1962

CHAPTER 10

1 James Douglas-Hamilton, After You, Prime Minister, Stacey International, 2009, p 10
2 Scottish Daily Mail, 1 September 1959
3 James Douglas-Hamilton, After You, Prime Minister, p.21
4 The Duke of Hamilton to J.Steven Watson, 25 November 1968, University of St Andrews Library, Special Collections, UY875/ Watson/107/2

5 J.Steven Watson to the Duke of Hamilton, 16 December 1970, Hamilton Papers

6 Ibid, 15 July 1971

7 The Duke of Hamilton to J. Steven Watson, 5 July 1972, University of St Andrews Library, Special Collections, UY875/Watson/107/2

8 The Times, 2 April 1973

9 Scotsman, 2 April 1973

10 East Lothian Courier, 6 April 1973

11 Address at the Duke of Hamilton's Memorial Service, 27 April 1973

CONCLUSION

1 The Duke of Hamilton to R.H.Melville, 26 May 1941, Hamilton Papers

LIST OF NEWSPAPERS, JOURNALS AND MAGAZINES CITED

American Mercury, Anglo-German Review, Belfast Telegraph, Cumberland News, Daily Express, Daily Herald, Daily Mail, Daily Record, Daily Telegraph, Democratic Action, Dundee Courier, East Lothian Courier, Eton Chronicle, Flight, Glasgow Evening News, Glasgow Evening Times, Glasgow Herald, Govan Press, Greenock Telegraph, Hansard, Home Journal, Isis, Lanarkshire, London Evening News, Los Angelone, Manchester Guardian, New York Times, News Chronicle, Omnibook, Paisley and Renfrewshire Gazette, Pearson's Weekly, Press and Journal, Renfrew Press, Reynold's Illustrated News, Salisbury Journal, Saturday Review, Scottish Daily Express, Scottish Daily Mail, Scotsman, Scots Observer, Strother's Glasgow, Lanarkshire and Renfrewshire Xmas and New Year Annual, Sydney Morning Herald, The Aeroplane, The Age, The Straits Times, The Student, The Times, Times of India, Venture, Weekly Record, World News and Views

*B*IBLIOGRAPHY

Allen, Martin, *The Hitler/Hess Deception: British Intelligence's best kept secret of the Second World War*, Harper Collins, 2003

Allen, Warner, *Lucy Houston DBE*, Constable and Company, 1947

Berry, Peter, *Prestwick Airport and Scottish Aviation*, Tempus, 2005

Blacker, Barnaby [ed], *The Adventures and Inventions of Stewart Blacker*, Pen and Sword Military, 2006

Bowd, Gavin, *Fascism in Scotland*, Birlinn, 2013

Cameron, Dugald, *Glasgow's Own, 602 {City of Glasgow} Squadron Royal Auxiliary Air Force 1925-1957*, Squadron Prints, 1987

Cameron, Dugald, *Glasgow Airport*, Holmes McDougall Ltd, 1990

Cannadine, David, *The Decline and Fall of the British Aristocracy*, London: Picador, 1992

Chisholm, Anne, and Davie, Michael, *Beaverbrook: A Life*, Pimlico, 1993

Churchill, Randolph, *They Serve the Queen*, Hutchinson, 1953

Churchill, Winston, *The Second World War, Vol 2, Their Finest Hour*, London, 1949

Churchill, Winston, *The Second World War, Vol 3, The Grand Alliance*, London, 1950

Colville, John, *Footprints in Time*, Collins, 1976

Colville, John, *The Fringes of Power. Downing Street Diaries 1939-1955*, London, 1985

Colvin, Ian, *Vansittart in Office*, London, 1965

Costello, John, *Ten Days That Saved The West*, London: Bantam, 1991

Clydesdale, The Marquis of, and McIntyre, David, *The Pilots' Book of Everest*, William Hodge and Company Ltd, 1936

Davenport-Hines, Richard, *An English Affair: Sex, Class and Power in the Age of Profumo*, Harper Press, 2013

Devine, T.M., *The Scottish Nation 1700-2000*, London: Allen Lane, 1999

Dilks, David [ed], *The Diaries of Sir Alexander Cadogan 1938-1945*, London, 1971

Dorril, Stephen, *Blackshirt: Sir Oswald Mosley and British Fascism*, London: Viking, 2006

Douglas-Hamilton, Alasdair, *Lord of the Skies: The Life of Lord Malcolm Douglas-Hamilton*, Lulu, 2011

Douglas-Hamilton, James, *The Air Battle for Malta: The Diaries of a Spitfire Pilot*, Mainstream, 1981, Airlife Publishing Ltd, 2000

Douglas-Hamilton, James, *Roof of the World: Man's First Flight over Everest*, Mainstream, 1983

Douglas-Hamilton, *The Truth about Rudolf Hess*, Mainstream, 1993

Douglas-Hamilton, James, *After You, Prime Minister*, Stacey International, 2009

Dudgeon, Jeffrey, *Sir Roger Casement: The Black Diaries*, Belfast Press, 2002

Eagan, Edward, *Fighting for Fun*, London: Lovat Dickson, 1932

Edgerton, David, *England and the Aeroplane*, Macmillan, 1991

Elliott, Geoffrey, *Gentleman Spymaster: How Lt Col Tommy 'Tar' Robertson Double-Crossed the Nazis*, Methuen, 2011

Ewart, Jim, *Prestwick Airport Golden Jubilee 1935-1985*, Scottish Airports, 1985

Fellowes Air Commodore P.F.M., *First over Everest: The Houston Mount Everest Expedition 1933*, John Lane, the Bodley Head Ltd, 1933

Ferguson, Ron, *George MacLeod: Founder of the Iona Community*, London: Collins, 1991

Gortemaker, Manfred [ed], *Britain and Germany in the Twentieth Century*, Berg, 2006

Gottlieb, Julie V., *Feminine Fascism: Women in Britain's Fascist Movement 1923-1945*, London: I.B. Tauris, 2000

Griffiths, Richard, *Fellow Travellers of the Right: British Enthusiasts for Nazi Germany 1933-1939*, London Oxford Paperbacks, 1983

Griffiths, Richard, *Patriotism Perverted: Captain Ramsay, the Right Club and British Anti-Semitism 1939-1940*, London: Constable, 1998

Harris, John, and Trow, M.J., *Hess: The British Conspiracy*, Andre Deutsch Ltd, 1999

Harvey, John [ed], *War Diaries of Oliver Harvey*, London: Collins, 1978

Hess, Wolf Rüdiger, *My Father Rudolf Hess*, London: W.H.Allen, 1987

Holt, Richard, *Sport and the British, A Modern History*, OUP, 1990

Hough, Richard, *First Sea Lord, An Authorised Biography of Admiral Lord Fisher*, George Allen and Unwin Ltd, 1969

Hutchison, I.G.C, *Scottish Politics in the Twentieth Century*, Palgrave, 2001

Hutton, J. Bernard, *Hess: The Man and his Mission*, David Bruce and Watson Ltd, 1970

Irving, David, *Hess, The Missing Years*, London Grafton Books, 1989

Johnstone, Sandy, *Where No Angels Dwell*, Cedric Chivers, 1974

Johnstone, Sandy, *Adventure in the Sky*, William Kimber, 1978

Johnstone, Sandy, *Spitfire into War*, William Kimber, 1986

Kershaw, Ian, *Making Friends with Hitler: Lord Londonderry and Britain's Road to War*, Allen Lane, 2004

Kilpatrick, John, *10 May 1941: Rudolf Hess's Flight to Britain. A bibliographical study*, Caledonian Philatelic Society, 2008

Kirkpatrick, Ivone, *The Inner Circle*, London, 1959

Kilzer, Louis C., *Churchill's Deception: The Dark Secret that destroyed Nazi Germany*, Simon and Schuster, 1994

Lake, Deborah, *Tartan Air Force: Scotland and a Century of Military Aviation*, Birlinn, 2007

Leasor, James, *Rudolf Hess, The Uninvited Envoy*, London, 1962

Lownie, Andrew, *John Buchan: The Presbyterian Cavalier*, Canongate, 1995

Lucas, Laddie [ed], *Wings of War*, Hutchinson, 1983

Lucas, Laddie, *Thanks for the Memory*, Stanley Paul and Co, 1989

Mackay, Ruddock, *Fisher of Kilverstone*, Clarendon Press Oxford, 1973

MacLean, Hector, *Fighters in Defence: Memories of the Glasgow Squadron*, Squadron Prints Ltd, 1999

MacLeod, Norman, *The Wallace Memorial Stone*, Pen Press Publishers Ltd, 2005

McCloskey, Keith, *Edinburgh Airport: A History*, Tempus Publishing Ltd, 2006

McGinty, Stephen, *Camp Z. How British Intelligence Broke Hitler's Deputy*, Quercus, 2011

McIntyre, Dougal, *Prestwick's Pioneer: A Portrait of David F.McIntyre*, Woodfield Publishing, 2004

McKechin, W.J., *A Tale of Two Airports*, Paisley, 1967

McRoberts, Douglas, *Lions Rampant: The Story of 602 Spitfire Squadron*, William Kimber, 1985

Manvell, Roger, and Fraenkel, Heinrich, *Hess*, MacGibbon and Kee, Granada Publishing Ltd, 1971

Marder, A.J., Fear God and Dread Nought: The Correspondence of Admiral of the Fleet Lord Fisher of Kilverstone: Vol 111 Restoration, Abdication, and Last Years, 1914-1920, Jonathan Cape, 1959

Masters, Brian, *The Dukes*, Frederick Muller, 1998

Mitchell, Angus, *Sir Roger Casement's Heart of Darkness: The 1911 Documents*, Irish Manuscripts Commission, 2003

Morris, Jan, *Fisher's Face*, Viking, 1994

Nesbit, Roy, and Van Acker, Georges, *The Flight of Rudolf Hess: Myths and Reality*, Sutton Publishing, 1994

O'Siochain, Seamas, *Roger Casement: Imperialist, Rebel, Revolutionary*, Dublin Lilliput Press, 2007

Olson, Stanley [ed], *Harold Nicolson. Diaries and Letters 1930-1964*, New York, 1980

Padfield, Peter, *Flight for the Führer*, London: Cassell, 2001

Penrose, Harald, *British Aviation- Widening Horizons 1930-1934*, London HMSO, 1979

Picknett, Lynn, and Prince, Clive, and Prior, Stephen, *Double Standards: The Rudolf Hess Cover-up*, Little Brown and Co, 2001

Pugh, Martin, *Hurrah for the Blackshirts!*, London: Pimlico, 2006

Pugh, Martin, *'We danced all night': A social history of Britain between the Wars*, London: Bodley Head, 2008

Reid, B.L., *The Lives of Roger Casement*, Yale, 1976

Rhodes James, Robert, *Bob Boothby, A Portrait*, Headline, 1992

Rhodes James, Robert [ed], *Chips: The Diaries of Sir Henry Channon*, Phoenix Grant, 1967

Robertson, Alan, *Lion Rampart and Winged: A Commemorative History of Scottish Aviation Limited*, William Kimber, 1986

Royle, Trevor, *A Time of Tyrants, Scotland and the Second World War*, Birlinn, 2011

Rubinstein, Christopher, [ed Daniel Rubinstein], *Royal Flourish*, Grosvenor House Publishing, 2010

Schwarzaller, Wolf, *Rudolf Hess, The Deputy*, London: Quartet, 1988

Skipwith, Sofka, *The Autobiography of a Princess*, Hart-Davis, 1968

Smith, Alfred, *Rudolf Hess and Germany's Reluctant War 1939-1941*, The Book Guild Limited, 2001

Stack, Prunella, *Movement is Life: An Autobiography*, Collins and Harvill Press, 1973

Stafford, David [ed], *Flight from Reality: Rudolf Hess and his Mission to Scotland 1941*, Pimlico, 2002

Stevenson, Frances, Lloyd George: A Diary {ed A.J.P.Taylor}, London: Hutchinson, 1971

Stewart, Neil M., *Fellow Travellers of the Right: Foreign Policy Debate in Scotland 1935-1939*, PhD Thesis, University of Edinburgh, 2001,[unpublished]

Thorpe, D.R., *Sir Alec-Douglas Home*, Sinclair-Stevenson, 1997

Tree, Ronald, *When the Moon was High: Memoirs of Peace and War*, Macmillan, 1975

Warner, Gerald, *The Scottish Tory Party: A History*, Weidenfeld and Nicholson, 1988

Wallace, William, *Hamilton Palace*, Hamilton District Council, 1995

Wentworth-Day, James, *Lady Houston DBE, The Woman who won the War*, Allan Wingate, 1958

West, Nigel [ed], The Guy Liddell Diaries, Vol 1, 1939-1942, Routledge, 2005

Zander, Patrick G., *Right Modern: Technology, Nation and Britain's Extreme Right in the Interwar Period*, PhD Thesis, Georgia Institute of Technology, 2009

Zander, Patrick G., *Wings over Everest: High Adventure, High Technology and High Nationalism on the Roof of the World 19321-1934*, 20th Century British History [2010], 21 [3], p.300-329

Zinovieff, Sofka, *Red Princess: A Revolutionary Life*, Granta Books, 2007

Printed in Great Britain
by Amazon.co.uk, Ltd.,
Marston Gate.